The Political Economy of Natural Resources and Development

The Political Economy of Natural Resources and Dev... ...ment offers a unique and multidisciplinary perspective on how the commodity boom of the mid-2000s reshaped the model of development throughout Latin America and elsewhere in the developing world. Governments increased taxes and royalties on the resource sector, the nationalization of foreign firms returned to the mainstream economic policy agenda, and public spending on social and developmental goals surged. These trends, often described as resource nationalism, have developed into a strategy for economic development, generated a re-imagining of the state and its institutional possibilities, and created a new but very significant political risk for extractive enterprises.

However, these innovations, which constitute the most dramatic change in development policy in Latin America since the advent of neoliberalism, have so far received little attention from either academic or policy-oriented publications. This book explores the reasons behind these policies, and their effects on states, firms, and development trajectories. This text brings together renowned experts to examine the political-economic causes of resource nationalism, as well as its manifestation in six Latin American countries. The causal variables considered by the contributors to this collection include a range of political-economic determinants of policy including commodity prices; the influence of ideology and national politics; ideas about industrial policy; relations between host governments and investors; and how countries respond to opportunities provided by regional initiatives and the new geography of the global economy.

This volume is essential reading in development economics, political economy, and Latin American studies, as well as for those who want to understand what economic development means after neoliberalism.

Paul A. Haslam is an associate professor in the School of International Development and Global Studies at the University of Ottawa, Canada.

Pablo Heidrich is an adjunct research professor in the Institute of Political Economy at Carleton University, Canada.

Routledge studies in development economics

For a complete list of titles in the series please visit www.routledge.com

The Political Economy of Natural Resources and Development

From neoliberalism to resource nationalism

Edited by
Paul A. Haslam and Pablo Heidrich

Routledge
Taylor & Francis Group

LONDON AND NEW YORK

First published 2016 by Routledge

2 Park Square, Milton Park, Abingdon, Oxfordshire OX14 4RN

52 Vanderbilt Avenue, New York, NY 10017

Routledge is an imprint of the Taylor & Francis Group, an informa business

First issued in paperback 2018

British Library Cataloguing in Publication Data

A catalogue record for this book is available from the British Library
Library of Congress Cataloging in Publication Data

The political economy of natural resources and development : from neoliberalism to resource nationalism / edited by Paul A. Haslam and Pablo Heidrich.
pages cm
1. Natural resources–Developing countries. 2. Economic development–Developing countries. 3. Nationalism–Developing countries.
4. Neoliberalism–Developing countries. I. Haslam, Paul Alexander, editor. II. Heidrich, Pablo, editor.
HC59.7.P577185 2016
333.709172'4–dc23
2015032337

ISBN: 978-1-138-91973-0 (hbk)
ISBN: 978-0-367-10977-6 (pbk)

Typeset in Times New Roman
by Cenveo Publisher Services, India

Contents

Figures

Tables

Contributors

Javier Arellano-Yanguas is research fellow and lecturer at the Centre for Applied Ethics at the University of Deusto (Bilbao, Spain). He is currently the director of the Centre. Javier holds a PhD in Development Studies from the Institute of Development Studies – University of Sussex. His work focuses on the political economy of natural resources led development, social conflicts, decentralization, transparency and accountability, and the political role of civil society and social movements. Most of this research is done in Andean countries and encompasses both quantitative and qualitative approaches.

Sebastián Bitar is assistant professor at the School of Government, Universidad de los Andes, Bogotá, Colombia. He holds a PhD in International Relations from the American University in Washington D.C. His areas of research include Foreign Policy, International Political Economy, and Security Studies. He has received funding for academic and research activities from Fulbright, the Tinker Foundation, the Kettering Foundation, the International Studies Association, the School of International Service at American University, the Colombian National Institute of Science (Colciencias), and the Universidad de los Andes in Colombia. Sebastian is the author of *US Military Bases, Quasi-bases, and Domestic Politics in Latin America* (Palgrave, 2015) and *The First Steps towards Human Rights in Colombia* (Universidad de los Andes, 2007).

Carlos Caballero Argáez is the Director of the Alberto Lleras Camargo School of Government at the Universidad de los Andes, Bogotá, Colombia. He holds a M.A. in Engineering from the the University of California-Berkely, a M.A. in Public Administration from Princeton University, and a M.A. in History from the Universidad de los Andes. He has held different possitions of leadership in the public and private sectors, including Minister of Energy and Mines, Director of the think tank Fedesarrollo, President of the Banker's Association, member of the Central Bank's Board of Directors, and President of Bogotá's Stock Exchange, among others. He co-authored the book *Historia del sector financiero colombiano en el siglo XX: ensayos sobre desarrollo y crisis* (2006, Norma), has edited several volumes on public policy and political economy, and published numerous articles in academic journals.

Eduardo Gudynas is senior researcher at the Centro Latino Americano de Ecología Social (CLAES), a NGO based in Montevideo (Uruguay), focusing on environment and alternatives to development. He has a degree in social ecology and his work involves different social movements and organizations in several Latin American countries. Latest books include one on environmental ethics and Nature's rights with a review of the situation in Ecuador and Bolivia, and another on extractivist development strategies in Latin America (both with editions in Peru, Bolivia, Colombia and Argentina). He is a regular contributor with op-eds in different newspapers and magazines in South America. He is also visiting professor in several universities, researcher at the Uruguayan national research system, research associate at the Department of Anthropology, University of California Davis, and Duggan fellow of the National Resources Defense Council (US). He can be followed on twitter at @EGudynas; and his blog, www.accionyreaccion.com.

Paul A. Haslam is an associate professor in the School of International Development and Global Studies at the University of Ottawa, Canada. His current research focuses on corporate social responsibility in the mining sector, and the regulation of foreign direct investment in Latin America through FTAs and bilateral investment treaties. He has co-edited *Introduction to International Development: Approaches, Actors and Issues* (Oxford University Press, 2011) and *Governing the Americas: Assessing Multilateral Institutions* (Lynne Rienner Press, 2007) as well as published in journals such as *World Development*, *The World Economy*, *Third World Quarterly*, and the *European Review of Development Studies*. He received his PhD from Queen's University.

Pablo Heidrich teaches research methods and international development in the Institute of Political Economy at Carleton University, Canada. His current research on extractive industries in Latin America is funded by Canada's Social Sciences and Humanities Research Council. He has published on international trade disputes, the World Trade Organization and economic policies of the New Left. Previously, he worked at The North-South Institute in Ottawa as a senior researcher on international trade and investment issues and at the Latin American Faculty of Social Sciences (FLACSO) in Argentina on regional integration issues. He got his PhD at the University of Southern California in Political Economy and Public Policy and his M.A. from Tsukuba University (Japan) on International Political Economy.

Daniel Hellinger is professor of International Relations at Webster University, in St. Louis, Missouri. He has published several books and many scholarly articles on Venezuelan politics, including *Global Security Watch: Venezuela*; *Venezuelan Politics in the Chávez Era: Class, Polarization and Conflict* (co-edited); *Venezuela's Bolivarian Democracy* (co-edited), and a text. *Comparative Politics in Latin America: Democracy at Last?* (2nd edition). He is past president of the Venezuelan Studies Section of the Latin American Studies Association. He is currently researching mining policies in Chile and Cuba, and also has published on conspiracy theory.

Anil Hira is professor of Political Science at Simon Fraser University in Vancouver, Canada. His specialisation is industrial, technological, and energy policies for development. His recent work includes States and High Tech: Cases from the Wireless Sector, a special edition of *International Journal of Technology and Globalisation*, 2012; *What Makes Clusters Competitive? Cases from the Global Wine Industry* McGill-Queens, 2013; Mapping out the Triple Helix: how institutional coordination for competitiveness is achieved in the global wine industry, special edition of *Prometheus: critical studies in innovation*, 2013; and *Three Perspectives on Human Irrationality: The Book of Rules*, Book Guild, 2014. His current research is focused on how developing countries can transform their energy sectors to respond to climate change in ways that balance labour, environmental, and economic concerns.

Samuel Kwami Gayi is currently director and head, Special Unit on Commodities (SUC). He holds a PhD in Development Economics from the University of Manchester, UK, and has taught in the Faculty of Social Sciences, University of Science and Technology, Ghana. Samuel has researched and published on a range of development issues including, Trade Diversification, Financial Sector Reforms, Domestic Financial Resource Mobilization, WTO issues, Structural Adjustment, Poverty Reduction, Commodity Dependence, Agriculture and Food Security. He has coordinated, and contributed to three UNCTAD flagship publications, including, *The Least Developed Countries Report* (1995-1999); *Economic Development in Africa* series (2003-2008). And, on becoming the Head of the SUC in 2011, he introduced and coordinated the production of a new biennial UNCTAD report on Commodities and Development (2013 and 2015). He is member of the Senior Steering Group of the UN Secretary General's High Level Task Force on the Global Food Security Crisis.

Eliza Massi recently completed her PhD at the School of Oriental and African Studies (SOAS) at the University of London. Eliza's research focuses on industrial policy, development banks and mobilization of finance for development, and political economy of industrialization in Latin American and East Asian middle income and newly industrialized countries. Previously, Eliza worked for the Pacific Basin Economic Council (PBEC) and as a research assistant for the French Development Agency-sponsored research program on "Institutions, Governance, and Long Term Growth." Eliza was also a fellow in the Asia Pacific Leadership Program at the Hawaii-based East-West Center and has recently been awarded a Fellowship from the Sheffield Institute for International Development and the Economic and Social Research Council in support of participation in a consultation on the post-2015 global development agenda for Latin America and the Caribbean.

Juan Carlos Moreno-Brid is full professor, Faculty of Economics, UNAM (National University of Mexico). From 2000 until April 2015, he was Deputy Director of ECLAC-Mexico, which he joined after years as a Research

Associate at the David Rockefeller Center for Latin American Studies (Harvard University). Dr. Moreno-Brid specializes in economic development and growth of Latin America. His recent books are *Structural change and growth in Central America and the Dominican Republic* (ECLAC, 2014) and *Development and growth in the Mexican economy: a historical perspective* (Oxford University Press, 2009). He is a member of the editorial committee of *El Trimestre Económico, ECONOMIAUNAM, ECLAC Review*, and is founding Member of the World Economics Association, with more than 14,000 affiliates. He holds a PhD (Cambridge University), M.A. Economics (CIDE), and B.A. Mathematics (UNAM).

Jewellord Nem Singh is a lecturer in International Development at the University of Sheffield, UK. His research focuses on the natural resource governance, theories of the state, and political economy of development. He is the co-editor of *Resource Governance and Developmental States in the Global South: Critical International Political Economy Perspectives* (Palgrave Macmillan, 2013) and *Demanding Rights: Claiming Justice in the Global South* (Palgrave Macmillan, In Press). He has also published in *Third World Quarterly, New Political Economy*, and *Citizenship Studies*. He has also served as Expert Consultant for the United Nations Research in Social Development (UNRISD) and United Nations Development Programme (UNDP) on natural resource governance issues.

Janvier Désiré Nkurunziza is the Chief of Research and Analysis Section in the Special Unit on Commodities, UNCTAD where he directs research on the interaction between primary commodities production and trade and economic development. Before his current position, Janvier was the Officer-in-Charge of the Africa Section, UNCTAD; Macroeconomic Policy Advisor at UNDP, New York; and an economist at UNCTAD and UNECA, as well as working at several prominent universities. He has published several articles and chapters in edited books and co-authored flagship reports, including UNCTAD's Economic Development in Africa Report; the *African Economic Outlook*; and UNECA's Economic Report on Africa. He holds a doctorate in Economics from the University of Oxford, where he is affiliated with the Center for the Study of African Economies. Janvier is a Fellow of a number of academic and research institutions. His recent research has focused on commodities and development; the economics of conflict; capital flight; and financial systems in Africa.

Lorenzo Pellegrini, PhD is associate professor of Economics of Environment and Development at the International Institute of Social Studies of Erasmus University (ISS) in The Hague, The Netherlands, and Adjunct Professor at the University San Francisco of Quito, Ecuador. He received his PhD from the VU University of Amsterdam. His research interests include the socio-environmental impact of extractive industries, environmental justice, impact evaluation, institutions and corruption. Recent publications have appeared in *World Development, The Extractive Industries and Society, Capitalism Nature Socialism* and

Conservation Letters. Countries of research experience include Bhutan, Bolivia, Ecuador, Honduras, India, Italy, Nicaragua, Pakistan, Peru, Rwanda, and Vietnam. Lorenzo has also led and participated in a number of capacity building projects in the Global South and is convenor of the Economics of Development Major of the ISS MA programme. He teaches courses on research methodology, development economics, sustainable development, and ecological economics.

Alicia Puyana Mutis is professor of Economics at the Latin American Faculty of Social Sciences (FLACSO Mexico), and member of the Mexican Academy of Sciences, and the Colombian Academy of Economic Sciences. She works on the effects of Latin America's insertion in the global economy, as well as the political economy of petroleum policy in Mexico and Colombia. Some recent publications include *Colombia y México: la economía política petrolera en un mercado global y politizado*, (FLACSO, Mexico, 2015); *América Latina. Problemas del Desarrollo en la Globalización 1980-2013* (FLACSO, Mexico, 2015); "Chinese Land Grabbing in Argentina and Colombia", in *Latin American Perspectives* (forthcoming). Dr. Puyana sits on the editorial boards of several international journals, and is member of the Board of Directors of the International Development Economics Association (IDEAS). She has consulted for Oxford Analytica, Cambridge Energy Research Associates (CERA), and British Petroleum on energy and petroleum issues in Latin America. Dr. Puyana holds a doctorate in Economics from Oxford University.

Vlado Vivoda is research fellow at the Centre for Social Responsibility in Mining, Sustainable Minerals Institute, The University of Queensland. He was previously based at the Griffith Asia Institute at Griffith University. Vlado holds a B.A. (Honours) from the National University of Singapore, and an M.A. (International Relations) from the Australian National University. He completed his PhD on the international political economy of oil at Flinders University in 2008. Since completing his doctorate, Vlado published extensively on a wide range of topics related to energy and minerals. His particular focus is on the international political economy of energy. He has published numerous articles with high profile journals which include *New Political Economy, Business and Politics, Journal of Contemporary Asia, Asian Survey, Journal of East Asian Studies, Resources Policy* and *Energy Policy*. His most recent book examines Japan's energy security challenges after Fukushima.

Preface and acknowledgements

This project began with our sense that a lot of the contemporary writing on the political economy of Latin America had missed the fundamental importance of the region's tilt towards resource nationalism. On the one hand, we felt that, despite interesting attempts to characterize the region as experiencing a post-neoliberal moment, there was not sufficient acknowledgment that the 2000s heralded an important return of the state, and even an institution-building project that was at variance with an academic discourse that continued to focus on liberalization and privatization. The exploitation of natural resources was at the centre of this transformation and was reflected in new combinations of policy, and the rising power of governments vis-à-vis firms, despite the "constraints" left over from neoliberalism. In a significant sense, resource nationalism is post-neoliberalism in Latin America.

To build this book, we have collaborated with a very diverse set of authors, who share an interest in how the exploitation of natural resources is being employed to fund Latin America's development, but who do not share a vision of how or even whether this be done. In fact, our authors look at resource nationalism from very different angles: some use developmentalism to critique the neoliberal perspectives that persist in the resource nationalist era, others focus on how the management of extractive industries fits with a wider post-neoliberal framework, and others reject the utility of the neoliberal or post-neoliberal frameworks, preferring to imagine alternatives to both. We very much want to thank our authors for being so willing to cross the theoretical, ideological, and methodological barriers among us, and commit themselves to producing work showcasing our communality of purpose within this intellectual diversity: understanding how resources fit into the Latin American political economy of development.

This book benefited from the generous (and often underpaid) support from our translators and research assistants: Sean Cornelissen and Kirsten Francescone, from Carleton University. Funding for the research assistance was generously provided by Canada's Social Sciences and Humanities Research Council through its research grant to Pablo Heidrich, as co-investigator, on Canadian mining investments in Latin America. Mentoring and guidance from the principal investigator of this grant, Laura Macdonald, is greatly appreciated. Additional support was provided from the International Development Research Council (IDRC). We'd also like to thank our editors at Routledge who saw the value in this project early on and helped us realize it: Emily Kindleysides and Lisa Thomson.

Abbreviations

AD	*Acción Democrática* (Democratic Action, Venezuela)
ALBA	*Alianza Bolivariana para los Pueblos de Nuestra América* (Bolivarian Alliance for the Peoples of Our America)
Ag	Silver
Al	Aluminum
ALCSA	*Área de Libre Comercio Sudamericana* (South American Free Trade Area)
ANH	*Agencia Nacional de Hidrocarburos* (National Hydrocarbons Agency, Colombia)
ANM	*Agência Nacional do Mineração* (National Mining Agency, Brazil)
ANP	*Agência Nacional do Petróleo, Gás Natural e Biocombustíveis* (National Petroleum Agency, Brazil)
AP	*Alianza País* (National Alliance, Ecuador)
APRA	*Alianza Popular Revolucionaria Americana* (American Popular Revolutionary Alliance, Peru)
Au	Gold
BADUCEL	Base de Datos Estadísticos de Comercio Exterior (Statistical Database on Foreign Trade)
BNDES	*Banco Nacional do Desenvolvimiento* (Brazilian Development Bank)
BNDESPAR	*BNDES Participações* (BNDES Participation)
B	billion
bbl	barrels
bpd	barrels/day
Bs.	Bolivars, Venezuela
CAN	Canadian
CARBOCOL	*Carbones de Colombia, S.A.* (Colombian Coal)
CCT	Conditional cash transfer
CEDIB	*Centro de Documentación e Información Bolivia* (Bolivian Centre for Documentation and Information)
CELAC	*Comunidad de Estados Latinoamericanos y Caribeños* (Community of Latin American and Caribbean States)

CENTROMIN	*Empresa Minera del Centro de Peru, S.A.* (Central Peru Mining Company)
CEPAL	*Comisión Económica para América Latina y el Caribe* (Economic Commission for Latin America and the Caribbean)
CFE	*Comisión Federal de Electricidad* (Federal Electricity Commission, Mexico)
CFEM	*Compensação Financiera pela Exploração de Recursos Minerais* (Compensation for Exploiting Mineral Resources)
CpC	*Cuidadanos por el Cambio* (Citizens for the Change, Peru),
CNPC	Chinese National Petroleum Corporation
CSN	*Comunidad Sudamericana de Naciones* (South American Community of Nations)
Cu	Copper
CVP	*Corporación Venezolana de Petróleos, S.A.* (Venezuelan Petroleum Corporation)
CVRD	*Companhia Vale do Rio Doce, S.A.* (Vale Company)
COMIBOL	*Corporación Minera de Bolivia* (Mining Company of Bolivia)
CONAGUA	*Consejo Nacional del Agua* (National Council on Water, Mexico)
CONAMA	*Conselho Nacional do Meio Ambiente* (National Council of the Environment, Brazil)
CONFIEP	*Confederación Nacional de Instituciones Empresariales Privadas* (National Confederation of Private Business, Peru)
CSR	Corporate Social Responsibility
CSUTCB	*Confederación Sindical Única de Trabajadores Campesinos de Bolivia* (Single Union Confederacy of Peasant Workers of Bolivia)
DNPM	*Departamento Nacional de Produção Mineral* (National Mineral Production Department, Brazil)
ECLAC	Economic Commission for Latin America and the Caribbean
ECOPETROL	*Empresa Colombiana de Petróleos, S.A.* (Colombian Petroleum Company)
EIA	Environmental Impact Assessment
ENI	*Ente Nazionale Idrocarburi* (National Hydrocarbon Organization, Italy)
ENOC	Oil-exporting National Oil Company
ETF	Exchange Traded Funds
EU	European Union
EU27	European Union excluding Croatia
FA	*Frente Amplio* (Broad Front, Uruguay)
FARC	*Fuerzas Armadas Revolucionarias de Colombia* (Revolutionary Armed Forces of Colombia)
FDI	Foreign Direct Investment
Fe	Iron
FEJUVE	*Federación de Juntas Vecinales de El Alto* (Federation of Neighbourhood Associations of El Alto, Bolivia)

FENCOMIN	*Federación Nacional de Cooperativas de Bolivia* (National Federation of Bolivian Cooperatives)
FMPED	*Fondo Mexicano del Petróleo para la Estabilización y el Desarrollo* (Mexican Petroleum Fund for Stabilization and Development)
FNR	*Fondo Nacional de Regalías* (National Royalty Fund, Colombia)
FONDEN	*Fondo de Desarrollo Nacional* (National Development Fund, Venezuela)
ft^3	cubic feet
FTA	Free Trade Agreement
FTAA	Free Trade Area of the Americas
GDP	Gross Domestic Product
ha	hectares
IDH	*Impuesto Directo a los Hidrocarburos* (Direct Hydrocarbons Tax, Bolivia)
IEA	International Energy Agency
IIRSA	Initiative for the Integration of Regional Infrastructure of South America
INOC	Oil-importing National Oil Company
IOC	International Oil Companies
IT	Information Technology
JV	Joint venture
Li	Lithium
MAS	*Movimiento al Socialismo* (Movement to Socialism, Bolivia)
Mb	Million barrels
mbd	million barrels per day
MEF	*Ministrio de Economía y Finanzas* (Ministry of Economy and Finance, Peru)
MEP	*Ministerio de Energía y Petróleo* (Ministry of Energy and Petroleum, Venezuela) Fund for Stabilization and Development)
MINAM	*Ministerio del Ambiente* (Ministry for the Environment, Peru)
MINEM	*Ministerio de Energía y Minas* (Ministry of Energy and Mines Peru)
MME	*Ministério de Minas e Energia* (Ministry of Mines and Energy, Brazil)
MNC	Multinational Corporation
MPPPM	*Ministerio del Poder Popular de Petróleo y Minería* (Ministry of the Popular Power for Oil and Mining, Venezuela)
Mm^3	Cubic metres
Mn	Manganese
Mo	Molybdenum
Mt	Million tonnes
NAFTA	North American Free Trade Agreement

n.d.	no data
NGO	Non-governmental Organization
Ni	Nickel
NOC	National Oil Company
OBM	Obsolescing Bargain Model
OECD	Organisation for Economic Cooperation and Development
OEFA	*Organismo de Evaluación y Fiscalización Ambiental* (Organization for Environmental Evaluation and Supervision)
OPEC	Organisation of Petroleum Exporting Countries
OPIM	*Organización del Pueblo Indígena Mosetén* (The Organization of Indigenous Mosetén People)
PAN	*Partido Acción Nacional* (National Action Party, Mexico)
Pb	Lead
PDVAL	*Producción y Distribución Venezolana de Alimentos* (Venezuelan Production and Distribution of Food)
PERCAN	Peru-Canada Mineral Resources Reform Project
PetroPerú	*Petróleos del Perú, S.A.* (Petroleum of Peru)
PNP	*Partido Nacionalista Peruano* (Peruvian Nationalist Party)
PPC	Petro-Political Cycle
PEMEX	*Petróleos Mexicanos, S.A.* (Mexican Petroleum Company)
PDVSA	*Petróleos de Venezuela, S.A.* (Petroleum of Venezuela Company)
Petrobras	*Petróleo Brasileiro, S.A.* (Brazilian Oil Company)
Petrosal	*Empresa Brasileira de Administração de Petróleo e Gás Natural, S.A. - known as Pré-Sal Petróleo, S.A* (Brazilian Administration Company for Oil and Natural Gas)
PMSP	*Programa Minero de Solidaridad con el Pueblo* (Mining Program of Solidarity with the People, Peru)
PND	*Plan Nacional del Desarrollo* (National Development Plan, Bolivia)
Previ	*Caixa de Previdência dos Funcionários do Banco do Brasil* (Employees of the Bank of Brazil Pension Fund, Brazil)
PT	*Partido dos Trabalhadores* (Workers' Party, Brazil)
PRD	*Partido de la Revolución Democrática* (Party of the Democratic Revolution, Mexico)
PRI	*Partido Revolucionario Institucional* (Institutional Revolutionary Party, Mexico)
PSA	Production-sharing agreement
R/P	Reserve-to-Production ratio
ROI	Return on Investment
SEMIP	*Secretaría de Energía, Minas e Industria Paraestatal* (Secretariat for Parastatal Energy, Mines and Industry)
SEMARNAT	*Secretaría de Medio Ambiente y Recursos Naturales* (Secretariat of Environment and Natural Resources, Mexico)
SGM	*Servicio Geológico Mexicano* (Mexican Geological Service)
Sn	Tin

SNMPE	*Sociedad Nacional de Minería, Petróleo y Energía* (National Society for Mining, Oil, and Energy, Peru)
SOE	State-owned enterprise
tboed	thousand barrels oil-equivalent per day
TIPNIS	*Territorio Indígena Parque Nacional Isiboro Sécure* (National Park and Indigenous Territory Isiboro Sécure)
TNC	Transnational corporation
US	United States
UN	United Nations
UNASUR	*Unión de Naciones Suramericanas* (Union of South American Nations)
UNCTAD	United Nations Conference on Trade and Development
USO	*La Unión Sindical Obrera de la Industria del Petróleo* (Workers' Union Syndicate of the Petroleum Industry, Colombia)
Vale	*Companhia Vale do Rio Doce, S.A.* (Vale Company)
VAT	Value-added tax
WTI	West Texas Intermediate light crude
WTO	World Trade Organization
YPF	*Yacimientos Petrolíferos Fiscales* (State Petroleum Company, Argentina)
YPFB	*Yacimientos Petrolíferos Fiscales Bolivianos* (Bolivian State Petroleum Company)
Zn	Zinc

1 From neoliberalism to resource nationalism

States, firms and development

Paul A. Haslam and Pablo Heidrich

Introduction

The nationalization of foreign firms has once again returned to the mainstream economic policy agenda in Latin America and elsewhere in the developing world – especially in the extractive sector. Between 2006 and 2014, the governments of Argentina, Bolivia, Ecuador and Venezuela announced full or partial nationalizations in the oil/gas and mining sectors for over several billion dollars of assets (Deloitte 2013; Ernest & Young 2013). In addition to these more extreme actions, a wider set of governments in the region expanded the tax and royalty burdens on foreign firms. This was accompanied by a rush of institution-building, as new regulatory agencies were created to manage the resource bonanza and its dysfunctions, and state-owned enterprises (SOEs) were created to capture rents and maximize developmental spillovers. These experiments have become reference points for other areas of the developing world that are beginning to move in the same policy direction, notably in Sub-Saharan Africa and East Asia (Gajigo et al. 2012), and many observers believe these trends will either continue at the current pace or even accelerate (UNCTAD 2012; ECLAC 2013a).

The term 'resource nationalism' is frequently used to capture this relatively diverse set of policies and practices. Although some associate the term with the ideological and nationalist opposition to private and foreign exploitation of natural resources that predominated in the 1960s and 1970s (Biersteker 1987; Chua 1995: 262), we use the term more neutrally, without prejudice to political orientation, to capture a wide range of actions and policies through which the state seeks to enhance its influence over the development of the resource sector. In this regard, we include as resource nationalism three categories of actions: the maximization of public revenue; the assertion of strategic state control (ability to set a political or strategic direction to the development of the sector); and enhancement of developmental spillovers from extractive activity.[1] Notwithstanding the possibility of joint gains, these actions generally come at the expense of firms, following Vernon's classic insight from *Sovereignty at Bay* (1971). Where states maximize government take, corporate profits are reduced; where states make strategic choices about resource development, corporate autonomy is curtailed; and where states manage developmental spillovers, corporate relationships with suppliers, consumers, and communities are pre-empted.

Furthermore, a wide variety of policy instruments are available to states: from flashy nationalizations and quasi-nationalizations (forced divestment of shares) that grab newspaper headlines and unsettle investors; royalty and taxation changes; the creation of state-owned enterprises to 'partner' with foreign firms; modifications to bureaucratic processes that affect property rights, administrative approval processes and environmental licensing regimes; and even informal (extra-legal) pressures (Duncan 2006: 86–7; Kobrin 1980). In some cases, the instrument may realize a single policy goal: a change to the royalty rate increases the government take without directly impacting the government's strategic control of the industry, or fostering developmental spillovers. In other cases, instruments such as the forced divestiture of shares, or the creation of a state-owned enterprise, offer the potential, although not the guarantee, of realizing multiple goals: appropriating rents; influencing strategic decision-making; and transforming the developmental contribution of the firm.

Overall, it is clear that governments in Latin America have switched, in varying degrees, from a *laissez-faire* attitude regarding foreign direct investment (FDI) in extractive industries, to actively seeking to maximize the contribution of foreign firms to government revenue and economic development. However, these nationalizations and regulatory changes, which constitute the most dramatic change in development policy in the region since the advent of neoliberalism, as of yet, have received little attention from either academic or policy-oriented publications. Most fundamentally, researchers have been slow to understand why resource nationalism has emerged, again, in the first decade of the twenty-first century, or explain the many different policies and practices it has manifested. In addition, the impact on states, firms and development trajectories is largely unknown. Is it a return to the failed import-substitution policies of the past (Gallagher and Porzecanski 2010; Moran 2001)? Is it a hybrid model in which neoliberal states become increasingly dependent on resource revenues for social spending (Gudynas 2012; Hujo 2012: 7)? Does it constitute a new set of policies for economic development in a post-neoliberal environment (Flores-Macias 2012; Grugel and Riggirozzi 2009; Macdonald and Ruckert 2009)? In this regard, fundamental questions about the relationship between states, firms, and development, are raised by the new resource nationalism.

Our principal concern in this book is to examine the variation in the policies that constitute resource nationalism. It is a long chain of causality from the political and economic factors that shape policies, to the success or failure of those policies in fomenting economic development. We have chosen to focus on the first part of the equation, believing that before we can address the consequences of policy, we need to understand the reasons behind the resource *nationalisms* that characterize the region, and their effects on the principal actors in economic development: states and firms. In this respect, the sets of policies that reflect different positions on the capture and use of resource rents, from limited, to moderate, to radical, are the dependent variables of our project. The independent variables considered by the contributors to this collection include a range of political-economic determinants of policy including commodity prices; the influence of ideology and national politics; ideas about industrial policy; relations between host governments and investors; and how countries respond to opportunities provided by regional initiatives and the new geography of the global economy.

This chapter seeks to contextualize our enquiry into the causes and nature of resource nationalism in Latin America. Firstly, we examine the relationship between resources and development, particularly the applicability to Latin America of claims that resources constitute a 'curse' for economic development. Secondly, we examine the 'institutional turn' in resource politics, focusing on the nature of the state and its importance for resource nationalism. Our examination of the how the state has transformed itself around the question of resource nationalism, permits us to contribute to theoretical debates about the conditions under which rent-seeking is curtailed or promoted, and whether sufficient institutional capacity and autonomy can be built to make the most out of resource endowments. Thirdly, we examine the legislative and regulatory changes that have been made over the last twenty-five years in the resource sector. This detailed analysis allows us to classify countries according to limited, moderate, and radical approaches to resource nationalism; a classification which is then reflected in the organization of the book. Finally, we conclude with a summary of the chapters found in this collection.

Resource nationalism and development

The questions, 'What role should natural resources play in the economy?, and 'What policies should be applied to maximize their contribution to economic development?', have been fundamental to the development trajectory of most Latin American countries. In this regard, the resource nationalism of the 2000s is not only a contemporary issue, but is also the latest iteration of a long debate that stretches back to the colonial period. This debate has oscillated between those who see reliance on natural resources as 'curse' that has hampered Latin America's development, and those who see it as an opportunity to be seized.

The debate over mining and hydrocarbons policy has also been one over the most appropriate growth and development strategy. It is well established that Latin America pursed a liberal and export-oriented strategy between 1870 and 1914, that gradually gave way to a period of resource nationalism, beginning in the late 1930s, as the region faced new political constituencies related to incipient import-substitution industrialization, new ideas about the importance of industrialization for development, and growing anti-imperialist sentiment (Bulmer-Thomas 1994: 56–7, 69; Cardoso and Faletto 1979; Galeano 1997). Latin America's first nationalization is widely considered to be Bolivia's (1937) takeover of Standard Oil; which was rapidly followed by Mexico's nationalization of its oil industry (1938) and the creation of state-owned *Petróleos de México* (PEMEX). Chua describes this as the first complete *privatization-nationalization* cycle, which was followed by a second cycle that began in the mid-1950s and ended with nationalizations in the late 1960s–1970s; and a third cycle that began with liberalization in the 1980–90s (Chua 1995: 228, 238; see Berrios et al. 2011: 676–9), and found its conclusion in the period of resource nationalism covered by this book.

While the existence of such cycles is still the subject of debate, we find this is a compelling way of underlining both the existence of a trend and its historical roots (see Moran 1974). It contrasts with most studies of state–firm relations in Latin America, which tend towards a linear interpretation: nationalizations in the 1970s were viewed by the dependency literature of the time as the result of a permanent increase in the state's autonomy and capacity that enabled it to put pressure on multinational corporations (Evans 1979; Jenkins 1977; Kobrin 1980: 76, 79). Conversely, in the 1990s, it was thought that the power of states to nationalize had been permanently debilitated by the retreat of the state, new kinds of cooperative and synergistic relationships between states and firms (Dunning 1991; Luo 2001; Stopford and Strange 1991; Wells 1998: 17), and international constraints on governmental policy autonomy (Gallagher 2005; Haslam 2010b; Sánchez-Ancochea and Shadlen 2008). The resource nationalism of the mid-2000s put paid to these ahistorical arguments, by showing that states had both the will and capacity to nationalize and regulate the extractive sector.

However, the ability of states to translate resource nationalism into a path to economic development remains in doubt. The literature that originated with Auty (1993, 2001) argued that natural resource endowments in developing countries were associated with slow growth, deindustrialization, and inequality and likely to 'impede rather than further balanced and sustainable development' (Humphreys et al. 2007: 1). The economic dysfunctions of the resource curse were usually associated with 'Dutch Disease' effects, when overvaluation of the currency contributed to falling competitiveness and re-allocation of resources away from, and crowding-out of, the domestic manufacturing sector (Sachs and Warner 2001: 828, 833). However, recent studies, have increasingly called Sachs and Warner's macro-economic findings into question, especially when institutional controls are included (Brunnschweiler 2007: 412; Mehlum et al. 2006: 1127).

Equally important are the political dysfunctions of the resource curse, which are mostly related to 'unproductive' rent-seeking (Deacon and Rode 2012: 9). Humphreys, Sachs and Stiglitz describe the issue as follows: 'Especially in the case of natural resources, a gap – commonly referred to as an economic rent – exists between the value of that resource and the costs of extracting it. In such cases, individuals, be they private sector actors or politicians, have incentives to use political mechanisms to capture these rents' (Humphreys et al. 2007: 4). The most parsimonious explanation of the political resource curse comes from Karl, who argues that when governmental budgets are financed through resource rents, governments have little incentive to tax their populations, and in the absence of taxation, civil society is less likely to demand fiscal accountability, representation or participation (Karl 1997: 14–17). When states are fiscally autonomous from the governed and civil society is politically disengaged, institutional weakness, patronage, corruption, and unresponsive policy-making become business-as-usual (Karl 2007: 264–8). When the pursuit of rents works to undermine a capable and professional institutional apparatus, 'a predatory state eclipses the developmental state' (Sachs and Warner 2001: 836). Limiting unproductive rent-seeking by society and wasteful rent appropriation by the state, therefore, is necessary for building the responsive and institutionalised state apparatus found in successful developers (Thorp et al. 2012: 9–10).

Despite the dysfunctions identified by Karl in Venezuela, Latin America seems to have escaped so far many of the most severe consequences of the resource curse: kleptocracy, dictatorship, and civil war (see Ross 2012; McFerson 2010: 340). Indeed, Lederman and Maloney show there is little evidence for a 'curse' in Latin America, especially between 1820 and 1950 (Lederman and Maloney 2008: 9). However, they also note that the region mostly failed to link resource exports to innovation and human capital formation, as resource-rich economies in the developed world did (Lederman and Maloney 2007: 7–8). Nonetheless, a recent literature has extended arguments about the macro-level resource curse to the micro-level, where it has become evident in the last ten years that resource extraction can fuel intense and sometimes violent disputes in the communities most affected by the extractive process (Arellano-Yanguas 2012; Bebbington 2012; Sawyer and Gomez 2012; Clark and North 2006). In this regard, it is possible to say that for much of its history, Latin America has relied on the exploitation and exportation of natural resources, but it has been relatively ineffective in converting these assets into broad-based economic development, nonetheless avoiding the worst pitfalls of the resource curse.

In theory, the resource nationalism of the mid-2000s offers a new opportunity to better use natural resources for development. Getting the most out of this resource boom is partly about the capture of resource rents; and secondarily about the use to which those rents are put (Boyd 2006: 153). Weak states blighted with the resource curse may be able to extract rents from the sector, but are often unable to use them productively. As Karl puts it, the ability to use rents well is 'at heart, political – a question of power, bargaining, and social justice' (Karl 2007: 258). In other words, resource-led development requires building appropriate institutions, and bargaining with other important social actors (Dietsche 2012: 131). However, most studies examine the historical and path-dependent processes of state-formation that culminated in a state apparatus capable of regulating natural resources in the public interest in some countries, but not in others (Kurtz 2009: 480–1; Crabtree and Crabtree-Condor 2012; Nem Singh 2014). In this regard, states have been categorized as *either* capable *or* incapable of managing their resource wealth, but there has been little consideration of the possibility of movement from one category to another (Kurtz and Brooks 2011: 749; Haber and Menaldo 2011: 2).

Consequently, one of the most theoretically exciting aspects of resource nationalism in Latin America is the extent to which it is the visible manifestation of a broader concern with rebuilding the developmental state, or at the very least, rebuilding the state's capacity to regulate and intervene in the economy. It is important, however, to keep in mind the diversity of policy responses that constitute resource nationalism in the region. At a minimum, countries have enhanced their capacity to capture, distribute, and consume rents through new taxation regimes and more-or-less universal social programmes, as expressed in the concept of *neo-extractivism* (Gudynas 2012). Other countries have pursued more ambitious institution-building programmes (Nem Singh 2014: 348). As Nem Singh and Bourgouin put it, 'Undeniably, the export bonanza represents a new opportunity for resource-abundant countries to rethink their models of development' (Nem Singh and Bourgouin 2013: 5).

In this respect, our focus on the causes and character of new configurations of resource policy is also a focus on the forces and constraints behind a nascent state-building project in the region. The resource sector is an ideal case study for examining the transformation of the state because policy changes in this sector have been particularly pronounced as governments have struggled to re-invent their relationships with firms in order to capture more surplus, push firms to integrate with the domestic economy, and manage the popular backlash and environmental fallout. In contrast to arguments about the resource curse, which focus exclusively on the link between resource abundance and various diseases of the state, this approach to resource nationalism in Latin America takes a more open-ended perspective. It interrogates whether the current policy outcomes in the sector are a window into Latin America's capacity to build capable, professional, embedded, and autonomous developmental states or whether the region will relive its historic dependence on erratic commodity booms without achieving this end (Bulmer-Thomas 1994). Consequently, the focus of this volume is on the state – and the particular nature of the policies that have emerged as a result of resource nationalism. We believe that this first step is necessary before it is possible to evaluate the impact of resource nationalism on economic development.

Two decades of legal and regulatory change

Much of the literature on mining and hydrocarbons policy in developing countries has painted a picture of persistent liberalization that was, by the mid-2000s, in obvious disagreement with the facts on the ground. Since that time, resource nationalism in Latin America has been in full swing, and characterized by re-regulation; new strategies for rent appropriation by the state; an increased role for the state in direct production; and an explicit concern for the developmental spillovers from foreign investment in the sector. The purpose of this section is not to interpret or explain these changes, but rather to set the stage for the ensuing discussion by the theoretical and country specialists united in this book. In this regard, we seek only to describe the trends over two decades of legal and regulatory changes in the resource sector that occurred between the early 1990s and 2014, particularly in the countries examined in this book: Bolivia, Brazil, Colombia, Mexico, Peru, and Venezuela.

However, we depart from the standard script, by identifying three distinct phases in the governance of natural resources since the early 1990s, that could

Table 1.1 Overview of mining; oil and gas in Latin America

Country	Mineral Production	Oil and Gas Production	Contribution to GDP	Value of Exports (Minerals and Hydro-carbons)	Mineral Rent as % of Fiscal Revenue‡
Bolivia	Ag = 1,214,025 kg Au = 6,973 kg Cu = 9,449 t Pb = 79,044 t Sn = 19,702 t Zn =389,911 t	Oil (crude) = 15.1 Mb Gas = 18,706 Mm^3	14.65% of GDP (2012) 8% of GDP (1994)	$US 7.6 B in exports (2012)	Mining: 4.2% (2010-12) 0.5% (2000-03) Oil and Gas: 31.8% (2010-12) 11.9% (2000-03)
Brazil	Ag = 36,400 kg Au = 56,670 kg Cu = 223,141 t Fe = 400.82 Mt Li = 7,084 t Pb = 16,953 t Ni = 14.749 Mt Zn = 164,258 t	Oil (crude) = 762.6 Mb Gas = 25,415 Mm^3 Coal = 12.7 Mt	4.5% of GDP (2012) 2% of GDP (1995)	$US 38.7 B in exports (2012)	Mining: 0.8% (2010-12) 0.3% (2000-03) Oil and Gas: 3.0% (2010-12) 2.3% (2000-03
Colombia	Ag = 19,368 kg Au = 66,178 kg Cu = 690 t Fe =173,000 t Ni = 70,000 t	Oil (crude) = 343.7 Mb Gas = 10,900 Mm^3 Coal = 89 Mt	7.7% of GDP (2012) 5% of GDP (1994)	$US 40.1 B in exports (2012)	Mining: 1.6% (2010-12) 0.6% (2000-03) Oil and Gas: 13.1% (2010-12) 5.4% (2000-03)
Mexico	Ag = 5,358,195 kg Bauxite= 96,000t Au =102,802 kg Cu = 439,531 t Fe = 8.047 Mt Mn = 188,294 t Mo = 11,366 t Pb = 238,091 t	Oil (crude) = 930 Mb Gas = 59,470 Mm^3 Coal = 29.9 Mt	8.7% of GDP (2012)* 9.33% of GDP in (1994)	$US 68.5 B in exports (2011)**	Mining: 1.5% (2010-12) 0.3% (2000-03) Oil and Gas: 35.1% (2010-12) 19.8% (2000-03)
Peru	Ag = 3,479,000 kg Au = 161,325kg Cu = 1.197 Mt Fe = 6.791 Mt Mo = 16,790t Pb = 248,659t Sn = 26,105t Zn = 1.280 Mt	Oil (crude) = 24.4 Mb Gas = 11,859 Mm^3 Coal = 0.23 Mt	11.8% of GDP in 2012* 2.7% of GDP in 1994*	$US 31.6 B in exports (2012)	Mining: 8.3% (2010-12) 1.0% (2000-03) Oil and Gas: 7.3% (2010-12) 3.2% (2000-03)
Venezuela	Bauxite= 2 Mt Au = 12,000 kg Fe = 17 Mt Ni = 10,400t	Oil (crude) = 900.9 Mb Gas = 33,800 Mm^3 Coal = 1.3 Mt	26% of GDP (2012)* 24.6% of GDP (1994)*	$US 96.9 B in exports (2012)	Mining (n.d.) Oil and Gas: 41.5% (2010-12) 48.0% (2000-03)

Sources: USGS, 1994–2013. Additional sources include: ‡ ECLAC, 2013b; *World Bank, 2015; **PEMEX 2015.

Notes: Figures from 2012, unless otherwise indicated. Unless explicitly indicated, mineral sector figures include both mining and oil and gas.

be considered a *privatization-nationalization* cycle. These phases partially overlap and cannot be easily periodized with specific dates, but nonetheless constitute identifiably distinct policy periods: a *liberalizing* phase in the early to late-1990s, in which state-dominated resource sectors were opened to foreign investment; a *regulating* phase in the late 1990s to mid-2000s, in which some of the excesses and lacunae of the liberalizing phase were corrected in some countries; and a *re-nationalizing* phase after the mid-2000s, in which states reasserted their role and presence in the sector. The *re-nationalizing* phase is particularly diverse, exhibiting a variety of resource nationalisms from limited (Colombia and Mexico), to moderate (Brazil and Peru), to radical (Bolivia and Venezuela). The explanation of these resource nationalisms is the principal purpose of this book, but here, we seek only to describe the legislative and regulatory framework that characterizes them. Table 1.2 (pp. 16–27) outlines the most important elements of this framework for each of the six country-cases in this book.

It is well established that the governance of natural resources experienced a profound liberalization in the early 1990s, as Latin America was emerging out of the worst decade for development in its independent history, and liberalization and privatization programmes were viewed by most governments as the best way to stimulate economic growth, control inflation, reduce government deficits, and generate the resources to pay down accumulated debt obligations (Bridge 2004). Extractive industries policy reform was part of this agenda, although in many countries of relatively peripheral importance. In this regard, reforms included an ambitious set of liberalization initiatives, intended to encourage new foreign direct investment in exploration and exploitation, and shift the engine of sectoral development from the state to the private sector. The similarity of reforms across the region, which were framed by new foreign investment statutes, and revisions to national mining and energy sector codes, have caused it to be labelled the 'Latin American Mining Law Model' in that industry (Bastida et al. 2005: 1).

New mining and hydrocarbon legislation in the early 1990s established incentives for private and foreign investment. Key components included the restriction of royalty rates; exemption from various duties, taxes, and administrative fees on imports of capital goods and exports of unprocessed raw materials; deduction of exploration expenses from profits; accelerated amortization (loan costs deducted from profits); and tax stability agreements that guaranteed no increases in taxation over a set period (usually 10 to 30 years). Where the exploitation of minerals or hydrocarbons was the reserve of the state, reforms opened a space for private sector participation. The exact nature of this space varied significantly across the region, but the policy options fall into three categories: the derogation of restrictions on the operation of foreign and private companies in the resource sector, or the limitation of the monopoly rights of state-owned firms; allowing contracting, licencing, or joint ventures between the state and private companies; and the direct privatization of state-owned firms. Privatization was, of course, the most visible element of this transformation.

These reforms had the effect of transferring the risks and rewards of exploration and exploitation activities from the state to the private sector. In conjunction with generous tax and royalty regimes, they provided the incentives for the private sector to invest in finding new reserves and bringing them to production – a task which the state had often failed to realize during the import-substitution period. The results were, in most countries, an important increase in proven and probable reserves, and increased capacity to exploit them. Consequently, mining and hydrocarbon exports increased in volume between 1990 and 2015 (see Table 1.1).

A second phase of reform, which we characterize as *regulating*, occurred principally from the mid-1990s to the mid-2000s, when it became apparent that the mining and hydrocarbon sector required an institutional framework. When the state held a monopoly rights in the extractive industry, which were executed through state-owned firms, regulatory functions were effectively performed by these same companies and the political decisions that affected them. In this regard, the arrival of privately-owned firms as important actors that were independent of state influence, created a need for more substantive regulation. In this regard, the *regulating* phase should be viewed as an attempt to perfect the incentives and address regulatory lacunae of the *liberalizing* phase – but within a broader commitment to liberal and open economies. In particular, legislation responded to growing concern about lack of state oversight in the sector, environmental and social externalities of extractive activities, as well as concerns over the contribution of these enclaves to local development.

By the late 1990s and early 2000s, concern over the environmental externalities of large-scale mining and hydrocarbon extraction had begun to build. Pressure from local and international activists on environmental issues, as well as increasing social conflict between industry and communities contributed to institutional experimentation, including efforts to legislate a more robust environmental licencing regime (Bebbington and Bury 2013; Jaskoski 2014). While it must be stated that concerns over the efficacy of this regime remain, most of the countries considered in this volume strengthened environmental oversight of the sector with new legislation, enhanced the Environmental Impact Assessment (EIA) process, and established requirements to consult affected populations.

The third phase we identify, and with which this volume is principally concerned, is what we call the *re-nationalization* phase. Resource nationalism is often associated with post-neoliberal policies in the region – although the exact nature of those policies has proved notoriously difficult to define (Beasley-Murray et al. 2010: 9; MacDonald and Ruckert 2009: 7). In most cases, macro-economic policies followed some of the prescriptions of the Washington Consensus while innovating in social policy provision and the extension of citizenship rights (Moreno-Brid and Paunovic 2010; Reygadas and Filgueira 2010). Despite the rhetoric of continued openness to foreign direct investment, governments also began to experiment with hard bargaining with private firms in a wide range of industries – including the extractive sector (Haslam 2010a). Indeed, the increasing dependence of governments on resource rents for social programming may be the defining feature of post-neoliberalism (see Gudynas 2012).

In Latin America, tax revenues as a percentage of GDP increased across the region, during the period from 2000 to 2011, thanks in part to a favourable economic environment and resource rents (ECLAC 2013a: 12–14). In the 2000s, most governments reformed royalties and other taxes in order to increase the 'take' from extractive industry, and in some cases distribute the benefits more widely to subnational governments (see Table 1.1). Important royalty reforms that increased the level of taxation occurred in Bolivia (2005), Brazil (2010), Ecuador (2010), Colombia (2011), Peru (2011), and Mexico (2014). Other countries have used special taxes, or changes to the income tax rate to extract more rent, notably Argentina through export duties (2005), and Chile and Peru with 'special taxes' specific to mining (ECLAC 2013a: 16). Additionally, some governments have used political pressure to encourage firms to increase their 'voluntary' contributions to economic and social development, often at the subnational level.

Governments also increased their appropriation of rent through equity stakes in extractive industries, particularly in hydrocarbons (ECLAC 2013a: 16). In some cases, this has meant outright nationalization, but in most cases, what is commonly called nationalization is in fact 'forced divestment' of privately-held shares to the government (Kobrin 1980). Some of the most prominent examples included Venezuela's 2001 requirement that private companies in petroleum exploitation 'migrate' to joint venture contracts with the state, transferring 50% (and in 2005, 60%) of the equity; Bolivia's nationalization of the hydrocarbon sector (May 2006), which required the transfer of 51% ownership; and Argentina's nationalization of 51% of YPF-Repsol in 2012.

Another significant component of the re-nationalization phase of the mid-2000s is the conscious effort to re-build the state and its role in the economy and society. This has been particularly evident in the creation of state-owned enterprises (SOEs) throughout Latin America. Public declarations by political figures have certainly associated forced divestment with the development of capable state-owned corporations, as was Bolivia's 2006 hydrocarbons nationalization with the re-creation of YPFB (Haslam 2010a: 223). It is less clear that state-owned companies like YPFB have been able to develop independent business capacity (Kaup, 2010, 126). Nonetheless, many governments have actively created new SOEs, or reactivated defunct ones, to manage existing or new resources.

It is important to recognize, however, that the creation of state-owned enterprises and joint ventures with SOEs, especially through the forced divestment of privately-held shares has been, predominantly, a rent-appropriating strategy. In this regard, we should be careful not to overestimate the importance of this policy for building a capable, autonomous, and developmental state. Furthermore, it is notable that efforts to rebuild the state through various state-owned enterprises have not substituted for private enterprise, as was the tendency in the ISI period. Instead, the private sector retains an important role, even in the 'radical' cases of resource nationalism, of providing the capital, technology and management expertise to exploit the resources. While, states have used SOEs to increase the 'government take', with few exceptions, they remain dependent on private capital, especially in the expertise-intensive exploration phase. From the state's perspective, the relationship between the state and private capital is complementary, and as a result, most governments continue to maintain sufficiently attractive conditions for private enterprise.

One of the most interesting transformations of the post-neoliberal period of resource nationalism is the state's increased role in directly managing the economic and social spillovers of extraction. While governments continue to respect some principles of the neoliberal package, arguments about the natural 'trickle down' of economic growth have been widely rejected in favour of approaches that see the state playing an active role in promoting economic spillovers and managing negative externalities. In terms of spillovers, we see a wide variety of policies in the region, including decentralization of mining revenues to subnational governments; the creation of funds to invest in alternatives to mining; the promotion of 'voluntary' contributions by firms to local economic development; and programmes to develop mining suppliers (including various degrees of legal obligation to substitute for imports).

The preceding section showed that within the broad tendency to resource nationalism in Latin America, it is also important to recognize the diversity of policy responses. The principal task of the chapters united in this book is to understand the factors that explain this diversity of resource nationalisms across the region. The following chapters analyse these factors in detail, and apply them to specific country-cases.

Structure of the book

This collection is structured into two main sections. The first section examines the political, institutional, and economic factors that affect the likelihood of nationalization and regulation in the oil/gas and mining sectors. This section examines the role of commodity prices; the new industrial policy in the post-neoliberal era; changes in the nature of state-firm bargaining; and the new context of regionalism and the left's rise to power. In the second section, Latin American country-cases have been organized according to groups exhibiting *limited change* (Colombia and Mexico); *intermediate change* (Brazil and Peru); and *radical change* (Bolivia and Venezuela). With two countries in each group we enhance direct comparability, as well as showing the diversity of responses to resource nationalism across the three groups.

In Chapter 2, Samuel K. Gayi and Janvier D. Nkurunziza examine the trends in mineral, ore and metal prices over the last decade. They underline the cyclical nature of resource nationalism and its association with the high point of the commodity price cycle. The authors show that price increases were driven by industrial growth and the need for minerals, particularly from China, although other factors such as low interest rates in the US and the 'financialization' of commodities markets remain relevant. Gayi and Nkurunziza set the stage for the ensuing discussion by showing how increases in commodity prices create a revenue management challenge for governments, as well as incentives to demand a 'fairer' distribution of revenue from companies.

In Chapter 3, Vlado Vivoda examines bargaining between host governments and multinational corporations, over the distribution of benefits from extractive industry. His chapter focuses on corporate responses to resource nationalism – and how the changing rules of the game undermined the power of international oil companies (IOCs). Drawing on the obsolescing bargain literature, Vivoda shows how the resurgence of resource nationalism in the 2000s was associated with a problematic conjuncture for IOCs of rising costs and declining returns on investment, competition with nationally-based oil companies, and declining access to reserves, which resulted in a shift of bargaining power towards host governments.

In Chapter 4, Anil Hira examines contemporary economic thinking about industrial policy in Latin America and its pertinence to resource nationalism. He calls this new thinking 'industrial policy lite'. Based on the new institutional economics, industrial policy lite legitimated combining neoliberal macro-economic fundamentals with social spending and limited interventions in areas of comparative advantage. Hira points to three kinds of industrial policy models in the region: a conservative (neoliberal) model based on existing comparative advantages in resources; a moderate middle ground which combines a liberal macro-environment with increased rent appropriation, and pro-poor public expenditure; and a 'Bolivarian' model based on enhanced control of the resource sector and redistributional politics. The changing economic ideas embodied in industrial policy lite have contributed to a greater role for the state in managing economic development, which characterizes many of the resource nationalisms in Latin America.

In Chapter 5, Pablo Heidrich looks at the interplay between the external and internal trends that have made possible in Latin America a resurgence of resource nationalism. The main external factor has been the rise of China and other Asian economies, configuring a different and more positive international context for Latin American commodity exporters, particularly those with comparative advantages in extractive industries. The internal factors include a clear change in political sign from neoliberal to populist and left-of-centre administrations with more state- and less market-oriented perspectives in regards to economic development. The combination of a common, more favourable external context and roughly similar political perspectives have translated into a post-hegemonic brand of regionalism that leverages natural resources to exercise diplomacy, as seen in the Petrocaribe and ALBA initiatives, as well as UNASUR's goal of infrastructure integration across South America.

In Chapter 6, Eduardo Gudynas examines the relationship between South America's progressive governments and resource nationalism. He shows that these new left governments struggle with balancing the contradictions inherent in extractivist models of development. Progressivism depends on natural resource extraction for growth, revenue and pro-poor social programmes, but it also has to face the negative consequences of this strategy. Thus, Gudynas shows that South America's extractivisms are characterized by a new form of state, the Compensatory State, which is obliged to compensate the population for the negative environmental and social consequences of extractive industry. This balancing act is inherently unstable and contradictory and the state must constantly struggle to reconcile growth with social legitimation through compensatory measures. The embrace of extractivisms is also problematic in ideological terms: it sustains contemporary progressivism, but it also represents an abandonment of the left's commitment, while in opposition, to do away with the commodification of social life under neoliberalism. Gudynas reminds us of the social dimension of resource nationalism, which constitutes a logic that pushes the state to extract more and more revenue from the exploitation of natural resources.

In the second part of the volume, we have organized the chapters according to the degree of resource nationalism experienced by each. Broadly speaking we have three categories: relatively liberal regimes that largely sidestepped the regional trends of resource nationalism (Colombia and Mexico); intermediate cases that pursued moderate programmes of resource nationalism (Brazil and Peru); and the radical cases (Bolivia and Venezuela), which not only sought to increase the government take, but which also engaged in state-building projects, and constitutionalized this transformation. The authors of these chapters explain why their countries adopted more or less radical approaches to resource national-ism. By bringing diverse cases together, we seek to explain the variation in resource nationalist policies seen across the region.

Liberal cases

The first two case studies included in this volume are countries that have been committed to liberal economic recipes, and which have only engaged, in a limited manner, the resource nationalism that swept the region. In Chapter 7, Carlos Caballero Argáez and Sebastián Bitar examine Colombia, a country with one of the strongest liberal traditions in Latin America, which has privi-leged respect for contracts with private actors. The state has been directly involved in extractive industry, through state-owned enterprises such as ECOPETROL. However, the authors explain that the Colombian government finds itself in a precarious position of being relatively dependent on resource exports (coal and petroleum), while being relatively poorly endowed with resources. For this reason, and despite rising commodity prices, the govern-ment committed to a liberal policy regime designed to encourage foreign investors to increase exploration activities in the hope of proving new reserves.

In Chapter 8, Juan Carlos Moreno-Brid and Alicia Puyana examine President Peña Nieto's reforms to the oil and mining sectors in 2013. Until these reforms, Mexico was largely out of step with the resource nationalism of the rest of the region. Similar to Colombia, the Mexican state was highly dependent on resource revenues, and faced the prospect of rapidly declining reserves and production. The authors show that concerns about the decline of production led to the *Pacto por Mexico*, which sought to make PEMEX more efficient, and allowed it to associate with foreign capital. Mexico also increased taxation on the mining sector in 2014, which brought taxation levels in line with international standards, but as Moreno-Brid and Puyana lament, too late to benefit from the commodities supercycle which peaked in 2008. Additionally, they underline that Mexico, despite the recent reforms, has been unable to integrate the resource sector into a broader policy for industrial transformation.

Intermediate cases

In Chapter 9, Jewellord Nem Singh and Eliza Massi examine Brazil's resource nationalism as a particular manifestation of post-neoliberal development policy. They point out the uniqueness of the Brazilian case, which has, through the creation of state-owned companies like *Petrobras*, *Companhia Vale do Rio Doce* (Vale) and *Petrosal*, sought to link resources to a national industrialization strategy. Nem Singh and Massi describe how, during the second term of President Luiz Inácio 'Lula' da Silva's government (2007–2011), state intervention was consolidated in natural resources. The result was a resource nationalist agenda which envisioned a new production-sharing regime for the newly discovered pre-salt reserves, the creation of the SOE *Petrosal*, a social fund, and plan for distributing rents across different levels of government. Brazil's liberalization of its resource sector built efficient, internationally competitive companies, while maintaining their role as contributors to the state's developmental and industrialization project.

In Chapter 10, Javier Arellano-Yanguas examines President Ollanta Humala's mining policy in Peru, and the limits to reform in a country that he describes as being caught between the dual imperatives of facilitating mining investment and better regulation. Arellano-Yanguas identifies both structural and conjunctural factors as important to the policies chosen. Humala's doubts about his own electoral partners and the absence of coherent proposals for change, led him to trust liberal voices in his cabinet, which saw increased mining investment as the sources of employment, revenue, and progressive social spending. Combined with the fragmented institutionality of the Peruvian state, in which the mining lobby and economic and mining ministries retained predominant influence, substantive change was limited to a 'patchwork of disjointed proposals'. In this regard, resource nationalism in Peru constituted a set of policies that were partly incoherent, and of relatively minor impact on the mining industry.

Radical cases

In Chapter 11, Lorenzo Pellegrini looks at the *discourse* of resource nationalism in Evo Morales' Bolivia. In particular he examines the tension between a government discourse that portrays resource nationalism as the culmination of an anti-imperialist struggle that seeks authentic and fairly-distributed development; and related efforts to promote indigenous values such as *vivir bien* (living well) and political autonomy. Pellegrini shows how these contractions were embodied in legislation such as the new Constitution (2009), which embraced *vivir bien*, while simultaneously pursuing increased extraction, processing and industrialization of natural resources. Pellegrini argues that the discourse of resource nationalism transcends, to a certain extent, these divisions and contradictions. In this regard, he shows that resource nationalism is not an economic strategy, *per se*, so much as a discursive strategy employed by proponents and opponents of extractivism to leverage legitimacy and influence.

In Chapter 12, Daniel Hellinger assesses the resource nationalism of the Chávez government in Venezuela. Taking issue with the conventional assessment of Bolivarian resource nationalism, he shows that it was not as radical as often believed. Despite the '21st century socialist project', which required foreign companies to 'migrate' into joint ventures with the state, Chávez increased the country's reliance on foreign capital, technology and financing in the oil sector. In this regard, Hellinger locates the resource nationalism of the Chávez government within a historically nationalist project that had previously culminated in the creation of *Petróleos de Venezuela* (PDVSA) in 1975, and which was partially undone by the opening and liberalization of the early-mid 1990s. In this regard, Chávez's project was an attempt to re-embed oil resources in a national space, where they directly served the interests of the nation. However, Hellinger questions the sustainability of a project that depends on high oil prices, and which is suffering from lack of investment from foreign companies and PDVSA.

Conclusion

We conclude the book in Chapter 13, with an attempt to draw these arguments together, and answer the question we posed at the beginning of this chapter: 'What explains the range of approaches (limited, moderate, radical) to resource nationalism in Latin America after the mid-2000s?' We develop a framework that emphasizes how changes in key factors, at the international, domestic, and industry level create constraints and opportunities to engage in resource nationalism. Through an analysis of the six country-cases included in this volume, we show that variation in resource nationalisms, from limited, to moderate, to radical, can be explained by a combination of factors. Resource nationalism in contemporary Latin America is the most important policy change that has occurred since liberalization in the 1990s, and many respects, defines the post-neoliberal model. Understanding the variations that occur in practice across the region, is fundamental to understanding the political economy of development.

Table 1.2 Key extractive sector regulation, 1990–2014 (selected countries)

Country	Liberalizing (protection and promotion of foreign investment in the sector)	Regulating (response to technical problems with liberal regime; extension of oversight)	Re-nationalizing (asserts state's right to own, tax and direct the extraction of natural resources for development)
Bolivia (mining and hydrocarbons)	Investment Statute, Law No. 1182 (1990) • Liberalized restrictions on FDI Supreme Decree 23230-A (1992) • Privatization of COMIBOL (Corporación Minera de Bolivia) assets Hydrocarbon Law 1689 (1996) • Privatized YPFB (Yacimientos Petroleros Fiscales de Bolivia) • Administers permits for exploration and export • Royalties reduced to 18% of gross production (from 50%) for new investments Mining Code, Law 1777 (1997) • Allowed state-owned companies to form joint ventures with private companies • COMIBOL mines leased to and operated by private interests • Tax code for companies reformed	Environment Law No. 1333 (1992) • General framework for conservation of the environment Popular Participation Law No. 1551 (1994) • Responsibilities transferred to municipalities and rural organizations; fiscal decentralization of tax revenue to municipalities (20%) and public universities (5%) EIAs required for new projects and upgrading (1996) National Development Plan (2006–2011), Supreme Decree 29,272 (2007) • Framework for use of revenues derived from nationalization (development, cultural, democratic decentralization) Framework Law No.300 of Mother Earth and Integrated Development for Living Well (2012) • Companies liable for damaging the environment	New Hydrocarbons Law No. 3058 (2005) • Replaces 1996 Legislation • Direct Hydrocarbons Tax (IDH) imposes a 50% royalty on hydrocarbon production • New contracts replace "risk-sharing" model • Revenue shared with Departments Supreme Decree No. 28701 (2006) • Nationalization of hydrocarbons (51% ownership and 4 of 7 seats on the board) COMIBOL restarts operations (2006) • 4,900 miners transferred from cooperatives to employees after taking over Huanuni tin mine Mining Code amendment Law No. 3787 (2007) • Royalty rates increased for all mining and industrial processes using minerals • Revenues distributed 85% to Department, 15% to municipality

Constitution (2009), Plurinational State of Bolivia

- *Natural resources belong to the people, administered by the state*
- *Mixed economy (state, private, community)*
- *Foreign investors cannot receive more favourable treatment than domestic[a]*

Nationalization of Mining, Supreme Decree No. 0726 (2010)

- *Companies required to move from concessions to public-private contracts*

Law on Investment Promotion, No. 516 (2014)[a]

- *Establishes principles for investor-state relationship that envision a developmental role for the firm, and state dominance in strategic sectors*

Mining and Metallurgy Law No. 535 (replaces Law No. 1777) (2014)

- *Multinationals cannot register deposits as assets*
- *Mining co-operatives cannot form partnerships with private companies*
- *Bolivians can form joint ventures with COMIBOL*

(Continued)

Table 1.2 Key extractive sector regulation, 1990–2014 (selected countries) (Continued)

Country	Liberalizing (protection and promotion of foreign investment in the sector)	Regulating (response to technical problems with liberal regime; extension of oversight)	Re-nationalizing (asserts of state's right to own, tax and direct the extraction of natural resources for development)
Brazil (mining and hydrocarbons)	Constitutional amendments No. 5 and No. 9 (1995) • *Restrictions on participation of foreign firms in natural resources removed* • *Petrobras can enter joint ventures and invest abroad* Law No. 9314 (1996) amends Mining Code • *Defines state role in granting concessions* • *Licencing restricted to industrial minerals* • *More prominent role for private firms* Decree No. 1510 (1995) • *Privatizatioin of Companhia Vale do Rio Doce (CVRD) (effected in 1997)* Decree No. 9478, Petroleum Law (1997) • *Petrobras monopoly limited* • *Opens sector to private investment (concession model)*	Decree No. 97632 (1989) – rehabilitation of areas affected by mining; use of mercury prohibited by artisanal operations CONAMA (National Council of the Environment) Resolution No. 9 and 10 (1990) – establishes environmental licencing regime CONAMA Resolution No. 237 – defines procedures for environmental licencing (1997) Law No. 9605 (1998) – sanctions against environmental damage Decree 4340 (2002) • *Establishes three kinds of environmental licences (preliminary; installation; operational)* Decree 6848 (2009) modifies Decree 4340 • *Sets a 0.5% limit on environmental impact fee*	1988 Constitution • *Only domestic firms to operate in all phases of resource exploration* Royalties established by Compensation for Exploiting Mineral Resources (CFEM) Law No. 7990 (1989) • *Establishes federal royalty rates (up to 3% of net income; rates vary by mineral)* • *Allocates shares of royalties to municipalities, states, and federal government* Law No. 9993 (2000) • *Federal share of CFEM directed to fund technological innovation and the Brazilian Environmental Agency (IBAMA)* Creation of Empresa Brasileira de Administração de Petróleo e Gás Natural S.A. - Pré-Sal Petróleo, S.A (Petrosal), Law No. 12304 (2010) to govern production-sharing agreements

- *Petrobras capitalization through grant of unlicenced offshore pre-salt oil reserves, Law No. 12276 (2010)*

Law 12.351 (2010), Production-sharing for offshore pre-salt reserves

- *State asserts subsoil rights*
- *30% minimum participation for the state*
- *Establishes a Social Fund to manage revenue from pre-salt reserves (2010)*

Mining Reform (under consideration in 2015)[b]

- *Creation of new regulatory agency*
- *Public auction of concessions*
- *Incentives for national content*
- *Increased royalties and transfers to municipal level*

- *Creates regulatory agency – National Petroleum Agency (ANH)*
- *Defines petroleum royalties, including standard 10% ad valorum tax; and higher "special participations" for highly productive fields[e]*
- *Royalties distributed to states and municipalities*

Colombia (mining and hydrocarbons)	Mining Code, Decree 2655 (1988)	Ministry of Environment created, Law No. 99 (1993)

- *Subsoil resources property of the state*
- *Cannot be exploited without title granted by the Ministry of Mines and Energy*

Law 141 (1994)**

- *Creates National Royalty Fund (FNR)*
- *Distribution of royalties to departments and municipalities*

(Continued)

Table 1.2 Key extractive sector regulation, 1990–2014 (selected countries) (Continued)

Country	Liberalizing (protection and promotion of foreign investment in the sector)	Regulating (response to technical problems with liberal regime; extension of oversight)	Re-nationalizing (asserts of state's right to own, tax and direct the extraction of natural resources for development)
Colombia (mining and hydrocarbons)	Promotion of FDI in oil and gas, Decree 266 (1999)	Environmental Management Plan, adopted by Ministry of the Environment (1999)	
	• Royalty relief, rapid environmental permits	• Covers prospecting (Res. 1167); mining and cement (Res. 1168); industrial minerals (Res. 1169); sedimentary materials (Res. 1170); gold (Res. 1171 and 1172)	
	• reduction in ECOPETROL's participation from 50–30%		
	Privatization of CARBOCOL (Empresa Colombiana de Carbón Ltda.) (2000)	National Hydrocarbon Agency (ANH) created (2003)	
	Mining Law No. 685 (2001)		
	• Subsoil resources property of the state	• Responsible for assigning concessions and contracts, collecting royalties	
	• Concessions to be granted for 30 years, with option to renew		
	• Allows est. of reserves for indigenous and artisanal mining	Ministry of Environment, Housing and Territorial Development created by Law No. 216 (2003)	
	Law No. 756 on royalties (2002) (modifies Law No. 141 of 1994)	• Authority responsible for the environment	
	• Eliminate fixed royalty of 20%, replaced with variable rate 8–25%		

Colombia	Presidential Decree 1760 (2003)	Amendment 22 of Law No. 685 (Mining Law) (2009)

Presidential Decree 1760 (2003)

- Strips ECOPETROL of regulatory functions which are transferred to ANH (Agencia Nacional de Hidrocarburos)
- Requirement for joint ventures with ECOPETROL eliminated

ANH presents new contract model for hydrocarbons (2004)

- Concession with royalty awarded to investors assuming total risk

Capitalization of ECOPETROL, Law No. 1118 (2006)

- Public offering of 11.5%; permits autonomous development of enterprise

Amendment 22 of Law No. 685 (Mining Law) (2009)

- Concession applicants must identify if artisanal mining exists in the zone

Legislative Act 05 (2011)**

- General System of Royalties (GSR) replaces (FNR)
- Centralizes royalty revenue, recognizes right of subnational territories to 10% of all revenue

MME resolution No. 180102 (2012)

- Defines strategic minerals and areas available for concession

---

Mexico (mining and hydrocarbons)

SEMIP (Secretariat for Parastatal Energy, Mines and Industry) Regulations (1990)

- Flexibilize foreign ownership restrictions in 1975 Mining Code by permitting exploration and production trusts

Elimination of mineral production tax (1991)

Mining Law (1992)

- Privatization of state-owned firms and their reserves

General Law of Ecological Balance and Environmental Protection (1988)

- Requires permits for mining and exploration
- EIAs required for major projects

Federal Law Concerning Water Rights (1992)

- Regulates water discharge from mining
- Fees not required if discharge meets CONAGUA (National Council on Water) quality standards

Mining Law Reforms (2014)

- Concession payments reformed to account for value of production (rather than area under concession)
- New tax of 7.5% on sales
- New tax of 0.5% on gross revenue of gold, silver and platinum mines
- Revenue sharing between federal government and states/municipalities [c]

(Continued)

Table 1.2 Key extractive sector regulation, 1990–2014 (selected countries) (Continued)

Country	Liberalizing (protection and promotion of foreign investment in the sector)	Regulating (response to technical problems with liberal regime; extension of oversight)	Re-nationalizing (asserts of state's right to own, tax and direct the extraction of natural resources for development)
Mexico (mining and hydrocarbons)	• Permitted FDI ownership of 100% through 30-year trusts • Greater legal security for concessions • Private participation in strategic minerals permitted (except oil and gas, uranium) Privatization of state-owned mining companies (1992-1993) Foreign Investment Law (1993) • Eliminated local content and technology transfer requirements [c] Reform to Implementing Regulation of Art. 27 of the Constitution (1995) • Permits private participation in gas transmission, distribution and storage (previously reserved to PEMEX) Mining Regulations (revisions) (1999) • Reduction of red-tape Pacto por México, Energy and Oil Reforms (2014)	SEMARNAT (Secretariat of Environment and Natural Resources) Norms 120-ECOL (1997) – establishes environmental protection for mining, clarified in 1999. SEMARNAT Regulation of EIAs (2000) • EIAs required for plant improvements, pipelines and mines, and must be approved by SEMARNAT Reform of Mining Law (2005) • Modernization of various procedures • Establishment of Mexican Geological Service (SGM)	

	Constitutional amendments,: • Art. 25 introduces concept of "productive state enterprise" • Art. 27. Elimination of PEMEX's monopoly in oil, associations allowed with private enterprise • Art. 28. Creation of a "Mexican Petroleum Fund for Stabilization and Development (FMPED)" to administer oil revenues Hydrocarbons Revenue Law (2014) • Sliding scale of royalties depending on profitability of the field and price of oil or gas.		Supreme Decree no. 015-2004-PGM (2004) • *Use mining revenue to promote local social development* Petróleos del Perú (PETROPERÚ) renovated, Law No. 28244 (2004) • *Authorized to explore and produce hydrocarbons (upstream activities)* Mining Royalties Law No. 28258 (2004) • *Establishes 1-3% royalty on sales (minus operational costs)* • *Revenues to be distributed in mining regions*
Peru (mining and hydrocarbons)	Legislative Decree No. 662 (1991) • *Protects and promotes FDI* • *Allows foreign investors unrestricted access to all sectors* Decree No. 708, Promotion of Investment in Mining (1991) • *Stability Contracts signed since 1993 based on Decrees 662, 708, 757.* General Mining Law, Supreme Decree No. 014 (1992)	Environmental Code, Legislative Decree No. 613 (1990) Supreme Decree No. 016-93-EM (1993) • *Regulation of 1990 Code, establishes emissions standards and sustainable development model in mining* Canon Law No. 27506 (2002) • *Transferred 50% of mining taxes to regions and municipalities (modified 2003–4)* Fiscal Decentralization, Legislative Decree 955 (2004)	

(Continued)

Table 1.2 Key extractive sector regulation, 1990–2014 (selected countries) (Continued)

Country	Liberalizing (protection and promotion of foreign investment in the sector)	Regulating (response to technical problems with liberal regime; extension of oversight)	Re-nationalizing (asserts of state's right to own, tax and direct the extraction of natural resources for development)
Peru (mining and hydrocarbons)	• Protection to mining ventures and contracts • Established "canon minero" (right of subnational jurisdictions to 20% of mining taxes) Constitution (1993) • Equal protection for foreign and domestic investors Privatization of CENTROMIN (Empresa Minera del Centro de Peru S.A.) (1993) Creation of Perúpetro S.A., Law No. 26221 (1993) • Promotes FDI, negotiates, signs and administers hydrocarbon contracts Law 26505 (1995) • Right to use land in exchange for compensation (Art. 7) • Permitted sale of communal lands (Art.11)	General Environment Law No. 28611 (2005) • Empowers Ministry of the Environment to coordinate with subnational governments Legislative Decree 1013 creates the Ministry of Environment, MINAM (2008) • Separates environmental functions from the Ministry of Mines and Energy (MINEM) Supreme Decree No. 28-2008-EM / Ministerial Resolution No. 304-2008 MEM/DM (2008) • Establishes regulations for citizen participation in EIAs National System of Environmental Evaluation and Supervision Law No. 29325 (2009) • Creates OEFA (Organization for Environmental Evaluation and Supervision)]	Strengthening and Modernizing PETROPERÚ Law No. 28244 (2006) • Institutional modernization and expansion into downstream activities (petrochemicals, derivatives, energy) Mining Program of Solidarity with the People (PMSP), Supreme Decree No. 071-2006-EM (2006) • State agrees on "voluntary" contributions by major mining firms in lieu of taxation Royalty Law Amendment No. 29788 (2011), modifying Law No. 28258 (2004) • New royalty regime to companies without existing tax stability agreements (from 1-12% depending on rate of operational profit, replacing ad valorem calculation) Special Tax on Mining Law No 29789 (2011) • 2-8.4% on operating income (windfall tax)

	Legislative Decree No. 818 (1996) • *Incentives for investing in resources* Hydrocarbons Law No. 26844 (1997) • *Elimination of PETROPERÚ monopoly* Law No. 27623 and Supreme Decree No. 047 (2002) • *Reduction of sales taxes and duties for capital goods imports*	Prior Consultation Law 29785 (2011) • *Indigenous communities have right to consultation before mining investment* Law No. 30011 (2013) • *Facilitates coordination between levels of government* • *Defines sanctions to be applied by OEFA*	Special Levy on Mining Law No. 29790 (2011) • *"Voluntary" tax on mining that applies to companies with tax stability agreements (4–13% on operating income)* "Infrastructure for Taxes" Law No. 30138 (2013) • *Allows companies to deduct investments in infrastructure (made in cooperation with regional authorities) from taxes*
Venezuela (mining and hydrocarbons)	Decree No. 2.095 (1992) • *Equal treatment for foreign and domestic investment, except sectors where the Venezuelan government should hold a majority stake* CVP (Corporación Venezolana de Petroleos S.A.), subsidiary of PDVSA, opens production agreements to the private sector, especially in heavy-crude Orinoco Belt (early 1990s) Privatization of various SOEs, including subsidiaries of state mining company Corporación Venezolana de Guyana (CVG) (1995-1998) Presidential Decree 5.532 (1998) • *Opens gas sector to private investment (processing; transportation; storage; distribution)*	Penal Environmental Law (1992) • *An ELA must be submitted and approved before a mining project can begin* Norms for Environmental Evaluation of Activities Susceptible to Degrading the Environment, Decree No. 1.257 (1996) • *Requires ELA for projects in hydrocarbon and mining sectors* Institutional reorganization (2005) • *Mineral sector responsibilities, including CVG, transferred to new Ministry of Basic Industry and Mining (MIBAM)* Organic Environmental Law No. 5.833 (2006)	Constitution (1999) • *Reserves primary activities in hydrocarbons for the state (Art. 302)* • *State retains all shares of PDVSA (Art. 303)* Mining Law, Decree No. 295 (1999) • *Mineral resources belong to the nation* • *Mining must involve direct participation by the state* • *Establishes royalties for specific minerals* Hydrocarbon Law, Decree No. 1510 (2001) • *Primary activity to be carried out by the state, or a joint venture owned 51% by the state* • *Secondary activities open to private sector under a license and permit regime* • *Arbitration to be conducted in domestic venues (Calvo clause)*

(Continued)

Table 1.2 Key extractive sector regulation, 1990–2014 (selected countries) (Continued)

Country	Liberalizing (protection and promotion of foreign investment in the sector)	Regulating (response to technical problems with liberal regime; extension of oversight)	Re-nationalizing (asserts of state's right to own, tax and direct the extraction of natural resources for development)
Venezuela (mining and hydrocarbons)	Organic Gaseous Hydrocarbons Law, Decree 310 (1999) • Permits domestic and foreign participation in all activities		Royalty payments are 20-30% of production (Orinoco Belt bitumen at lower rate) • Corporate income tax rate raised from 34% to 50% (retroactive to 2000)
	Constitution (1999) • International standards, and national treatment for private investors (Art. 301)		Creation of state mining company: Empresa de Produccion Social Minera Nacional, C.A. (EPS Nacional Minera), Decree No. 4201 (2005)
	Decree 3110 (2004) – redefines Itacama Forest to permit mining (Las Cristinas gold project)		Migration of oil contracts, Decree Law 5.200 (2006) • Contracts signed under "apertura petrolera" deemed illegal under Constitution • Forced migration to 60% state ownership and increase in royalty rates
			Nationalization of cement and steel industry (2008); takeover of Crystallex gold mines (2008); petrochemicals (2009); gold mining (2011)

Organic Law governing Crude Oil Goods and Services (2009)

- *Reserves service activities connected to primary hydrocarbon activity to the state; basis for expropriation of oil services companies*

Windfall profits tax (2008)

- *Increase to royalties to 50% above $70/bbl; 60% (above $100)*
- *Goes to National Development Fund (FONDEN) to fund social programs*
- *Revised in 2011 and 2013*

Sources: USGS, Country Reports, 1994–2013. Other sources include: ** Vargas and Escobar (2011); [a] Brauch, 2014; [b] STRATFOR, 2015; [c] STRATFOR, 2013; [d] Negroponte, 2014; [e] Postali, 2009, 2006.

Note

1 Thanks to anonymous reviewer for this categorization scheme.

Bibliography

Arellano-Yanguas, J. (2012). Mining and conflict in Peru: Sowing the minerals, reaping a hail of stones. In Bebbington, A. (ed.). *Social Conflict, Economic Development and Extractive Industry: Evidence from South America.* London: Routledge, pp. 89–111.

Auty, R. (1993). Sustaining Development in Mineral Economies: The Resource Curse. New York: Routledge.

Auty, R. (2001). Conclusions: resource abundance, growth collapses, and policy. In Auty, R. (ed.). *Resource Abundance and Economic Development.* Oxford: World Institute for Development Economics Research and Oxford University Press, pp. 315–28.

Bastida, A., Irarrázabal, R., and Labo, R. (2005). Mining investment and policy developments: Argentina, Chile and Peru. Unpublished Paper. Available from: http://www.dundee.ac.uk/cepmlp/gateway/index.php?news=28246. [Accessed 30 June 2015].

Beasley-Murray, J., Cameron, M.A., and Hershberg, E. (2010). Latin America's left turns: A tour d'horizon. In Cameron, M.A., and Hershberg, E. (eds). *Latin America's Left Turns: Politics, Policies & Trajectories of Change.* Boulder: Lynne Rienner, pp. 1–20.

Bebbington, A. (2012). Extractive industries, socio-environmental conflicts and political economic transformations in Andean Americas. In Bebbington, A. (ed.). *Social Conflict, Economic Development and Extractive Industry: Evidence from South America.* Milton Park: Routledge, pp. 3–26.

Bebbington, A. and Bury, J. (2013). Political ecologies of the subsoil. In Bebbington, A. and Bury, J. (eds). *Subterranean Struggles: New Dynamics of Mining, Oil and Gas in Latin America.* Austin: University of Texas Press, pp. 1–25.

Berrios, R., Marak, A., and Morgenstern, S. (2011). Explaining hydrocarbon nationalization in Latin America: Economics and political ideology. *Review of International Political Economy* 18 (5), pp. 673–97.

Bierstecker, T.J. (1987). *Multinationals, the State, and Control of the Nigerian Economy.* Princeton, NJ: Princeton University Press.

Boyd, R. (2006). Modes of rent-seeking and economic outcomes: A comparison of Japan and Mexico. In Boyd, R., Galjart, B., & Ngo, T-W. (eds). *Political Conflict and Development in East Asia and Latin America.* New York: Routledge, pp. 148–201.

Brauch, M.D. (2014). Opening the door to foreign investment? An analysis of Bolivia's new investment promotion law. [Online]. Winnipeg: International Institute for Sustainable Development (IIDS). Available from: http://www.iisd.org/itn/2014/08/11/opening-the-door-to-foreign-investment-an-analysis-of-bolivias-new-investment-promotion-law/ [Accessed: 26 July 2015].

Bridge, G. (2004). Mapping the bonanza: Geographies of mining investment in an era of neoliberal reform. *The Professional Geographer* 56 (3), pp. 406–21.

Brunnschweiler, C.N. (2007). Cursing the blessings? Natural resource abundance, institutions, and economic growth. *World Development* 36 (3), pp. 399–419.

Bulmer-Thomas, V. (1994). *The Economic History of Latin America since Independence.* Cambridge: Cambridge University Press.

Campbell, B. (2010). Revisiting the reform process of African mining regimes. *Canadian Journal of Development Studies* 30(1–2), pp. 197–217.

Cardoso, F.H., and Faletto, E. (1979). *Dependency and Development in Latin America.* Berkeley, CA: University of California Press.

Chang., R., Hevia, C., and Loayza, N. (2009). Privatization and nationalization cycles. NBER Working Paper No. 16126. Cambridge, MA: The National Bureau of Economic Research, pp. 57.

Chua, A.L. (1995). The privatization-nationalization cycle: The link between markets and ethnicity in developing countries. *Colombia Law Review* 95(2), pp. 223–303.

Clark, T.D., and North, L. (2006). Mining and oil in Latin America: Lessons from the past, issues for the future. In North, L, Clark, T.D., and Patroni, V. (eds.). *Community Rights and Corporate Responsibility: Canadian Mining and Oil Companies in Latin America.* Toronto: Between the Lines Press, pp. 1–16.

Crabtree, J., and Crabtree-Condor, I. (2012). The politics of extractive industries in the Central Andes. In Bebbington, A. (ed). *Social Conflict, Economic Development and Extractive Industry: Evidence from South America.* Milton Park: Routledge, pp.46–64.

Deacon, T., and Rode, A. (2012). Rent seeking and the resource curse. Working Paper. Santa Barbara: Department of Economics, University of California, pp. 34.

DeLoitte. (2012). *Tracking the Trends 2013. The Top 10 Issues Mining Companies May Face in the Coming Year.* Toronto: DeLoitte.

Dietsche, E. (2012). Institutional change and state capacity in mineral-rich countries. In Hujo, K. (ed.). *Mineral Rents and the Financing of Social Policy.* Basingstoke: Palgrave Macmillan and UNRISD, pp.122–54.

Duncan, R. (2006). Price or politics? An investigation of the causes of expropriation. *The Australian Journal of Agricultural and Resource Economics* 50, pp. 85–101.

Dunning, J.H. (1991). Governments and multinational enterprises: From confrontation to cooperation? *Millennium Journal of International Studies* 20 (2), pp 225–44.

ECLAC (2012). *Panorama de la inversión extranjera directa en América Latina y el Caribe.* Santiago: United Nations and Economic Commission of Latin America and the Caribbean.

ECLAC (2013a). *Fiscal Panorama of Latin America and the Caribbean: Tax Reform and Renewal of the Fiscal Covenant.* Santiago: United Nations and Economic Commission of Latin America and the Caribbean.

ECLAC. (2013b). Natural Resources: Status and Trends towards a Regional Development Agenda in Latin America and the Caribbean. Santiago: United Nations.

Ernst & Young. 2013. *Business Risk Facing Mining and Metals, 2012–2013.* New York, London and Toronto: Ernst & Young.

Evans P.B. (1979). Dependent Development: The Alliance of Multinational, State, and Local Capital in Brazil. Princeton, NJ: Princeton University Press.

Flores-Macias, G. (2012). After Neoliberalism? The Left and Economic Reforms in Latin America. New York: Oxford University Press.

Gajigo, O., Mutambatsere, E., and Ndiaye, G. (2012). Royalty rates in African mining revisited: Evidence from gold mining. *Africa Economic Brief* 3 (6), pp. 1–12.

Galeano, E. (1997). Open Veins of Latin America: Five Centuries of the Pillage of a Continent. New York: New York University Press.

Gallagher, K.P. (2005). Globalization and the nation-state: Reasserting policy autonomy for development. In Gallagher, K.P. (ed.). *Putting Development First: The Importance of Policy Space in the WTO and International Financial Institutions.* London: Zed Book, pp. 1–14.

Gallagher, K.P., and Porzecanski, R. (2010). *The Dragon in the Room: China and the Future of Latin American Industrialization.* Stanford: Stanford University Press.

Grugel, J., and Riggirozzi, P. (2009). The end of the embrace? Neoliberalism and alternatives to neoliberalism in Latin America. In *Governance after Neoliberalism in Latin America*. Basingstoke: Palgrave Macmillan, 1–23.

Gudynas, E. (2012). Estado compensador y nuevos extractivismos: Las ambivalencias del progresismo sudamericano. *Neuva Sociedad* 237, pp. 128–46.

Haber, S., and Menaldo, V. (2011) Do natural resources fuel authoritarianism? A reappraisal of the resource curse. *American Political Science Review* 105 (1), pp. 1–26.

Haslam, P.A. (2010a). Foreign investors over a barrel: Nationalizations and investment policy. In Cameron, M.A., and Hershberg, E. (eds.). *Latin America's Left Turns: Politics, Policies & Trajectories of Change*. Boulder: Lynne Rienner, pp. 209–30.

Haslam, P.A. (2010b). The evolution of the foreign direct investment regime in the Americas. *Third World Quarterly* 31 (7), pp. 1181–203.

Hujo, K. (2012). Introduction and overview: Blessing or curse? Financing social policies in mineral-rich countries. In Hujo, K. (ed.). *Mineral Rents and the Financing of Social Policy*. Basingstoke: Palgrave Macmillan and UNRISD, pp. 3–25.

Humphreys, M., Sachs, J.D., and Stiglitz, J.E (2007). Introduction: What is the problem with natural resource wealth? In Humphreys, M., Sachs, J.D., and Stiglitz, J.E. (eds). *Escaping the Resource Curse*. New York: Colombia University Press, pp. 1–20.

Jaskoski, M. (2014). Environmental licensing and conflict in Peru's mining sector: A path-dependent analysis. *World Development* 64, pp. 873–83.

Jenkins, R.O. (1977). Dependent Industrialization in Latin America: The Automotive Industry in Argentina, Chile, and Mexico. New York: Praeger Publishers.

Karl, T.L. (1997). *The Paradox of Plenty: Oil Booms and Petro-States*. Berkeley: University of California Press.

Karl, T.L. (2007). Ensuring fairness: The case for a transparent fiscal social contract. In Humphreys, M., Sachs, J.D., and Stiglitz, J.E. (eds). *Escaping the Resource Curse*. New York: Colombia University Press, pp. 256–85.

Kaup, B.Z. (2010). A neoliberal nationalization? The constraints on natural-gas-led development in Bolivia. *Latin American Perspectives* 37(3), pp. 123–38.

Kobrin, S.J. (1980). Foreign enterprise and forced divestment in LDCs. *International Organization* 34 (1), pp. 65–88.

Kurtz, M.J. (2009) The social foundations of institutional order: Reconsidering war and the 'resource curse' in third world state building. *Politics & Society* 37 (4), pp. 480–81.

Kurtz, M.J., and Brooks, S. (2011) Conditioning the 'resource curse': Globalization, human capital and growth in oil-rich nations. *Comparative Political Studies* 44 (6), pp. 747–70.

Lederman, D., and Maloney, W.F. (2007). Neither curse nor destiny: Introduction to natural resources and development. In Lederman, D., and Maloney, W.F. (eds.). *Natural Resources: Neither Curse Nor Destiny*. Washington DC: The World Bank and Stanford University Press, pp. 1–12.

Lederman, D., and Maloney, W.F. (2008). In search of the missing resource curse. *Economía* 9 (1), pp. 1–57.

Luo, Y. (2001). Toward a cooperative view of MNC-host government relations: Building blocks and performance indicators. *Journal of International Business Studies* 32 (3), pp. 401–19.

Macdonald, L., and Ruckert, A. (2009). Post-neoliberalism in the Americas: An introduction. In Macdonald, L., and Ruckert, A. (eds.). *Post-neoliberalism in the Americas*. Basingstoke: Palgrave Macmillan, pp. 1–18.

Mcferson, H.M. (2010). Extractive industries and African democracy: Can the 'resource curse' be exorcised? *International Studies Perspectives* 11, pp. 335–53.

Mehlum, H., Moene, K., & Torvik, R. (2006) Cursed by resources or institutions? *The World Economy* 29 (8), pp. 1117–31.

Moran, T.H. (1974). Multinational Corporations and the Politics of Dependence: Copper in Chile. Princeton: Princeton University Press.

Moran, T.H. (2001). Parental Supervision: The New Paradigm for Foreign Direct Investment and Development. Washington DC: The Peterson Institute.

Moreno-Brid, J.C., and Paunovic, I. (2010). Macroeconomic policies of the new left: Rhetoric and reality. In Cameron, M.A., and Hershberg, E. (eds.). *Latin America's Left Turns: Politics, Policies & Trajectories of Change*. Boulder: Lynne Rienner, pp. 193–208.

Negroponte, D.V. (2014). Mexico's energy reforms become law. Brookings Briefs, 14 August. [Online]. Available from: http://www.brookings.edu/research/articles/2014/08/14-mexico-energy-law-negroponte. [Accessed: 26 July 2015].

Nem Singh, J.T. (2014). Towards post-neoliberal resource politics? The international political economy (IPE) of oil and copper in Brazil and Chile. *New Political Economy* 19 (3), pp. 329–58.

Nem Singh, J.T., and Bourgouin, F. (2013). Introduction: Resource governance at a time of plenty. In Nem Singh, J.T., and Bourgouin, F. (eds). *Resource Governance and Developmental States in the Global South*. Basingstoke: Palgrave Macmillan, pp. 1–18.

PEMEX (2015). *Indicadores Petroleros*, 27(2), pp. 29. [Online]. Available from: http://www.ri.pemex.com/index.cfm?action=content&sectionID=16&catID=12155&media=pdf. [Accessed 29 July 2015].

Postali, A.S. (2009). Petroleum royalties and regional development in Brazil: The economic growth of recipient towns. *Resources Policy*, 34, pp. 205–13.

Reygadas, L., and Filgueira, F. (2010). Inequality and the incorporation crisis: The left's social policy toolkit. In Cameron, M.A., and Hershberg, E. (eds.). *Latin America's Left Turns: Politics, Policies & Trajectories of Change*. Boulder: Lynne Rienner, pp., 171–91.

Ross, M.L. (2012). The Oil Curse: How Petroleum Wealth Shapes the Development of Nations. Princeton: Princeton University Press.

Sachs, J.D., and Warner, A.M. (2001) The curse of natural resources. *European Economic Review* 45, pp. 827–38.

Sánchez-Ancochea, D., and Shadlen, K. (2008). Introduction: Globalization, integration, and economic development in the Americas. In Sánchez-Ancochea, D., and Shadlen, K. (eds.). The Political Economy of Hemispheric Integration. Basingstoke: Palgrave Macmillan, pp. 1–25.

Sawyer, S., and Gomez, E.T. (2012). Transnational governmentality in the context of resource extraction. In S. Sawyer and E.T. Gomez (eds). The Politics of Resource Extraction: Indigenous Peoples, Multinational Corporations, and the State. Basingstoke: Palgrave Macmillan and UNRISD, pp. 1–8.

STRATFOR (2015). Why Brazil cannot afford to stall its mining law any longer. [Online]. Available from: https://www.stratfor.com/analysis/why-brazil-cannot-afford-stall-its-mining-law-any-longer. [Accessed: 26 July 2015].

STRATFOR (2013). Mining in Mexico faces reforms. STRATFOR, 22 May [Online]. Available from: https://www.stratfor.com/analysis/mining-mexico-faces-reforms. [Accessed: 26 July 2015].

Stopford, J., and Strange, S. (1991). Rival States, Rival Firms: Competition for World Market Shares. Cambridge: Cambridge University Press.

Thorp, R., Battistelli, S., Guichaoua, Y., Orihuela, J.C., and Paredes, M. (2012). Introduction. In Thorp, R., Battistelli, S., Guichaoua, Y., Orihuela, J.C., and Paredes, M. (eds). The Developmental Challenges of Mining and Oil. Basingstoke: Palgrave Macmillan, pp. 1–18.

UNCTAD (2012). World Investment Report, 2012. Towards a New Generation of Investment Policies. Geneva: United Nations Commission for Trade and Development.

USGS (US Geological Survey) (various years). Minerals Yearbook, Vol. III. Area Reports: International. (Washington D.C.: US Geological Survey). Available from: http://minerals.usgs.gov/minerals/pubs/country/sa.html. [Accessed: 19 April 2015].

Wells, L.T. Jr. (1998). Good and fair competition: Does the foreign direct investor face still other risks in emerging markets? In Moran, T.H. (ed.). Managing International Political Risk. Malden, Mass: Basil Blackwell Publishers, pp. 15–43.

Vargas, M.H., and Escobar, F.A. (2011). El Federalismo Fiscal y El Proceso de Decentralización Fiscal en Colombia. Available from: http://aprendeenlinea.udea.edu.co/revistas/index.php/red/article/viewFile/18416/15836. [Accessed 29 July 2015].

Vernon, R. (1971). Sovereignty at Bay. New York. Penguin.

World Bank (2015). Data. Total natural resources rents (% of GDP). [Online]. Available from: http://data.worldbank.org/indicator/NY.GDP.TOTL.RT.ZS. [Accessed: 29 July 2015].

PART I

The political economy of resource nationalism

2 Trends in minerals, ores and metals prices

Samuel K. Gayi and Janvier D. Nkurunziza[1]

Introduction

Commodity dependence, defined as the ratio of commodities exports to total merchandise exports, appears to have increased over time. Whereas 64 per cent of countries had a ratio of commodity exports to total merchandise exports of at least 50 per cent in 2009–2010, the proportion of countries with this ratio had increased to 70 per cent by 2012–2013. Out of 133 developing countries[2] analysed, 93 countries derived 50 per cent of their merchandise export earnings from commodities in 2009–2010 (UNCTAD 2014a). By 2012–2013, the number of developing countries deriving at least 50 per cent of their merchandise export earnings from commodities had increased to 100. If this cut-off point is increased to at least 80 per cent of merchandise exports derived from commodities, 45 per cent of developing countries under review could be classified as commodity dependent in 2009–2010, increasing to 47 per cent by 2012–2013. The situation in Latin America and the Caribbean region reflects this pattern.

The economics literature has generally associated commodity dependence, a feature characterizing most developing economies, with negative development outcomes. The literature argues that commodities affect development through three main channels: negative terms of trade, the Dutch Disease phenomenon, and political instability often resulting from struggles over the control of rents associated with commodity windfalls (Humphreys et al. 2007; UNCTAD 2013a).

In spite of the negative association between the reliance on commodities and economic development, commodity sectors are of strategic interest not only to resource-rich developing countries but also to other stakeholders including multinational companies and their host countries, which regard them as high-return destinations for their financial capital. On the one hand, commodity exports are the major source of foreign exchange in a number of developing countries in Latin America and Africa. On the other hand, developed countries such as Switzerland, where about 570 companies are involved in commodity trading alone, derive substantial benefits from commodities trade. It has been estimated that commodity trading in Switzerland, for example, has a workforce exceeding 10,000 employees, and represents 3.6 per cent of the country's GDP. In 2010, commodity trading contributed to about 50 per cent of the country's economic growth (SwissBanking 2013). Therefore, the way that rents, generated in the commodity sectors, are shared by the different stakeholders along the value chain is an important determinant of the sector's growth and development, including its stability.

In some ways, resource nationalism may be considered as a response from resource-rich developing countries to the perceived inequitable distribution of the resource rents generated along the commodities value chain. The efforts of this group of countries to obtain what they consider as a 'fair' share of the rents generated by natural resource extraction have often been frustrated by TNCs' tough negotiating stance, derived from a power asymmetry between them and host countries. Resource nationalism has, however, not been limited to resource-rich developing countries. Natural resource-rich developed countries such as Australia, Canada and the United Kingdom have also renegotiated contracts with mining companies controlling the value chains to increase their share of the rents derived from these resources (Bremmer and Johnston 2009).

Resource nationalism comes in different guises: increases of the government's ownership stake; increases in taxes and royalties, which could be introduced as part of a broader reform in the mining sector; and restrictions on imports and exports[3] (Ernst & Young 2013). In its extreme form, the exploitation of a natural resource is nationalized, as was the case in Chile, when the state-owned copper company gradually took over copper operations from private companies starting in 1964, and culminating in full nationalization, '*estatización*' in 1971 (Léniz n.d.; Meller and Simpasa 2011).

In general, resource nationalism does not only derive from the need to increase the share of rents accruing to host countries. It is usually underscored by a combination of factors, such as cultural, historical, political, or economic motivations (Domjan and Stone 2010). It has also been argued that rising energy prices underscored by geopolitical and market conditions, could instigate nationalistic resource policies. In this regard, resource nationalism is identified as a cyclical phenomenon, the intensity of which '...is felt far more acutely at the upper end of the resource cycle than at the lower end when it begins' (Maniruzzaman 2009: 81). Indeed, the recent rise in resource nationalism seems to have coincided in the last decade or so with the longest commodity boom across virtually all commodity groups. In its update on resource nationalism, Ernst & Young (2013, 2014), for instance, identified a total of 27 resource-rich countries (both developed and developing) that implemented different forms of resource nationalism policies:[4] government ownership (7), increases in taxes and royalties (2), restrictions on imports and exports (5), and mining reforms (13).

Historically, commodity markets have been characterized by boom and bust cycles; thus the size of resource rents fluctuates with commodity price fluctuations. During periods of high prices, investors pour their resources into the production and trading of commodities as they anticipate high returns. At the same time, depending on the terms of the contracts binding investors and resource-rich countries, high commodities prices should be associated with higher export earnings for the exporting country. Low prices, on the other hand, may result in disinvestment and shrinking resources in producing countries. It has been established that many resource-rich countries engage in costly investment programmes, often with low returns, during boom periods (Bevan et al. 1993; Hirschman 1977).

When prices decline, countries are unable to maintain the same consumption and investment patterns. Hence, they either abandon their projects or borrow to complete them, sometimes driving their debt stocks to unsustainable levels as a result. Thus, booms and busts in commodity markets have had a substantial effect on macro-economic performance of resource-rich developing countries. The long-term downward trends in commodity prices observed during the 1980s and 1990s negatively affected economic performance in many resource-rich developing or least-developed countries (Deaton 1999). Therefore, understanding the general trends in commodity prices can help shed some light on the behaviour of resource-rich countries with respect to the management of their commodities sectors, including, where relevant, the occurrence of resource nationalism.

This chapter analyses the general trends in commodity prices since the 1970s, with a particular focus on minerals, ores and metals. It provides background information that could help to understand why countries, particularly in Latin America, resorted to resource nationalism policies at some specific period in their commodities price cycle. The underlying question, even though this chapter will not attempt to address it, is whether high commodity prices, particularly those observed since the 2000s, might have contributed to motivating some producing countries to adopt resource nationalism policies, allowing them to capture more of their natural resource rents. Retaining value locally, in order to increase the share of commodity rents accruing to them, remains a challenge facing most commodity-dependent developing countries.

The rest of the chapter proceeds as follows. The second section reviews the trends in global metals markets, identifying some of the major driving factors. The third section analyses the interaction between commodities prices and some key macro-economic variables. The cases of 3 mineral-rich countries in Latin America are used as an illustration. The fourth section concludes.

Global metals markets: an overview since the 1970s

Since the 1970s, commodity markets have been characterized by price cycles with higher fluctuations than in preceding decades (Chu and Morrison 1984). Such cycles have usually seen shorter boom periods followed by longer periods of bust (Cashin et al. 2002; UNCTAD 2003), except for the upswing in the 2000s, which has been recorded as the longest in history.

Trend of minerals, ores and metals prices

From 1970 to the 2000s, nominal prices of minerals and metals, as depicted by their price index, show a generally upward trend with intermittent fluctuations. However, in real terms, they have trended downwards until the early 2000s (see Figure 2.1).

Figure 2.1 Nominal and real price indexes of minerals, ores and metals, 1970–2013 (2000=100)

Source: UNCTADStat

Notes: The real price index was obtained by deflating the nominal price index by the unit value index of manufactured goods exported by developed market-economy countries with 2000 as the base year. The manufactured goods included in the index cover: chemicals and related products, manufactured goods classified chiefly by material, machinery and transport equipment and miscellaneous manufactured articles (sections 5 through to 8 of the Standard International Trade Classification (SITC)).

The United Nations Conference on Trade and Development (UNCTAD) Minerals, Ores and Metals Price Index,[5] in nominal terms, increased by roughly 90 per cent from 1972 to reach 88 points in 1974. This corresponds to a 68 per cent increase in real terms.[6] It was not only oil prices that experienced a dramatic increase in 1973–74 but also commodity prices across the board, leading to a major commodity boom. For example, prices of agricultural commodities such as cereals more than tripled over the period 1972–74. Afterward, the index showed relative stability in nominal terms until the early 2000s, save for some short-term fluctuations, particularly during 1979–80, 1988–89, 1995 and 1997 due to various macro-economic shocks. In the early 2000s, dramatic increases in commodity prices ushered in another commodity boom. Between 2003 and 2008, the nominal index for minerals, ores and metals increased more than threefold. The dip in 2009 was the result of the financial crisis but prices recovered quickly to reach their peak in 2011, although they have eased in the last three years. Nevertheless, the nominal index shows that the current prices are still much higher than their levels before the beginning of the commodity boom in 2002.

For most of the period since 1970, the real value of the index trended downwards. From 1974 to 2000, the nominal value of UNCTAD Minerals, Ores and Metals Price Index increased by 13 per cent whereas the unit value index of manufactured goods exported by developed market-economy countries increased by about 122 per cent, leading to a decrease in the real value of the index by 50 per cent. This means the slight upward trend recorded in nominal prices of minerals, ores and metals could not match increasing prices of manufactured products over the same period. This confirms the unfavourable evolution in the terms of trade of countries that export minerals, ores and metals but mostly import manufactured products. The long-term decline in real prices is illustrative of the relevance of the Prebisch-Singer hypothesis, even taking into account the recent commodity boom (Harvey et al. 2010) and the effect of cheap imports from China on the terms of trade (Kaplinsky 2006).

From the end of 2003 to 2004, commodity prices in global markets rose gradually but the pace intensified between 2004 and 2008. For example, the UNCTAD Minerals, Ores and Metal Price Index rose to 137 points in 2004 peaking at 332 points in 2008. Thereafter, the boom was interrupted by the 2008 financial crisis. The price index lost 100 points between 2008 and 2009. However, subsequently, as demand recovered from emerging economies such as China, amid supply constraints, commodities prices rebounded to reach new peaks in 2010 and 2011. Moreover, intensified speculative trading, boosted by low interest rates and weak oversight of financial derivatives transactions, (the so-called 'financialization of commodities') amplified upward price movements and increased price volatility. In 2011, the UNCTAD Mineral, Ores and Metal Index reached an historical peak of 375 points. In real terms, minerals and metals prices also recorded significant increases in the 2000s, unlike the trend through the 1980s and 1990s.

The recent boom in commodity markets has been recorded as the longest in the history of commodities prices. It also has been the broadest, as it has affected almost all commodity classes including agricultural, mining and energy commodities. In 2013, commodity prices eased in comparison to their 2011 level but minerals and metals prices remained high compared to their long-term trend. The UNCTAD Minerals, Ores and Metals Index averaged 306 points in 2013, as demand remained strong.

It is worth noting that even as commodity prices dropped, in some cases dramatically, after reaching peaks during upswing periods, they have not returned to their pre-boom levels. It would, however, be simplistic to conclude that current levels of prices are likely to be a new phase of minerals, ores and metals prices. As highlighted by UNCTAD in its 2013 *Trade and Development Report* (2013b: 59–60) there are differing views. First, one school of thought contends that we have actually entered in a new phase of calmer and more stable growth where commodity prices will remain at relatively high levels compared to their pre-2003 levels. For these observers, the pre-2003 levels of commodity prices are behind us. Second, some observers think that the expansionary phase of the commodity supercycle, started a decade ago, still has some years to run. This school of thought argues that emerging economies including China and India will continue an intensive growth trajectory that will keep commodity prices firm. Finally, some others believe that the expansionary phase has come to an end and further price drops should be expected. The ongoing restructuring of China's economy, which to some extent is shifting from investment to consumption, may sustain this point.

The main drivers of minerals, ores and metals price trends

Several factors explain the general trend in the price index of minerals, ores and metals. The most important drivers relate to 'fundamentals', or demand and supply factors. Other factors include macro-economic policy stances in developed economies, most particularly US monetary policy, as well as financialization of commodities.

Effect of economic fundamentals on the prices or minerals, ores and metals

Minerals, ores and metals have specific properties that make them valuable for industrial use. These properties include high strength, durability, capacity to conduct heat and electricity, use in the manufacturing of mechanical tools, and in infrastructure development. Iron ore, for example, is the primary commodity used for steelmaking. Steel is also known to be used in many industrial and infrastructural projects. These properties imply that this class of commodities would be in high demand in regions and countries where economies are growing and in need of such raw materials. Hence, to understand the trend in the prices of minerals, ores and metals, one needs to look at the economic performance and outlook in major industrialized economies, the United States, the Eurozone, and growth prospects in emerging economies. In the 1970s, although the surge in minerals and metals prices has often been associated with the 1973 oil crisis, it was also a response to strong industrial growth and expansionary monetary policy in the United States beginning in 1971 (Barsky and Kilian 2002).[7] More recently, in the 2000s, the commodity boom was driven by strong global economic growth led by developing economies and, particularly, the group of emerging economies among them (see Figure 2.2).

It is clear from Figure 2.2 that if economic growth is an indicator of commodity prices, most of the effect in the period from 2000–2001 to 2011–2012 originated in emerging economies, which posted growth rates systematically higher than those achieved by developed economies, with the exception of the period 2000–2001, before the onset of the commodity boom. The difference in growth rates was more pronounced at the end of the period as developed economies continued to experience very low rates of economic growth following the 2007–2009 financial and economic crises during which they recorded negative rates of economic growth.

It would, however, be misleading to lump emerging countries together and assume that each country has had an equal effect on commodities prices. Most of the increases in the prices of minerals, ores and metals have been due to one country: China. It accounted for a large share of the demand in these commodities. For example, in the period 2011–2012, China alone accounted for about 60 per cent and 30 per cent, respectively, of total imports of iron ore and copper. In the same period, the shares accruing to the 27 countries of the European Union as a group were about 10 per cent and 28 per cent, respectively (Figure 2.3).[8]

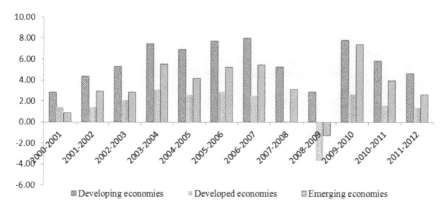

Figure 2.2 GDP Growth by country groups (in 2005 US dollars*)

Source: Data from UNCTADStat.

Note: US dollar at constant exchange rate.

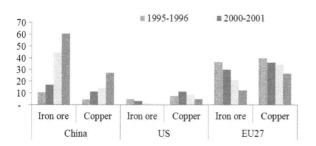

Figure 2.3 Share in world imports of copper and iron ores (%), selected countries, 1995/96–2011/12

Source: UNCTADStat database.

It is interesting to note that China's demand for iron ore and copper increased exponentially over the period 1995–2012, whereas that of the EU27 and the US declined steadily. China's dominant position in the demand for primary commodities extended beyond iron ore and copper. In 2012, the country accounted for about 52 per cent of cotton, 46 per cent of nickel ores, 24 per cent of natural rubber, 23 per cent of aluminium ores, 17 per cent of coal and 13 per cent of crude petroleum (Figure 2.4).[9]

Considering that additional Chinese demand for commodities was not matched by an equal increase in their supply, the result was an increase in the prices of these commodities. It is clear, therefore, that China's strong demand for commodities, needed to fuel the country's fast-growing economy, was responsible for a major part of commodity price increases. So, there appears to be a positive

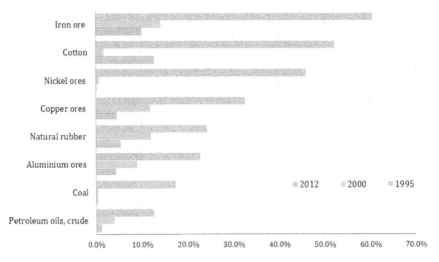

Figure 2.4 China's share in world imports, selected commodities, 1995–2012 (current US dollars)

Source: UNCTADStat database.

correlation between economic growth in emerging economies, particularly China, and the demand for minerals, ores and metals.

The role of China in the recent commodity boom is not uncontested. Some analysts argue that the United States plays an even bigger role in shaping international commodities markets. In his analysis of two types of demand shocks that affect commodities prices,[10] Roache (2012) contends that China's impact on commodities prices increased, but that it remained smaller than that of the United States. First, China's increase in industrial production had a large and significant impact on oil and copper prices, but the impact of the United States was greater and across all commodities because China's activity growth rate shock was weak and not as persistent as that of the United States. Second, the United States' industrial growth had stronger spillover effects on the rest of the world's economic activity, and was important both for world commodity demand and consumption (Roache 2012; UNCTAD 2013a).

Supply factors have also contributed to driving commodity price trends. The supply of minerals depends, in part, on the speed with which new production comes on stream, with the understanding that several years are often necessary for new projects to reach the production stage. For example, the long-term negative trend of the real price index of minerals, ores and metals (1980–2002) depicted in Figure 2.1, might have contributed to the commodity boom of the 2000s. Low prices throughout the 1980s and 1990s discouraged producers to invest in capacity expansion. As a result, the mining industry was not able to respond quickly to strong demand, especially from emerging economies, since the early 2000s.

Conversely, as the commodity boom unfolded, the commodity sector attracted large investments by investors expecting high returns on their investments, both before and after the 2007–2009 crises. As a result, as these projects reached their production stage, there was an over-supply, which led many commodities to experience reversals in their price trends starting from about 2011. However, commodity price levels remained much higher than their values before the boom.

Other supply and demand factors that have affected commodity prices include transport costs, as well as import and export restrictions. A recent case about the export of rare earth metals from China illustrates the latter point. Between the end of 2010 and mid-2011, the price of rare earth metals reached historic highs mainly as a result of a decision by Chinese authorities to drastically reduce exports from the country, which accounted for most of the global exports of rare earth metals. Hence, relative to the year before, import prices by mid-2011 were about five times their previous levels in the United States, four times in Japan and four times in the European Union (UNCTAD, 2014b). When used by major commodity exporters, export quotas reduce supply on the international market leading to price increases.

Other factors affecting commodities prices

Traditionally, monetary policy in the United States has been an important determinant of commodities prices in the international market. Indeed, expansionary monetary policy in the United States and other major economies has resulted in low interest rates, which in turn have affected commodity prices in several ways. Low real interest rates derived from the monetary policy stance of the United States over the last decade not only increased liquidity in the United States, but also in global commodity markets. As commodities are traded in dollars, this increased liquidity generated upward pressure on commodities prices. Three other channels through which a low real interest rate increases commodity prices are by: (i) reducing the incentive for extraction today rather than tomorrow, thereby decreasing supply; (ii) lowering the cost of holding inventories, thus stimulating demand; and (iii) shifting financial investment away from United States Treasury bills into commodity-related portfolio investments and commodity index funds, causing an overshooting of commodities prices, as discussed below (UNCTAD 2013a).[11] Empirical results have confirmed this negative relationship between real interest rates and commodities prices (Frankel 2008).

Moreover, the depreciation of the United States dollar has tended to push currency investors solely motivated by profit maximization towards Exchange Traded Funds (ETF) and notes with short maturity, destabilizing the commodities market. Therefore, as commodities become higher-return assets relative to traditional investment instruments, the flight of institutional investors, in particular, from financial instruments to commodities led to the 'financialization' of commodities, a phenomenon that gained prominence during the latest commodity boom (Basak and Pavlova 2014; Henderson et. al. 2014; Tang and Xiong 2012). For example, in 2008, volume growth in futures markets increased five-fold compared with a decade earlier (CFTC 2008). In April 2013, speculative investment in commodity indices was estimated to have reached $451 billion up from $15 billion in 2003 (United Nations 2013). Gold, one of the commodities most preferred by investors (Dwyer et al. 2011), saw its price more than double between early 2008 and September 2011 when it reached its all-time monthly average high of $1,772 per troy ounce.[12]

Since about 2012, commodity prices have been easing as a result of changes in fundamentals (see previous section) but also due to the acceleration of outflows from exchange traded funds (ETFs) in anticipation of a change in the macro-economic policies of developed countries, particularly the expected tapering of quantitative easing by the US Federal Reserve. For example, ETFs were 33 per cent lower in June 2013 than their peak level in April 2011 (United Nations 2013). It should also be noted that pressure on commodity prices has eased as a result of measures put in place in some countries, including the United States, to limit the size of speculators' positions in commodity derivatives markets. Following the Dodd-Frank Wall Street Reform and Consumer Protection Act, some financial institutions have closed down their commodity warehouses that had been previously used to engage in speculative commodity hoarding. The recently agreed Third Basel Accord (Basel III), requiring banks to hold more liquidity as a way of strengthening the stability of the banking sector, might have forced some banks to reduce their speculative investments in commodities in order to comply with the Accord, easing pressure on commodities prices.

Trends in selected minerals, ores and metals prices (1960–2012)

Prices for most minerals, ores and metals have evolved following the path of their global index. However, taken individually, some departures from the main index can be noted. Moreover, for most commodities discussed below, there are stark differences in the trends of nominal prices (Figure 2.5) and those of real prices (Figure 2.6), particularly if the observation is limited to the period before the commodity boom.

Copper

From 1970 to 2003, the nominal prices of copper were characterized by high volatility with occasional bumps in some years. The price of copper went through three different phases. On average, prices were lowest from the 1960s up to the mid-1980s (Figure 2.5); there was a short lived boom in 1973–74; and from the mid-1980s to the early 2000s, the price, on average, increased by about 50 per cent. However, the most dramatic increase in price occurred during the commodity boom, when it more than doubled in a period of just three years, from US $2,865 per tonne in 2004 to US $7,117 per tonne in 2007. Thereafter, the upward trend was interrupted by the 2008 financial crisis, with the price retreating to US $5,127 per tonne in 2009.

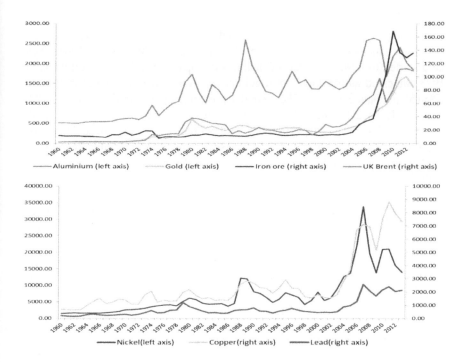

Figure 2.5 Nominal prices of selected commodities

Source: Authors' calculations based on UNCTADStat and IMF, International Financial Statistics.

The price recovered quickly as a result of strong demand from emerging economies, ending the year 2013 at US $7,325 per tonne.

Iron ore

Until recently, iron ore prices were very low. From 1960 to 2004, iron ore traded under US$20 per tonne. After reaching US$28 per tonne in 2005, the price increased exponentially, reaching its historic high of US$167 per tonne in 2010. This drastic movement in prices in the second half of the 2000s was due to increased demand particularly from emerging economies such as China with critical needs for steel in construction and manufacturing industries (Figure 2.4). Interestingly, unlike most other metals, the upward trend in iron ore in the 2000s was not interrupted by the 2008 financial crisis as China, the major importer, was not as negatively affected by the crisis as mature economies like the European Union and the United States. By 2013, the price increase had eased, but iron ore was still trading at US$136 per tonne, which was very high compared with the historical average.

Gold

Historically, gold prices have gone through different regimes. Before 1967, the monetary value of gold was constant. Prices started to fluctuate in 1967 when gold started to trade in markets (Shafiee and Topal 2010). The first oil crisis in 1973 coincided with a doubling of gold prices from US$58 per ounce in 1972 to US$156 per ounce in 1974. The second historical jump occurred over 1979–1980 in the wake of the Iranian Revolution as gold prices increased nearly fourfold, from US$193 per ounce in 1978 to US$613 per ounce in 1980. Indeed, in periods of political and economic uncertainty, as was the case with the Iranian Revolution, gold is used as a safe-haven asset for investors. As this period also experienced high inflation, led by high prices of crude oil, gold was used to hedge against the effect of inflation, putting pressure on the gold market.

The 1980s and 1990s were mostly uneventful for the gold market. Prices declined, slowly, reaching US$310 in 2002. Thereafter, in the midst of the commodity boom, gold markets became bullish. By 2012, relative to its level in 2002, the price of gold had increased more than fivefold to reach an all-time high annual average price of US$1668 per ounce. In addition to the huge investments in gold in the form of ETFs discussed earlier, the surge in gold prices was mainly attributed to economic uncertainty resulting from the financial and economic crises and unstable macro-economic policy in developed economies. This may explain why, as Figure 2.5 shows, the increasing trend of gold prices was uninterrupted by the 2007–2008 crisis. High prices were also due to reduced production underpinned by increased mining costs and difficulties in finding new deposits (Shafiee and Topal, 2010).

Commodities and economic performance in selected resource-rich countries

The index-based analysis carried out so far gives an overall picture of commodity prices in the specific commodity group captured by the index. However, it does not show how changes in minerals and metals prices affected specific exporting countries. This section briefly illustrates the effect of the prices of minerals, ores and metals on a range of macro-economic variables using the examples of three Latin American resource rich-countries, namely Bolivia, Chile and Peru. Each of these countries derives a large share of its export earnings from the mining sector (Table 2.1).

Between 2007 and 2012, Chile and Peru derived more than a half (54 per cent) of their total export earnings from minerals, ores and metals. And on average, the sector represented 21 per cent and 14 per cent of GDP respectively in Chile and Peru. In Bolivia, the mining sector represented about 26 per cent of total exports, and 11 per cent of GDP over the same period. As depicted in Table 2.1, the size of export earnings derived from minerals, ores and metals,

Table 2.1 Minerals, ores and metals exports as a share of total exports and GDP (nominal US dollars, percentage)

Period	Chile		Peru		Bolivia	
	Total exports	GDP	Total exports	GDP	Total exports	GDP
1995–2000	35	10	39	5	23	5
2001–2006	45	18	50	11	16	5
2007–2012	54	21	54	14	26	11

Source: Authors' calculations based on UNCTADStat.

increased steadily in all three countries, in particular over the decade associated with the boom in global commodity markets. This suggests that changes in values of export earnings were primarily the effect of elevated commodity prices rather than quantities. For example, the correlation between international prices and export revenues for copper was as high as 98 per cent in Chile and 95 per cent in Peru during the period 2004–2013. In contrast, the correlation between export revenues and production of copper in the two countries is lower (see Table 2.2).

As depicted in Table 2.3, just a few commodities dominate the mining sector in these countries. Chile, for example, derived almost 90 per cent of its mining export revenues from just copper during the period of 2007–2012.

The health of the commodities sector in resource-rich developing countries, which greatly depends on international prices, affects the overall economic performance and development of these countries. For example, the coefficients of correlation between export revenues from minerals, ores and metals and fixed capital investment are very high, exceeding 90 per cent in the three countries over the period 1995–2012. Similarly, for all three countries, the correlation between export revenues and household consumption is elevated, exceeding 94 per cent for all three resource-rich countries over the same period. The situation is exacerbated by the fact that the export earnings of most resource-rich countries are derived from a limited range of commodities (as discussed above). Furthermore, overall economic performance seems to be strongly associated with the boom recorded in commodities prices between 2003 and 2011 (Figure 2.6).

The most interesting feature of Figure 2.6 is the evolution of GDP which appears to mirror the evolution of commodity prices. For all three countries, there is a turning point in the trend of GDP in the period from about 2002 to about 2004, which corresponds with the time when most commodities prices started to accelerate. As discussed earlier, the acceleration in copper prices started in 2004, which is more or less when Chile, for example, started experiencing an exponential increase in GDP.

Table 2.2 Correlation matrix between export revenues, international price and production of copper in Chile and Peru (2004–2013)

	Chile			*Peru*		
	Copper export revenues	*Copper prices*	*Copper production*	*Copper export revenues*	*Copper prices*	*Copper production*
Copper export revenues	1.00	0.98	0.25	1.00	0.95	0.81
Copper prices		1.00	0.13		1.00	0.67
Copper production			1.00			1.00

Source: Authors' calculations using data from UNCTADStat and the United States Geological Survey.

Table 2.3 Share of main commodity exports in total mining exports in Chile, Peru and Bolivia (average values over the period 2007–2012)

Chile	Copper* (88%)
Peru	Gold (33%); Copper* (41%)
Bolivia	Ores and concentrates of base metals (41%); Gold (14%); Tin (13%)

Source: Authors' calculations based on data from UNCTADStat.

Note: *including copper ores and concentrates.

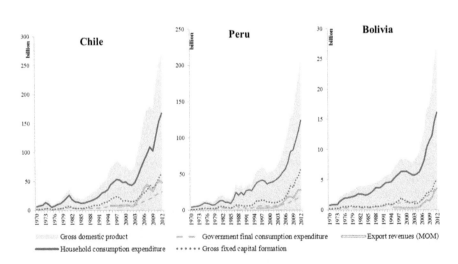

Figure 2.6 Evolution of GDP and other macro-economic variables for selected countries (in current US dollars)

Source: Compiled by authors using data from UNCTADStat

Conclusion

There is ample evidence in the economic literature, and in practice, that very few natural resource-rich countries have managed to make the transition from heavy reliance on their natural resource endowments to sustainable economic growth and development. In these countries, structural transformation to greater value-added activities in the secondary and tertiary sectors remains elusive. This has been identified as the 'paradox of plenty' or simply as a 'natural resource curse'. Indeed, one observation from the analysis carried out in this chapter is that natural resource-rich developing countries face two major constraints. The first is that as price takers, their development performance depends on unpredictable revenues in view of the booms and busts characterizing commodities markets over the long term. This calls for improved macro-economic management skills that prioritize inter-temporal management and investment of resource rents and revenues over current consumption expenditures. Few countries have these skills. The second constraint, although not specifically discussed in this chapter but well covered in others, and which has become topical in the context of the recent commodity boom, is that judging from a producing country's perspective, resources from the exploitation and trading of commodities are not fairly shared among all the stake-holders in the commodities value chains.

In view of the high dependence of many developing countries on natural resource exploitation and exports, not getting a fair share of the resource rents could have far-reaching effects on their populations that have to live in poverty in spite of their natural resource endowments. In many cases, this context has led to discontent, particularly during periods of commodity booms such as the recent one when massive rents are generated in the commodities sector. This might have encouraged politicians in a number of countries to adopt nationalistic policies, including the nationalization of their natural resources sectors. While these policies are not new, whether or not nationally-controlled natural resources are more pro-developmental than multinational-controlled resources remains an empirical question.

Notes

1 Respectively, Head, Special Unit on Commodities (SUC), and Chief, Commodities Research and Analysis Section, SUC, UNCTAD. Excellent research assistance from Komi Tsowou, Associate Economic Affairs Officer, SUC, UNCTAD, is highly appreciated. The views expressed in this chapter do not represent those of the UNCTAD secretariat or those of its Secretary General, and should therefore not in any way be attributed to either.
2 Developing countries which are UN member states only.
3 These three types of resource nationalism could be described as variants of 'economic resource nationalism'. The other three main categories of resource nationalism identified in the literature are revolutionary, legacy, and soft resource nationalism (Bremmer and Johnston, 2009).

4 Only five countries were identified as having implemented what was termed 'retreating resource nationalism', i.e., return focus to investment attraction. These are Australia, China, India, Ukraine and Vietnam.

5 The UNCTAD minerals, ores and metals price index covers copper, aluminium, iron ore, nickel, lead, zinc, tin, phosphate rock, manganese ore, and tungsten ore. Gold is not included in the price index.

6 Real prices were obtained by deflating nominal prices by the unit value index of manufactured goods exported by developed market-economy countries (United Nations Statistical Division). Use of this index as a deflator – although not entirely uncontroversial – is common as the resulted deflated prices reveal the terms-of-trade effects.

7 The effect of monetary policy will be discussed in the next section.

8 Chinese imports of soybeans as a share of world imports also doubled over the period, 2002/03 to 2010/11, from 11.2 per cent to 22.3 per cent (UNCTAD 2013a, 48–9).

9 The share in crude oil imports in 2013 had increased to 20 per cent of total world imports.

10 These are aggregate economic activity shocks (measured by industrial production) and commodity-specific demand shocks (measured by apparent consumption) that are unrelated to aggregate activity,

11 Each of these three explanations has inherent caveats. For these details and a discussion of the implications of United States exchange rate for commodities prices see (UNCTAD, 2013a, 34–9).

12 The daily all time high was recorded on 6 September 2011 when the price of gold reached US$ 1922 per troy ounce.

Bibliography

Basak, S., and Pavlova, A. (2014). A model of financialization of commodities. *Working Paper*, London Business School.

Barsky, R.B., and Kilian, L. (2002). Do we really know that oil caused the great stagflation? A monetary alternative. *NBER Macroeconomics Annual 2001*, 16. MIT Press, pp. 137–98.

Bremmer, I., and Johnston, R. (2009). The rise and fall of resource nationalism. *Survival*, 51(2), pp: 149–58.

Bevan, D., Collier, P. and Gunning, J.W. (1993). Controlled open economies: A neoclassical approach to structuralism. *Journal of Development Economics*. 41 (1), pp. 209–211.

Cashin, P.C., Mcdermott, C.J. and Scott, A. (2002). Booms and slumps in world commodity prices. *Journal of Development Economics*, 69, pp. 277–296.

CFTC (Commodity Futures Trading Commission) (2008). Staff Report On Commodity Swap Dealers & Index Traders with Commission Recommendations. Commodity Futures Trading Commission, September [Online]. Available from: http://www.loe.org/images/content/080919/cftcstaffreportonswapdealers09.pdf. [Accessed: 3 March 2015].

Chu K.-Y. and Morrison T.K. (1984). The 1981–82 recession and non-oil primary commodity prices. Staff Papers. *International Monetary Fund*, 31(1), pp. 93–140.

Deaton, A. (1999). Commodity prices and growth in Africa. *The Journal of Economic Perspectives*, 13 (3), pp. 23–40.

Domjan, P. and Stone, M. (2010). A comparative study of resource nationalism in Russia and Kazakhstan 2004–2008. *Europe-Asia Studies*, 62 (1), pp. 35–62.

Dwyer, A., Gardner, G., and Williams, T. (2011). Global commodity markets–price volatility and financialisation. *RBA Bulletin*, June, pp. 49–57.

Ernst & Young (2013). Resource nationalism update.[Online]. Available from: www.ey. com/Publication/vwLUAssets/EY-M-and-M-Resource-nationalism-update-October-2013/$FILE/EY-M-and-M-Resource-nationalism-update-October-2013.pdf [Accessed: 3 March 2015].

Ernst & Young (2014). Resource nationalism update, July 2014 [Online]. Available from: www.ey.com/Publication/vwLUAssets/EY-Resource-nationalism-update-July-2014/$File/EY-Resource-nationalism-July-2014.pdf [Accessed: 3 March 2015].

Frankel, J. (2008). The effect of monetary policy on real commodity prices. In J. Campbell (ed.). *Asset Prices and Monetary Policy*. Chicago: University of Chicago Press, pp. 291–327.

Harvey, D., Kellard, N., Madsen, J., and Wohar, M. (2010). The Prebisch-Singer hypothesis: Four centuries of evidence. *Review of Economics and Statistics*, 92 (2), pp. 367–77.

Henderson, B.J., Pearson, N.D., and Wang, L. (2014). New evidence on the financialization of commodity markets. *Review of Financial Studies*. Corrected proof [Online]. Available from: http://rfs.oxfordjournals.org/content/early/2014/12/25/rfs.hhu091.full.pdf.

Hirschman, A.O. (1977). *A Generalized Linkage Approach to Development, with Special Reference to Staples*. Chicago: Chicago University Press.

Humphreys, M., Sachs, J. D., and Stiglitz, J.E. (2007). *Escaping the Resource Curse*. New York: Columbia University Press.

IMF (International Monetary Fund) (n.d.). International financial statistics [Online] Available from: http://www.imf.org/external/data.htm. [Accessed March 17th, 2015].

Kaplinsky, R. (2006). Revisiting the revisited terms of trade: Will China make a difference? *World Development*, 34 (6), pp. 981–95.

Léniz, F.C. (n.d.). Histories of nationalization and privatization: The cases of the Chilean and Zambian. Copper Industries [Online]. Available from: www.eisourcebook.org/cms/Histories%20of%20Nationalization%20and%20Privatization.pdf. [Accessed: 3 March 2015].

Maniruzzaman, A.F.M. (2009). The issue of resource nationalism: Risk engineering and dispute management in the oil and gas industry. *Texas Journal of Oil, Gas, and Energy Law*, 5(1), pp. 79–108.

Meller, P., and Simpasa, A.M. (2011). Role of copper in the Chilean and Zambian economies: Main economic and policy issues. Global Development Network Working Paper Series, 43 (June), pp.133.

Roache, K.S. (2012). China's Impact on world commodity markets. IMF Working Paper, WP/12/115, Washington, DC: International Monetary Fund.

Shafiee, S., and Topal E. (2010). An Overview Of Global Gold Market And Gold Price Forecasting. *Resources Policy*, 35(3), pp. 178–89.

SWISSBANKING (2013). La Suisse, place de négoce de matières premières. SwissBanking Factuals. March.

Tang, K., and Xiong, W. (2012). Index investment and the financialization of commodities. *Financial Analysts Journal*, 68 (5), pp. 54–74.

UNCTAD (n.d.). UNCTADStat database [Online]. Available from: http://unctadstat. unctad.org/wds/ReportFolders/reportFolders.aspx. [Accessed: 17 March 2015].

UNCTAD (2003). Economic development in Africa: Trade performance and commodity dependence. UNCTAD/GDS/AFRICA/2003/1. United Nations Conference on Trade and Development. New York and Geneva.

UNCTAD (2013a). Commodities and development report: Perennial problems, new challenges and evolving perspectives. UNCTAD/SUC/2011/9. New York and Geneva: United Nations Conference on Trade and Development.

UNCTAD (2013b). Trade and development report. UNCTAD/TDR/2013. New York and Geneva: United Nations Conference on Trade and Development.

UNCTAD (2014a). The State of Commodity Dependence 2014. New York and Geneva: United Nations Conference on Trade and Development.

UNCTAD (2014b). Commodities at a glance: Special issue on rare earths. New York and Geneva: United Nations Conference on Trade and Development.

UNITED NATIONS (2013). World Commodity Trends and Prospects. Report of the Secretary General. General Assembly. Document A/68/204. New York.

USGS (United States Geological Survey) [Online]. Available from http://minerals.usgs.gov/minerals/pubs/commodity/copper/. [Accessed: 2 March 2015].

3   Rise of state–firm bargaining in the 2000s

Vlado Vivoda

Introduction

In the world of international business, negotiation rather than the perfect market equilibrium solution is the rule (Agmon 2003). Nowhere is this more pronounced than in extractive industries, due to the cyclical and highly volatile nature of the markets. Since 1986, crude oil, refined petroleum and natural gas prices have been more volatile than prices for about 95% of other producer price index commodities (Regnier 2007). The price of West Texas Intermediate (WTI) light crude climbed from US\$ 50/barrel in January 2007 to a peak of US\$ 147/barrel in July 2008, subsequently dropping to under US\$ 34/barrel in December 2008. Frequently changing market conditions result in changes in relative bargaining power between host states and foreign investors, and changes in relative (potential or actual) bargaining power lead to (re)bargaining.

This chapter analyses the changing balance of power in the international oil industry in the 2000s. A particular focus is on five major international oil companies – IOCs (BP, Chevron, ExxonMobil, Royal Dutch/Shell, and Total). The chapter demonstrates that the international oil industry has shifted from a cooperative phase in the 1990s, when the IOCs managed numerous 'sweetheart' deals, to a conflictive phase characterized by resurgent resource nationalism and unfavourable bargaining outcomes for IOCs in the 2000s. Although the majors have made unprecedented profits during the past decade, this does not imply that they have been successful in bargaining with host states. As illustrated by the example of Venezuela, high oil prices have endowed oil-exporting states with increased bargaining power, which has been one of the drivers of the resurgence in resource nationalism. The majors have also been faced with a high degree of industry competition from national oil companies from importing countries. As a result, they have struggled to secure access to new oil reserves and, consequently, their production has dropped.

The evolution of state–firm relationships in the international oil industry

The raison d'être of the firm is the ongoing search for and sustainability of economic rents (Mahoney 1995). Host governments aim to transfer economic rent from foreign investors to domestic factors of production without reducing the inflow of beneficial foreign investment (Globerman and Shapiro 1998). Conflicts between host governments and multinational corporations (MNCs) usually centre on the issue of division of rents (Mikdashi 1976). In the international oil industry, typically, large economic rents can be earned, because the market price is well above the price required to keep the factor of production in active use, and is above the price required to earn profits. While this chapter focuses exclusively on the developments in the oil (and gas) industry, the overall dynamic also applies in the broader extractive sector, including the mining industry. Bargaining and negotiation between host states and oil and gas, and mining companies determine the division of these rents. Bargaining between the oil companies and host governments is positive sum, as the objectives of the two sets of actors are never exclusively conflictive. Although the goals of international oil companies (IOCs) and governments are different, there is always a range of complementarity or overlap and thus there is scope for each party to achieve its goals through cooperation (Eden et al. 2005).

During a period of high commodity prices, when large rents can be earned, the phenomenon of resource nationalism comes to the surface, as it is a by-product of high prices (Wälde 2008). This state of affairs corresponds to Ernest J. Wilson's model of the politics of the world oil market – the petro-political cycle (PPC) (Wilson 1986, 1987). The PPC model posits that the likelihood and the direction of market politicization are a direct function of the boom-and-bust phase of that market. Thus, petro-politics at the peak of the market will differ substantially from politics in a trough. In rising markets, sellers, such as energy-exporting governments, gain leverage. In falling markets, buyers, such as IOCs or oil-importing governments, gain leverage. In addition, during periods of rising commodity prices, the governments of developing states, which occupy a subordinate position in the international system, have real incentive to alter the basic rules of the game and reverse this status quo (Wilson 1987).

Historically, there has been cyclical change in the relative balance of power between host states and national oil companies of exporting countries (ENOCs) and major IOCs, reflective of the cyclical nature of the oil and gas industry (Joffé et al. 2009; Stevens 2008; Vivoda 2009a, 2011). Some periods, such as the 1970s and the early 1980s, can be classified as 'conflictive'. During these periods, rising and relatively high oil prices endowed host states with more capital, which helped them to renegotiate the agreements with the IOCs and to gain larger shares of the economic rent. These were also periods characterized by a low degree of compatibility between host state and IOC interests. Other periods, such as the late 1980s and 1990s, can be referred to as 'cooperative'. During these periods, falling markets and low prices resulted in the balance of power shifting to IOCs, which in turn allowed them to gain attractive investment terms in oil-exporting countries. Consequently, these periods were characterized by a higher degree of compatibility between host state and IOC interests. In short, the larger the rents to be divided, the more intensive the bargaining relationship becomes, and vice versa.

Vernon's obsolescing bargain model (OBM) has occupied the central stage in explaining host state–MNC bargaining dynamics in the late 1970s, 1980s and early 1990s. Such is the importance of this explanatory model that some have referred to it as the accepted paradigm of host government–MNC relations in the international political economy (Kobrin 1987; Nebus and Rufin 2010). The OBM explains the changing nature of bargaining relations between an MNC and host country government as a function of goals, resources and constraints on both parties (Kobrin 1987; Moran 1974; Vernon 1971). In the OBM, which is conceptualized as a positive sum game in which the goals of the MNC and host state are assumed to be in conflict, the initial bargain favours the MNC, but as MNC assets are transformed into hostages, relative bargaining power shifts to the host state over time. Once bargaining power shifts to the host state, its government imposes more conditions on the MNCs, ranging from higher taxes to asset expropriation. Thus, the original bargain obsolesces, giving the OBM its name. The OBM was originally applied as an explanation for widespread expropriation and nationalization in the 1970s of MNC natural resource subsidiaries located in developing countries (Vernon 1977). Rising oil prices motivated host states to renegotiate their agreements with the IOCs, and renegotiation often took the form of outright expropriation. In line with the general trends, the 1970s and early 1980s saw oil produced for the international oil market progressively brought under state control. The IOCs lost control of numerous 'sweetheart' deals with oil-exporting governments and their initial bargains obsolesced.

Relations between MNCs and host governments in developing countries changed from the 1970s, when they were predominantly confrontational, to being largely cooperative in the 1980s and 1990s (Dunning 1998; Luo 2001). With greater overall acceptance of foreign direct investment (FDI) in developing countries and transitioning economies, and privatization replacing public-sector ownership at a rapid pace around the globe, foreign investors in the extractive industries were treated just like FDI in any other sector (Moran 1998). The change in government attitudes was accompanied by economic liberalization, deregulation, privatization, less expropriation and the loosening of rules governing FDI – which created unprecedented opportunities for MNCs (Ramamurti and Doh 2004). In the international oil and gas industry, the openness to FDI that characterized the 1980s and 1990s replaced the nationalistic behaviour of the 1970s. In line with general trends, in the late 1980s and 1990s, the oil industry experienced both deregulation and privatization (Grosse 2005; Stevens 1998). As a consequence of low oil prices in the 1990s, various oil-exporting states offered relatively attractive deals to major IOCs. Reflective of the general sentiment of the 1990s, Edward Morse argued that 'resource nationalism has disappeared from the discourse of international relations' (Morse 1999: 14).

Three basic underlying factors influenced the relative balance of power in the international oil industry in the second part of the 1980s and in the 1990s. First, low oil prices provided the underlying conditions in which host countries became desperate for foreign investment. Second, IOCs had no competition from national oil companies (NOCs) from oil-importing countries. NOCs can be divided into oil-importing, such as those from China and India (INOCs), and oil-exporting, such as those from Brazil, Malaysia, Norway, Russia and Saudi Arabia (ENOCs). In the 1980s and 1990s, the technological and managerial capability of IOCs was unmatched by industry competitors. Third, IOCs were able to pursue alternative investment options if not permitted favourable entry to a particular host state. As a result, IOCs, after two decades resumed a dominant role in the international oil industry, as their market control had increased and joint ventures, strategic alliances and mergers had served to balance risk and control (van der Linde 2000).

The resurgence of resource nationalism in the 2000s

However, with rising oil prices since the turn of the century, bargaining episodes between host states, IOCs and other stakeholders have once again intensified. Driven by rising oil prices, many host states have renegotiated their agreements with IOCs. The investment terms for IOCs have worsened in Russia, Venezuela and numerous other countries. The major IOCs were faced with a high degree of industry competition from national oil companies from importing countries– China and India in particular. These INOCs have been challenging IOCs world-wide and have provided fierce competition for oil-production agreements in the Middle East, Latin America, the former Soviet Union and Africa. During the 2000s, the major IOCs have struggled to secure access to new oil reserves and consequently, their oil production has dropped (Vivoda 2009a). High oil prices, increased industry competition and the lack of alternative investment options for IOCs have translated into unfavourable bargaining outcomes. In the past decade, the oil industry once again shifted from a cooperative phase to a phase characterized by resurgent resource nationalism, increased competition and regulation of foreign investment, and expropriations (Joffé et al. 2009; Stevens 2008; Vivoda 2009a).

Resurgent resource nationalism in the international oil and gas industry has been the underlying factor for the demise of major IOCs in the past decade. The main reason for this resurgence has been the high price of oil. As demonstrated in the previous section, during a period of low oil prices, as in the late 1980s and for much of the 1990s, IOCs gain leverage, and are courted by commodity-rich states to develop their national resources. However, during a period of high oil prices, as in the first decade of the new millennium, host governments gain leverage and rethink their contracts and seek higher taxes and royalties.

Governments of Latin American states, such as Venezuela, are 'old hosts' to FDI and have much experience with multinationals. Rapid privatization of key politically sensitive sectors in Latin America in the 1990s caused a backlash from governments and the general public as the number of foreign takeovers increased. The openness to FDI in Latin America in the 1990s generated sufficient resentment required to swing the pendulum in the other direction. Whereas MNCs in general were offered subsidies and tax cuts to invest in Latin American econo-mies in the 1990s – for instance, one per cent royalties paid by IOCs producing in Venezuela's Orinoco Tar Sands – these generous terms have been eliminated and governments increasingly regulated their politically sensitive industries.

The Russian Federation, a transition economy, has had little experience with inward FDI, similar to other transition economies. In the 1990s, following the collapse of communism, Russia's economy opened to investment, which has been an important component of the economic reform programme. Its initial openness, evident in pro-FDI policies and privatization, was 'the calm before the storm', which started with President Putin's crackdown on Yukos in mid-2003. What followed was a renationalization of much of Russia's oil industry, increased regulation and higher taxes and an increasingly anti-FDI climate, as Russia retreated from liberalization and returned to high levels of state control. By realising how important it is for a transition economy to control its oil industry, and with an understanding that relying on global market forces alone did not serve its interests, Russia has quickly learned how to deal with the presence of IOCs. Putin understood that the goals and interests of IOCs do not fully coincide with those of Russia and, thus, the investment conditions for major IOC participation in the Russian oil industry have worsened, and they quickly became junior partners to Gazprom and Rosneft. This was evident in Shell's exit from Sakhalin-II project in 2006 and BP's 2008 dispute with its Russian joint venture partners. During the 2000s, Putin largely accomplished his goal of renationalizing hydrocarbon resources and the new subsoil legislation introduced in May 2008 made foreign investment in the country's oil and gas industry much more difficult (Panov 2008).

In addition, similar developments occurred in Kazakhstan, another former Soviet republic and a transition economy. In January 2004, Kazakhstan toughened its contract terms, limited foreign ownership in ventures, removed tax stability clauses and introduced a new escalator tax and, in October 2007, it amended its subsoil law (Panov 2008). The resurgence of resource nationalism during the 2000s was not confined to Latin America and the former Soviet Union. In many African oil-exporting countries, governments have been bargaining for more attractive conditions. For example, Nigeria and Angola have linked access to upstream assets to investments in other parts of the economy and have continued to demand large signature bonuses. In virtually every oil-exporting country, ENOCs, which had in the 1990s ceded ground to IOCs in the wake of globalization, have reclaimed lost ground. During the 2000s, the majors were struggling to hold on to their position in most states in which they operate (Johnston 2008).

The balance of power between governments and firms is determined by the particular circumstances of the times. In the 2000s, when considering exclusively empirical evidence from the international oil and gas industry, the nation-state appeared robust as a regulator of MNCs. There is no evidence to demonstrate that, in the first decade of the new millennium, governments were fading away in the face of the power of IOCs. On the contrary, IOCs' bargaining power was fading away vis-à-vis that of host states. Resource nationalism returned back to the forefront of relations between host governments and IOCs and it translated into an anti-Western IOC campaign (Stevens 2008). During the mid-to-late 2000s, oil-producing and -exporting states owned and controlled between 77% and 90% of total proven world oil reserves (Marcel 2006).

As a result of resurgent resource nationalism, during the 2000s, new IOC investment was not welcome in the major oil-producing region of the world, the Middle East, nor in North Africa, and much of Latin America and the former Soviet Union. The regions in which IOCs most wanted to operate became extremely difficult operating environments due to political and regulatory constraints. During the past decade, the greatest share of majors' oil production was from the North Slope in Alaska, the Gulf of Mexico and the North Sea; areas which have experienced rapid decline and where production was becoming increasingly cost-prohibitive. During the 2000s, North America and the North Sea accounted for 60% of the majors' oil production and these are the regions where more than 50% of the reserves have been extracted. In those areas, production costs have continued to climb throughout the 2000s and every new investment to extend the life of the reservoirs was becoming more marginal. In the North Sea, the average extraction cost for a barrel of oil increased by 42% from 2000 to 2005 (Bozon et al. 2005). Other states and 'safe zones' that were open to IOC investment were those in which, due to technical challenges, production was profitable only if oil prices remained very high (Alberta, Siberia, offshore West Africa), or in alternative energy sources (oil shale, tar sands, renewables). Many of these options have represented high risk to major IOCs as they may be unprofitable in the longer term if oil prices fall. Moreover, increased industry competition has further reduced their access to reserves. As a consequence, in the mid-2000s, major IOCs have had full access to countries with only 6% of global oil reserves, mainly in North America and Europe. They were also welcome to invest in countries that owned an additional 11% of reserves through joint ventures (JVs) or production-sharing agreements (PSAs) (Mouawad 2006).

The wave of largest publicly traded IOC consolidations in the 1990s, particularly through the merger of BP and Amoco, Exxon and Mobil, and Chevron and Texaco, has resulted in high concentration of large private oil companies. However, the international oil industry has become less concentrated in the 2000s as a result of market entry of new players. Major IOCs have been facing increasing competition, primarily from INOCs. Importing NOCs offered technology, capital and access to markets, the lack of which was often seen as a reason to privatize NOCs. Many NOCs had grand ambitions and started competing with the majors by developing new oil reserves overseas and investing in international refining and retail activities with a long-term business perspective (Marcel 2006). The ENOCs have been an emerging threat to the majors inasmuch as they have increased their downstream presence in the IOCs' traditional markets, and, in tandem with their governments, have further limited IOC access to oil reserves in their countries.

At the same time, INOCs have directly competed with the majors for access to new oil reserves. Competition for untapped energy deposits with INOCs, primarily from China and India, has been described as fiercer than ever (Bozon et al. 2005). For example, Chinese NOCs have throughout the 2000s spent billions of dollars on a global scramble for oil to feed China's booming economy. They have had the ability to obtain government loans at little or no interest. The government's energy security policy was aimed at diversifying import sources and routes and building up reserves to avoid unexpected interruption (Vivoda 2009b). Driven by the government's policy, China's NOCs have acquired growing equity oil stakes and long-term crude oil contracts and have signed strategic alliances with oil producers in all of the world's major oil-producing regions. In doing so, they have emerged victorious vis-à-vis major IOCs in various bidding and bargaining episodes and have provided IOCs with unwanted competition in many oil-producing countries, particularly in Angola, Iran, Kazakhstan, Nigeria and Venezuela.

The success of the INOCs has been made possible by their access to cheap home government finance, which has provided an unfair advantage against the major IOCs in bidding for concessions. Moreover, unlike the majors, many INOCs are not constrained by human rights norms imposed by their home governments (Vivoda 2009a). For example, throughout the past decade, Chinese NOCs have courted various oil-exporting states that do not or only barely meet minimum human rights standards (Chen 2007). The poor corporate social responsibility (CSR) standards adopted by Chinese NOCs have provided them with an operational advantage against the majors given that they have operated under considerably different 'rules of the game' imposed by their home governments and international institutions, by which the People's Republic of China does not necessarily abide.

The emerging trend of downstream and upstream internationalization of NOCs has been a particular threat for major IOCs. In addition to the INOCs' downstream and upstream monopoly in their home countries, many NOCs have challenged the IOCs on their own turf, as they have international activities and have established downstream presence in major Western markets, such as the US and the European Union (EU). This has made them increasingly competitive with IOCs. As a result, it has become increasingly difficult for IOCs to provide a value proposition to the owners of natural resources and their ENOCs (Oxford Analytica 2008). Historically, high levels of technology and project management skills were the value-added propositions, which were exclusive to the majors. However, during the 2000s, even the most technologically complex resources have no longer been exclusively at their purview (Johnston 2008). Given the IOCs' limited value-adding properties in oil exploration and production, the potential for cooperation with NOCs and oil-exporting states has been limited during the past decade, and has taken place only under unfavourable terms and conditions for the majors. Undoubtedly, the rise of the NOCs has been a significant challenge for the majors.

The case of Venezuela

The case of Venezuela under Hugo Chávez best exemplifies the change in the state–firm balance of power during the 2000s. Between 1993 and 1999, the policy of *la apertura*, under the direction of Luis Giusti, the chairman of Petróleos de

Venezuela, S.A. (PDVSA), Venezuela's NOC, set Venezuela on a course which incentivized foreign investment by exempting certain projects from the basic petroleum fiscal regime (Giusti 1999). In January 1996, PDVSA launched the largest round of international bidding on oil exploration and production rights since nationalization in 1975, making it possible for IOCs to return to the country (Maugeri 2006). As a consequence, until 1999, Venezuela's oil industry maintained an anti-statist and MNC management culture. Following *la apertura*, Venezuela arguably defected from OPEC into the opposite camp (Mommer 1998).

In 1998, Bernard Mommer suggested that Venezuela 'underlines the spread of the new liberal governance structure of international oil elsewhere. Hence, the trend in the governance of international oil at present is in precisely the opposite direction to that in the decades before the "OPEC revolution".' Nationalization, according to Mommer, 'has already been defeated, definitively, radically, and irreversibly' (Mommer 1998: 76–7). His predictions were to be proven incorrect by 1999 when Chávez, explicitly targeting *la apertura*, became Venezuela's president. During the 2000s, under the influence of President Chávez, Venezuela's oil industry was reformed, PDVSA's autonomy was reduced and the rules regulating the country's hydrocarbons sector amended. The changes brought up by *la apertura*, were reversed. PDVSA was placed under the jurisdiction of the Ministry of Energy and Petroleum (MEP), in practice controlled by Chávez, and lost all of its earlier independence. The reform encompassed four main areas: solidification of state ownership of the oil industry, tax reform, subordination of the oil industry to national interests, and the strengthening of OPEC.

Venezuela's 2001 Hydrocarbons Law, which came to effect in January 2002, discouraged IOCs from investment. This law replaced the Hydrocarbons Law of 1943 and the Nationalization Law of 1975. The 2001 Hydrocarbons Law raised royalties paid by private companies to 20–30% from the previous 1–16.7%, and from 1% to 16.7% for those producing from the tar sands (for example, in the Orinoco Belt). At the same time, the government increased a corporate tax rate for oil companies from the preferential rate of 34% to 50% (Vivoda 2008). The tax rate was applied retroactively to profits made between 2000 and 2005. As a consequence, Venezuela renegotiated the contracts with IOCs present in the country. By shifting its emphasis from income taxes to royalties, the government closed loopholes in the tax collection process. The law also guaranteed PDVSA at least a 51% stake in any exploration, production, transportation and initial storage of oil. With the new measures, the government forced all foreign companies, including Total, ENI, Repsol, Statoil, BP, ConocoPhillips, Chevron, and Exxon Mobil, with existing operating agreements to change over to the new regime.

The new law entered into practice in October 2004 when Chávez surprised the IOCs by announcing on his weekly radio broadcast that he was increasing royalties paid to the state by companies involved in heavy crude production in the Orinoco Tar Belt. The affected companies had signed strategic association agreements in the mid-1990s for the production in the Orinoco Belt. These strategic associations, as well as 32 other operating service agreements with private companies, had been signed on very favourable terms for the companies, and they reflected *la apertura* and the overall cooperative FDI climate of the 1990s. In addition, the low corporate tax rates and royalties associated with the initial contracts were designed to offset the high investment costs needed to set up the upgrading and conversion process for this type of production (Giusti 1999).

A telling sign of the emerging adverse political climate in Venezuela arrived in January 2005 when PDVSA officials ordered the Houston-based firm Harvest Natural Resources to cut production by one third, a step that sent the company's stock price tumbling (Schwartz 2005). Moreover, on 14 April 2005, Energy Minister Ramírez announced that operating strategic agreements between PDVSA and foreign companies would be terminated from 31 December 2005, with a grace period of six months for companies who were parties to operating contracts. Upon termination, operating strategic agreements were converted into joint ventures in which the government assumed a 51–70% stake of the equity, and in addition, there was an increase in the income tax for the IOCs (Freshfields Bruckhaus Deringer 2005).

There was no shortage of disturbing news for the IOCs, as it came out in May 2005 that the IOCs operating in the country were ordered to pay between $2 and 3 billion in back taxes for the previous ten years. For illustration, in early August 2005, Royal Dutch/Shell's office in Maracaibo, a city in western Venezuela, was closed by the Venezuelan tax agency for challenging its $132 million tax bill, which was levied on Shell in July 2005 (BBC News, 12 August 2005). High oil prices meant that other IOCs had to acquiesce, or face similar problems. Minister Ramírez said, 'Most companies are willing to pay, and they are paying' (Schwartz 2005). By 2006, the government collected $266 million in back taxes from the IOCs for the period between 2001 and 2004 (*Petroleum Economist* 2006).

By October 2005, 22 of the 32 operating agreements signed by foreign oil companies with PDVSA had been migrated to the new regime, and in late 2005, Caracas reaffirmed that future investments in the Orinoco Tar Belt were to be subject to higher royalties and that the contractual terms were to be renegotiated at some point. Initially, the affected IOCs said publicly that they were studying the matter and that they were unlikely to pull out of the projects. However, the 2001 Hydrocarbons Law clearly discouraged the IOCs from any new investment in Venezuela, as higher royalties and the limitations placed on JVs made FDI very unattractive (Freshfields Bruckhaus Deringer 2005).

On 1 April 2006, Venezuela's government took control of two oil fields, one operated by France's Total and the other by Ente Nazionale Idrocarburi (ENI) of Italy, after the companies refused to sign up to new arrangements converting their operating contracts into JVs in which PDVSA had a majority stake. Ramírez claimed that Venezuela did not need companies that have refused to adjust to the new terms, and that Total and ENI would not be compensated for the fields they lost. ENI, which invested $1.65 billion in its 60,000 bpd field, lost $900 million, while Total lost approximately $320 million. ExxonMobil earlier sold a minority stake in a small, 15,000 bpd field to Repsol, the field's operator, to avoid the change and confrontation with the government, but it remained active in a bigger, heavy oil project (*The Economist*, 6 April 2006).

In late April 2006, after all 32 oil fields were shifted to joint ventures, there were rumours that four heavy oil projects in the eastern Orinoco River basin, where Exxon Mobil, Chevron, Total, BP, ConocoPhillips and Statoil convert extra heavy crude into 600,000 bpd of synthetic crude using specialized refineries, were to follow suit in near future. It was suggested that the companies involved could see income taxes increased to 50% from 34% and royalties increased to 30% from 16.7%, as according to the new law (*Washington Post*, 23 April 2006).

Indeed, it did not take long for these rumours to materialize. On 8 May 2006, Chávez increased royalties for all companies involved in the country not to 30%, but to 33.3%. This measure was to affect the abovementioned companies extracting heavy crude in the Orinoco Tar Belt, as this area had been exempt from higher royalties in past due to higher investment needs. The income tax was also raised, as predicted, to 50% from 34%. Energy Minister Rafael Ramírez indicated that the new policies were not open for negotiations: 'We don't have anything to discuss with the companies ... The companies have to adjust' (cited in Forero 2006). Finally, in late February 2007, Chávez signed a decree for the government to take a majority (60%) stake in four heavy crude upgrading projects in the Orinoco River basin by 1 May 2007 (Pretel 2007).

All the measures taken by Venezuela in the mid-2000s provide evidence that the 2001 Hydrocarbons Law was applied in practice, and that Venezuela was in a strong bargaining position vis-à-vis the IOCs. With demand for oil growing at a rapid pace and the majority of reserves out of reach to foreign investment in the Middle East, the IOCs had no choice but to accept the new terms in Venezuela. However, Minister Ramírez was not just setting his sights on foreign firms in Venezuela. He wanted PDVSA to work with NOCs in countries such as Iran, Saudi Arabia and Algeria so that the NOCs could wrest even more power away from the likes of ExxonMobil and other IOCs. Thus, PDVSA found new partners for Orinoco JVs – NOCs from political allies, including Brazil, Iran, Russia, Argentina, Spain, China, India, Uruguay, Bolivia, Ecuador, Belarus and Vietnam, operated with technology purchased off the shelf (Mares and Altamirano 2007). For example, one of the NOCs involved, the Chinese National Petroleum Corporation (CNPC), received a best production technology award for its achievements in heavy oil recovery during 2006 (Xu 2007). While PDVSA was to develop 14 blocks in the Orinoco Tar Belt on its own, the other 13 blocks were to be developed through JVs with other NOCs, such as CNPC, who would have at most 49% ownership.

This development served as a sign that any IOC that exits Venezuela would be replaced by a Chinese, Indian, Russian or some other country's NOC. Caracas placed specific emphasis on nurturing its relationship with Beijing. In January 2005, upon Chávez's visit to Beijing, Venezuela signed 19 bilateral oil and gas agreements with China in order to increase exports to Beijing in exchange for the promise of future Chinese investment in Venezuelan oil fields. In May 2005, the first tanker with 1.8 million barrels of crude left Venezuela for China, and in August 2005, Venezuela opened its first oil office in China (Dumbaugh and Sullivan 2005). After exporting only 12,300 bpd in 2004, the following year

Venezuela exported 65,500 bpd of crude oil and products to China. However, after two sales contracts between CNPC and PDVSA were signed in November 2005, Venezuela was to double oil sales to China, to 160,000 bpd in 2006. The plans aimed at increasing the export volumes to 300,000 by the end of 2006, 500,000 bpd by 2010, and 1 million bpd by 2012 (Mares and Altamirano 2007).

In May 2006, PDVSA also announced that it planned to buy 18 oil tankers from Chinese shipyards at a cost of \$1.3 billion to allow for increased shipments to China. Moreover, in March 2007, Chávez said the two countries would start a joint oil shipping company with its own tankers to carry crude and other products between Venezuela and China (Wilson 2007). China also committed to building a number of refineries along its coast in order to process more of Venezuela's high-sulphur crude. For example, in March 2007, Chávez announced plans for Venezuela and China to build three refineries in China that will process a total of 800,000 bpd of heavy Venezuelan crude. Against the backdrop of these commitments, Venezuela's oil exports to China have been on the constant rise since the mid-2000s. As of 2014, China was Venezuela's largest oil customer, replacing the United States.

Chávez's actions against the IOCs had a domino effect as they contributed to similar developments in Bolivia and Ecuador (Philip 2008). In early May 2006, Bolivia's President Evo Morales, a close friend of Chávez, signed a decree placing his country's energy industry under state control, claiming that 'the pillage of our [Bolivia's] natural resources by foreign companies is over' (BBC News, 2 May 2006). He also said that foreign energy firms must agree to channel all their sales through the Bolivian state-run firm, Yacimientos Petrolíferos Fiscales Bolivianos (YPFB), or else leave the country. Although he set the firms a six-month deadline, by May 2006, the military and state energy officials took control of the oil fields and 56 energy installations (Glaister 2006). In the same month, Ecuador nationalized oil fields operated by Occidental, an American IOC (*The Economist*, 18 May 2006).

The consequences of resurgent resource nationalism for major IOCs

The developments in the international oil industry during the 2000s have had a negative effect on the health of IOCs as viable business entities. Ostensibly, it is hard to believe that major IOCs may be facing difficult times ahead. The six major IOCs are some of the world's largest and most powerful corporations. In 2010, their combined profits amounted to US\$79 billion and their sales revenues close to US\$1.5 trillion (*Fortune* 2011). Without a doubt, high oil prices have assisted major IOCs in generating unprecedented profits. At the same time, however, high oil prices fuelled the resurgence of resource nationalism, which imposed severe limits to the areas open to IOC investment and had negative effects on their operations. By the 2010s, it had become increasingly difficult for IOCs to find attractive ways to reinvest their profits due to limited drilling prospects.

The lack of investment opportunities has been a significant challenge for major IOCs in the past decade as they have been unable to replace their reserves. In the oil industry, reserve replacement is the best guide to whether a company will be able to maintain or grow production in the future. It is a key performance measure, which is critical to the way financial markets value a company's stock as it measures a company's ability to continue to operate as a viable business entity (Wright and Gallun 2008). A healthy reserve replacement ratio should always be over 100%. Between 1998 and 2002, the five majors 'replaced' 99.7% of oil produced, which was at the 'break-even' point. However, a composite ratio for five major IOCs has been below that level in the second half of the 2000s. Between 2003 and 2007 they 'replaced' only 51.7% of oil produced (OPEC 2003; OPEC 2008). In 2004, Royal Dutch/Shell's announcement that it had revised down their proven oil reserves by 20% suggested that oil majors have faced significant difficulties in booking new reserves during the past decade. Their poor reserve replacement performance is in contrast to the 1970s and 1980s when strong IOC exploration spending spurred a large increase in non-OPEC production, promoting diversity of supply and enhancing US energy security for two decades (Myers Jaffe and Soligo 2007). These non-OPEC assets have transitioned toward natural, geologic decline.

The biggest obstacle the majors have faced in replacing their reserves is the ultimate peculiarity of the oil business. Oil is the only industry in which the cheapest to produce oil reserves and largest assets, those located in Russia and OPEC states, are not in the hands of the most efficient and best capitalized firms, the oil majors. Instead, they are controlled by NOCs, and in most cases the government owns and self-finances the whole operation from reserves to pipelines. As illustrated in the previous section, in numerous countries, foreign investment in oil exploration and production (upstream) activities is banned or saddled with strong disincentives. Desperate majors have been looking for growth in West Africa, the Caspian, Russia's Far East, Canada's oil sands and the ultra-deep waters off the coastal Brazil. Nevertheless, this new wave of oil exploration has proven to be difficult and dangerous, due to complex oil formations and unforgiving environments that have required much up-front capital expenditure; and unreliable legal frameworks and political risks associated with investing in some of these areas. As a result, analysts have suggested that major IOCs have been confronted with their most far-reaching test in decades (Bozon et al. 2005).

As a consequence of their inability to replace reserves, the five majors' booked oil reserves, oil production and Reserve-to-Production (R/P) ratio have all dropped during the 2000s (Table 3.1). For example, their booked oil reserves dropped by over 20% between 1999 and 2009 and their R/P ratio dropped from 12 years to 9 years during the same period. In contrast, the top ten NOCs in 2006 have had an R/P ratio of 78 years (Pirog 2007). Moreover, major IOCs' composite oil production dropped by 7.6% between 1999 and 2009. In 2009, they owned only 2.4% of the world's total oil reserves (down from 3.8% in 1999) (OPEC 2010). In 2010, in the world's list of top 20 oil companies by reserves ExxonMobil was ranked eleventh, the top ranked major (*The Economist*, 29 October 2011). In 2009, the five majors

Table 3.1 Major IOCs' composite reserve, production, sales and financial data (1999, 2004, and 2009)

	1999	2004	2009
Reserve size (billion bbl)	40.9	34.7	32.3
Reserve size (share of global)	3.8%	2.9%	2.4%
Production (mil. bpd)	9.4	10.7	9.7
Production (share of global)	12.9%	13.3%	12.2%
R/P ratio (years)	12.0	8.9	9.1
Refined products sold (mbpd)	28.3	29.2	25.3
Return on investment	$19.7 bn	-$26.2 bn	-$66.7 bn

Sources: OPEC (2003, 2008, 2013); BP (2000, 2005, 2010).

Note: bbl (barrels); mbpd (million barrels per day).

produced only 12.2% of globally produced oil (OPEC 2010). In contrast, in 1972, the majors controlled 91% of Middle Eastern production and 77% of the non-communist world's oil reserves outside the United States (Bromley 2005).

In the capital-intensive oil industry, return on investment (ROI) is a key measure as it reflects not just how much profit a company made, but the cost of making it. As a result of high oil prices, major IOCs generated unprecedented profits during the 2000s, and had positive ROI in some years during the first half of the decade. However, in the second half of the decade, they spent much more to maintain their profit levels. For example, although they spent an unprecedented $135 billion in 2008, in 2009 their cumulative profits were only $68 billion (OPEC 2010). The bottom line is that value creation by oil companies had stagnated in the second half of the 2000s. While major IOCs have been profiting more than ever before, they have also been spending unprecedented amounts to generate those profits. The majors have been severely affected by rising costs in exploration and extraction, and the inability to access oil-rich regions. The cost of labour, supplies and the energy needed to explore for and produce oil have all soared throughout the 2000s, driving up the investment needed to find and develop new fields.

Conclusion

By focusing on major IOCs, this chapter examined the changing balance of power in the international oil industry in the 2000s, which has been characterized as conflictive. Due to their weak relative bargaining power, in the 2000s the IOCs have been unsuccessful in bargaining with host states and their NOCs. High oil prices, increased industry competition from NOCs, and the lack of alternative investment options for IOCs have translated to weaker bargaining power and unfavourable outcomes.

As illustrated by the Venezuelan example, during the 2000s, the country's former leader Hugo Chávez marginalized the private sector by changing Venezuela's hydrocarbon legislation. The heavy-oil projects, which were previously under private control, have fallen under state control. Besides the oil industry in Venezuela, increased regulation and/or nationalization followed in Bolivia and Ecuador. There have been similar developments in other major oil-producing regions. The major IOCs have been unable to effectively address the serious issues caused by the resurgence in resource nationalism. As illustrated in this chapter, they have struggled to replace their reserves and have been unable to effectively respond to increasing competition from INOCs.

Bibliography

Agmon, T. (2003). Who gets what: The MNE, the national state and the distributional rffects of globalization. *Journal of International Business Studies*, 34 (5), pp. 416–27.

BBC News (12 August 2005). Venezuela-Shell tax row heats up. Available from: http://news.bbc.co.uk/2/hi/business/4147622.stm. [Accessed: 12 June 2015].

BBC News (2 May 2006). Bolivia gas under state control. Available from: http://news.bbc.co.uk/2/hi/americas/4963348.stm. [Accessed: 12 June 2015].

Bozon, I.J.H., Hall, S.J.D., & Øygard, S.H. (2005). What's next for big oil? *The McKinsey Quarterly*, 2, pp. 94–105.

BP (2000). *BP Statistical Review of World Energy 2000*. London: BP.

BP (2005). *BP Statistical Review of World Energy 2005*. London: BP.

BP (2010). *BP Statistical Review of World Energy 2010*. London: BP.

Bromley, S. (2005). The United States and the control of world oil. *Government and Opposition*, 40 (2), pp. 225–55.

Chen, M.E. (2007). Chinese national oil companies and human rights. *Orbis*, 51 (1), pp. 41–54.

Chen, M.E., and Myers, Jaffe, A. (2007). Energy security and national oil companies. *The Whitehead Journal of Diplomacy and International Relations*, 8 (1), pp. 9–21.

Dumbaugh, K., and Sullivan, M.P. (2005). China's growing interest in Latin America. *CRS Report for Congress*. Washington, D.C.: Congressional Research Service, The Library of Congress, April 20.

Dunning, J.H. (1998). An overview of relations with national governments. *New Political Economy*, 3 (2), pp. 280–84.

The Economist (6 April 2006). Leaving the door ajar. Available from: http://www.economist.com/node/6775120. [Accessed: 12 June 2015].

The Economist (18 May 2006). Grabbing occidental. Available from: http://www.economist.com/node/6954013. [Accessed: 12 June 2015].

The Economist (29 October 2011). Big oil's bigger brothers. Available from: http://www.economist.com/node/21534794. [Accessed: 12 June 2015].

Eden, L., Lenway, S., and Schuler, D.A. (2005). From the obsolescing bargain to the political bargaining model. In Grosse, R.E. (ed.). *International Business and Government Relations in the 21st Century*. Cambridge, MA: Cambridge University Press, pp. 251–71.

Forero, J. (2006). Venezuela seizes control of two oil fields. *The New York Times*, 4 April. Available from: http://www.nytimes.com/2006/04/04/business/worldbusiness/04oils.html. [Accessed: 12 June 2015].

Fortune (2011). Global 500 2011. Available from: http://www.ft.com/cms/s/0/bd675ba2-98d5-11e0-bd66-00144feab49a.html#axzz3coHOFjKF. [Accessed: 12 June 2015].

Freshfields Brukhaus Deringer (2005). Venezuela: Proposed measures against oil and gas investors. *Briefing*, May. Available from: http://www.freshfields.com/uploadedFiles/SiteWide/Knowledge/Venezuela%20-%20proposed%20measures%20against%20oil%20and%20gas%20investors.pdf. [Accessed: 12 June 2015].

Giusti, L.E. (1999). La apertura: The opening of Venezuela's oil industry. *Journal of International Affairs*, 53 (1), pp. 117–28.

Glaister, D. (2006). How Morales took on the oil giants – and won his people back. *The Guardian*, 5 May. Available from: http://www.theguardian.com/world/2006/may/06/oil.business. [Accessed: 12 June 2015].

Globerman, S., and Shapiro, D. (1998), Canadian government policies toward inward foreign direct investment. Working Paper 24, Industry Canada.

Grosse, R.E. (2005). The bargaining view of government–business relations. In Grosse, R.E. (ed.). *International Business and Government Relations in the 21st Century*. Cambridge, MA: Cambridge University Press, pp. 273–89.

Joffé, G., Stevens, P., George, T., Lux, J., and Searle, C. (2009). Expropriation of oil and gas investments: Historical, legal and economic perspectives in a new age of resource nationalism. *Journal of World Energy Law & Business*, 2 (1), pp. 3–23.

Johnston, D. (2008). Changing fiscal landscape. *Journal of World Energy Law & Business*, 1 (1), pp. 31–54.

Kobrin, S.J. (1987). Testing the bargaining hypothesis in the manufacturing sector in developing countries. *International Organization*, 41 (4), pp. 609–38.

Luo, Y. (2001). Toward a cooperative view of MNC-host government relations: Building blocks and performance implications. *Journal of International Business Studies*, 32 (2), pp. 401–19.

Mahoney, J.T. (1995). The management of resources and the resource of management. *Journal of Business Research*, 33 (1), pp. 91–101.

Marcel, V. (2006). *Oil Titans: National Oil Companies in the Middle East*. London: Chatham House.

Mares, D.R., and Altamirano, N. (2007). Venezuela's PDVSA and world energy markets: Corporate strategies and political factors determining its behavior and influence. Paper prepared in conjunction with an energy study sponsored by Japan Petroleum Energy Center and the James A. Baker III Institute for Public Policy, Rice University, March. Available from: http://bakerinstitute.org/media/files/page/9c4eb216/noc_pdvsa_mares_altamirano.pdf. [Accessed: 12 June 2015].

Maugeri, L. (2006). *The Age of Oil: The Mythology, History, and Future of the World's Most Controversial Resource*. New York: Praeger.

Mikdashi, Z. (1976). *The International Politics of Natural Resources*, Ithaca, NY: Cornell University Press.

Mommer, B. (1998). *The New Governance of Venezuelan Oil*. Oxford: Oxford Institute for Energy Studies. Working Paper, No. 23, April. Available from: http://www.oxfordenergy.org/1998/04/the-new-governance-of-venezuelan-oil/. [Accessed: 12 June 2015].

Moran, T.H. (1974), *Multinational Corporations and the Politics of Dependence: Copper in Chile*, Princeton, NJ: Princeton University Press;

Moran, T.H. (1998). *Foreign Direct Investment and Development: The New Policy Agenda for Developing Countries and Economies in Transition*. Washington, DC: Institute for International Economics.

Morse, E.L. (1999). A new political economy of oil? *Journal of International Affairs*, 53 (1), pp. 1–29.

Mouawad, J. (2006). Western firms feel a pinch from oil nationalism. *International Herald Tribune*, 7 May. Available from: http://www.nytimes.com/2006/05/07/business/worldbusiness/07iht-OIL.html?_r=0. [Accessed: 12 June 2015].

Myers Jaffe, A., and Soligo, R. (2007). IOCs: Investment and Industry Structure. Paper prepared in conjunction with an energy study sponsored by Japan Petroleum Energy Center and the James A, Baker III Institute for Public Policy, Rice University, March. Available from: http://bakerinstitute.org/media/files/event/373c4d98/Hou-Soligo-IOC.pdf. [Accessed: 12 June 2015].

Nebus, J.F., and Rufin, C. (2010). Extending the bargaining power model: Explaining bargaining outcomes among nations, MNEs, and NGOs. *Journal of International Business Studies*, 41 (6), pp. 996–1015.

OPEC (Organization of the Petroleum Exporting Countries) (2003). *Annual Statistical Bulletin 2002*. Vienna: Ueberreuter.

OPEC (Organization of the Petroleum Exporting Countries) (2008). *Annual Statistical Bulletin 2007*. Vienna: Ueberreuter.

OPEC (Organization of the Petroleum Exporting Countries) (2010) *Annual Statistical Bulletin 2009*. Vienna: Ueberreuter.

OPEC (Organization of the Petroleum Exporting Countries) (2013). Annual Statistical Bulletin 2012. Vienna: Ueberreuter.

Oxford Analytica (2008). IOCs face increasing NOC challenge, 11 September. Available from: https://www.oxan.com/display.aspx?ItemID=DB145455. [Accessed: 12 June 2015].

Panov, I. (2008). Constraints of foreign investment to subsoil use in Russia. *Journal of World Energy Law & Business*, 1 (3), pp. 224–38.

Petroleum Economist. (2006). News in brief. *Petroleum Economist*, (1), p. 10.

Philip, G. (2008). *Oil and Politics in Latin America: Nationalist Movements and State Companies*. Cambridge: Cambridge University Press.

Pirog, R. (2007). The role of national oil companies in the international oil market. *CRS Report for Congress*, 21 August. Available from: http://fas.org/sgp/crs/misc/RL34137.pdf. [Accessed: 12 June 2015].

Pretel, E.A. (2007). Exxon to cede oil project ops to Venezuela by May. *Reuters*, March 1. Available from: http://www.canada.com/story.html?id=5de162e9-ebf0-431b-8687-bb59a3c7b699. [Accessed: 12 June 2015].

Ramamurti, R., and Doh, J.P. (2004). Rethinking foreign infrastructure investment in developing countries. *Journal of World Business*, 39 (2), pp. 151–67.

Regnier, E. (2007). Oil and energy price volatility. *Energy Economics*, 29 (3), pp. 405–27.

Schwartz, N.D. (2005). Oil's new Mr. Big. *Fortune*, 3 October, p. 57.

Stevens, P. (2008). National oil companies and international oil companies in the Middle East: Under the shadow of government and the resource nationalism cycle. *Journal of World Energy Law & Business*, 1 (1), pp. 5–30.

Stevens, P. (1998). *Strategic Positioning in the Oil Industry: Trends and Options*. Abu Dhabi, UAE: Emirates Center for Strategic Studies and Research.

Van Der Linde, C. (2000). *The State and the International Oil Market: Competition and the Changing Ownership of Crude Oil Assets*, Boston, MA: Kluwer Academic Publishers.

Vernon, R. (1971). *Sovereignty at Bay: The Multinational Spread of US Enterprises*. New York: Basic Books.

Vernon, R. (1977). *Storm Over the Multinationals: The Real Issues*. Cambridge, MA: Harvard University Press.

Vivoda, V. (2008). *The Return of the Obsolescing Bargain and the Decline of Big Oil: A Study of Bargaining in the Contemporary Oil Industry.* Saarbrücken, Germany: VDM Verlag.

Vivoda, V. (2009a). Resource nationalism, bargaining and international oil companies: Challenges and change in the new millennium. *New Political Economy,* 14 (4), pp. 517–34.

Vivoda, V. (2009b). China challenges global capitalism. *Australian Journal of International Affairs,* 63 (1), pp. 22–40.

Vivoda, V. (2011). Bargaining model for the international oil industry. *Business and Politics,* 13 (4), pp.1–34.

Wälde, T.W. (2008). Renegotiating acquired rights in the oil and gas industries: Industry and political cycles meet the rule of law. *Journal of World Energy Law & Business,* 1 (1), pp. 55–97.

Washington Post (23 April 2006) Venezuela to expand joint oil ventures, *Washington Post.* Available from: http://www.washingtonpost.com/wp-dyn/content/article/2006/04/23/AR2006042300051.html. [Accessed: 12 June 2015].

Wilson, E.J. (1986). The petro-political cycle in world oil markets. In Enders, R.L., and Kim, J. (eds.). *Energy Resource Development: Politics and Policies.* Westport, CT: Greenwood Press, pp. 1–20.

Wilson, E.J. (1987). World politics and international energy markets. *International Organization,* 41 (1), pp. 125–49.

Wilson, P. (2007). Chavez: China to become a top client. *Associated Press,* 23 March. Available from: http://www.globalexchange.org/news/chavez-china-become-top-oil-client. [Accessed: 12 June 2015].

Wright, C.J., and Gallun, R. (2008), *Fundamentals of Oil & Gas Accounting.* Tulsa, OK: Pennwell.

Xu, X. (2007). Chinese NOCs' overseas strategies: Background, comparison and remarks. Paper p in conjunction with an energy study sponsored by Japan Petroleum Energy Center and the James A. Baker III Institute for Public Policy, Rice University, March. Available from: http://bakerinstitute.org/media/files/page/94235e0c/noc_chinesenocs_xu.pdf. [Accessed: 12 June 2015].

4 The emergence of industrial policy lite

Latin America's blind spot

Anil Hira

Introduction

History repeats itself in Latin America. As at the turn of the twentieth century, in the 1920s, and in the 1960s, we are just exiting another commodity boom during which Latin American exports soared. In the 1920s and 1960s, incipient industrialization took place, but in a haphazard way that yielded limited success. To date, there are very few independent competitive manufacturers and little in the way of serious industrial policy in the region. Instead, a movement towards market reliance or incoherent policymaking has prevailed. Such policies seemed fine when commodity prices were high, but once they declined, as was the case following the 2008 global recession, Latin America found itself struggling with perennial issues of volatile growth, macro-economic instability, and low levels of social mobility (Prebisch 1950).

In this chapter, we examine the results of the latest wave of policy entrepreneurship, resulting from perceived failures of the most recent return to the market under neoliberal policies in the 1980s. Some countries have entered into a post-neoliberal period with bold experiments in both industrial policy and redistribution. However, we find that despite these efforts, the historical patterns appear to hold. The limitations on industrial policy experiments suggest the need for increased attention to the timing of policies, and state autonomy and capacity.

How the Washington consensus came to be questioned

As described in detail elsewhere, Latin America engaged in a prolonged industrialization process that began when it was cut off from foreign trade during the Great Depression, choking its export markets and ability to import manufactures (Thorp 1998). The heavy resource dependency of the region on minerals and/or agricultural exports was exposed, and led to a 'natural' phase of import substitution, requiring minimal state intervention, as World Wars I and II meant few manufactured imports were available. Industries such as food processing, household goods, and textiles were fairly easily established by local entrepreneurs. The development of such industries changed the political landscape of Latin America, with rising workers' movements coinciding with a wave of nationalism, as typified by the nationalization of Mexican oil fields by President Lázaro Cárdenas in 1938.

The second wave of import substitution occurred from the early 1960s and 1970s, this time with the support of state planning, borrowing, and protectionism. However, because the Latin American state was unable to gather either the resources or the knowhow to manage the process, in short order, multinational companies and finance were sought, resulting in the 'Triple Alliance' of states, multinationals, and domestic capital (Evans 1979). The results, in general, were industries that required ongoing state subsidization and protection (Hira 1998).

It is hard to tell if these industries would have eventually become competitive. Much of the region was mired in armed civil strife or dictatorship throughout the 1970s. The global problems of stagflation, in the context of OPEC oil price increases, helped to create increasing macro-economic imbalances in the form of budget and trade deficits, leading to unmanageable external debts by the 1980s, when global interest rates were ratcheted up as the United States attempted to control inflation. Almost all of the debt was dollarized.

In this context, the Washington Consensus took hold, emphasising fiscal discipline, trade and financial liberalization, and privatization, reflecting a desire to move to a more market-based economy (Williamson 1989). International organizations such as the IMF promoted the Consensus through creating conditionalities in exchange for help in servicing debts. These conditionalities came to be known as 'structural adjustment programs' (Hira 2011). The Washington Consensus is still promoted by the World Bank, as Wade notes (2013: 227).

Neoliberalism led to lower inflation, and more rapid growth in some cases, but that growth was more volatile. Meanwhile inequality continued to increase (Hira 2007a). As (Schamis 2002) describes, the net effect of neoliberalism in many cases was private interest capture given the weak ability, both in technical and political terms, of the state to regulate markets, as well as the limited size and/or concentration of economic activities. Moreover, as developing countries opened their economies, they risked the possibility of becoming swamped by foreign companies with better access to capital, technology, and economies of scale. Reflecting the lack of attention to distributive concerns in economics, such issues were largely ignored.

The emergence of 'industrial policy lite'

When there is a crisis of faith in the prevailing wisdom, space is opened for policy experiments, but only when a paradigmatic alternative presents itself (Hira 1998). It is hard to put an exact date on the re-opening of the debate about industrial policy, but we can see clear signs from the mid-2000s onwards. We should not exaggerate any revival; most mainstream economists continue to deny the value of industrial policy, which they deride as 'picking winners', implying that one also creates losers in the process (Williamson 2008: 27). They are sometimes open to public policies such as the elimination of tax loopholes and the provision of research and development funding through competition, but prioritizing particular industries is anathema. Thus, their new agenda centres on policies such as ensuring property rights and judicial reform, as reflected in the World Bank's indices for good governance, and creating the 'institutions' that allow free markets to function well (World Bank, n.d.). The other areas of the new prescription relate to export promotion and free trade agreements to reduce trade barriers. We can call this package of market friendly adjustments 'industrial policy lite'.

Douglass North's early research into the role of institutions in economic history is the foundation for this new perspective (North 1981). Authors such Acemoglu, et al. (2001) have become professional heroes by running large-n regressions showing that institutional stability is correlated with historical economic growth; findings that have been corroborated in Latin America by researchers from the Inter-American Development Bank (Chong and Zanforlin 2004). However, this level of analysis misses why the same institutions sometimes lead to successful industries and sometimes to failures. For example, Japan has long struggled with getting an aerospace industry off the ground, though it has been highly successful in promoting industries in a variety of other sectors. Furthermore, the attack on picking winners ignores the hypocrisy of what has worked in the history of Northern industrialization from railroads to aerospace – namely government promotion of industry in a variety of ways (Hira 2003).

This approach to treating institutions as a residual variable is evidently limited when one goes beyond the world of large-n regressions towards practical policy advice, and has opened the way for revisiting a more active industrial policy. As Rodrik states (2006b, 979–80), 'the focus on institutions has potentially debilitating side effects.... Institutions are by their very nature deeply embedded in society. If growth indeed requires major institutional transformation ... how can we not be pessimistic about the prospects for growth in poor countries?'. Thus, he concludes that the updated version of the Washington Consensus, including targeted poverty reduction, flexible labour markets, and corporate governance, is a dead-end. The reasons he gives for this reinforce our observations. First, he notes that the cross-national growth literature deals with general correlations on long-run growth, rather than any specific test of different types of institutional design and its effects on growth, so the only policy implication is for developing countries to become more developed. Secondly, he points out that the myth of market superiority persists because the developing country is always blamed for not implementing the programe correctly, thus rendering such theories 'unfalsifiable' (2006b: 980).

The financial collapse of 2008 further turned the tables on the premise that unfettered markets would create stable growth. Just as the Keynesian paradigm could not explain stagflation, the neoliberal paradigm cannot explain how low interest rates could lead to the irrational speculation that causes asset bubbles, or the lack of response by the economy to cheap money after the crisis ensued. This has opened the door for a Keynesian revival, which focuses on the need for temporary stimulus, as championed by celebrated economist Paul Krugman (2014).

Within this theoretical confusion, there was an opening for discussing industrial policy. Contained within the 2009 stimulus bill in the US were a variety of supports for industries, including individual companies. Some of these efforts went beyond bailing out the too-big-to-fail banks and big three auto firms. For example, the US government also supported electric vehicle maker Tesla.

Rodrik has become the de facto champion of the new industrial policy conversation. Yet, he is ambiguous about when and where it works. For example, he expresses doubts about 'picking winners' and correcting market failures by pointing to the limited information and incentives available to bureaucrats, in comparison to the private sector (Rodrik 2006a). He calls instead for a 'diagnostic' approach to be applied to economic growth issues, which includes an examination of government failures, infrastructure and human capital deficits, market failures, and financial systems (Hausmann et al. 2008). This is echoed at the micro-level by economists who believe that industrial clusters can be created using a flowchart or similar type of checklist (Kuchiki and Tsuji 2010). It is hard to see this as a major improvement. Carrying out such a diagnosis will lead to predictably unhelpful results, not unlike the large economic growth studies which 'reveal' positive correlations between growth and education or stable institutions. In a sense, this approach moves towards a 'do everything' approach, which makes prioritization exceedingly difficult when everything needs attention.

Development organizations have taken note of the change in the economics discourse and have begun to reconsider the acceptability of industrial policy. However, this reconsideration occurs within the constraints of the existing orthodoxy. In 2001, World Bank economists De Ferranti, Perry and Lederman signalled the opening of the door with a study of comparative advantage that began, 'we must reiterate that rich endowments of natural resources, combined with the aggressive pursuit and adoption of new technologies, are a proven growth recipe. Further, the evidence strongly indicates that their development does not preclude the development of manufacturing or other activities in the "knowledge" economy' (2001: 10). In fact, they interpreted Latin American history during the post-World War II import substitution phase as evidence of the negative effects of ignoring resource endowments, when comparing economic achievement between this period and the neoliberal period reveals a mixed picture with higher economic growth rates under ISI.[1] In addition, income distribution did not improve during this period, and further deteriorated during the neoliberal era (Hira 2007a). Echoing the World Bank's East Asian Miracle report (1993), ascribing growth to institutions that allowed markets to function well, they called for complementary policies related to education, infrastructure, and institutions.

The World Bank held a conference entitled 'Implementing Policies for Competitive Industries', in October 2013, which entertained some Rodrik-like versions of market-friendly industrial promotion. This followed the appointment of some new officials in the World Bank who were more open to limited and highly constrained government interventions in industries in which a country already had a comparative advantage. However, one such official suggested that less than 10% of World Bank economists were sympathetic to any kind of intervention. Similarly, the constraints on direct interventions imposed by the World Trade Organization in recent years directly curtailed the instruments of East Asian success (Wade 2013: 235, 237). Nonetheless, some economists have begun to argue that the state has a role to play given the increasing importance of knowledge content in new goods that support competitiveness in emerging industries. This lies behind the strong support for educational reform found in some analyses (Bianchi and Labory 2011: 142).

The new market-friendly approach to industrial policy is palatable because it does not represent a major contradiction to neoliberalism. In the abstract, it is not far from Robert Wade's seminal work on East Asia, where he calls state intervention 'market-conforming' (1990: 24). However, unlike Wade, most economists remain vehemently opposed to targeting. Industrial policy lite economists such as Rodrik limit the role of the state to that of 'pathfinder', 'catalyst', or 'coach' (Bianchi and Labory 2006: 20). Many economists focus on labour reform, for example, such as reducing unionization and workers' rights, in order to increase labour force participation, especially among young workers. Similarly, increasing educational choice and improving the fit between education and market needs are seen as a way to improve competition among educational institutions. Despite its success in picking winners, China is often dismissed as a model for other developing countries because of its unusual features – size of population and internal market, control by the Communist Party and the military, and mixture of capitalist and planning features. More importantly, China is seen as highly vulnerable to collapse from political, economic, or even environmental sources.

Within this opening, then, there is room for a redefinition of the state, between planning and the market, towards what Levy (2006: 386) calls 'the constructive state'. He refers to the state playing a role of midwife of new technologies and industries through financial support, regulation, and other means. This is termed 'horizontal' support, meaning that efforts are not focused on particular companies, but are indirect in their approach. However, unlike the neoliberal period, such policies do sometimes target specific sectors (Warwick 2013: 8). World Bank economists Lederman and Maloney (2012: 5-9, 106) carefully bridge the gap between the religious acceptance of free market tenets and the minor transgression of limited horizontal intervention. Using a large-n empirical approach, they conclude, with regard to the resource curse, that the *average* effect of natural resource endowments (measured by mining output as a share of GDP) on growth appears to be positive, although they raise concerns about export concentration - oddly enough, not seeing the natural link between the two. They also conclude that 'a combination of orthodox pro-trade policy and rather soft industrial policies in support of exporting activities could be useful in raising the skill premium within countries. This, in turn, could raise private incentives to invest in education and skills that would help national development through the social spillovers of education' (Lederman and Maloney 2012: 7). Again, they fail to see the inherent contradiction between industrial policy and orthodox pro-trade policy: Which industries are to be favoured?

Moreover, one can think of any number of highly-educated countries in the developing world that still struggle economically, such as Argentina and Sri Lanka.

In terms of value added, and the importance of improving quality, they state that 'certain goods have greater potential for quality growth due to longer "quality ladders" that offer stronger convergence effects toward higher unit values', yet 'there is no obvious market failure that suggests that countries are incorrectly specialized should they find themselves in goods, such as commodities, with shorter ladders' (Lederman and Maloney 2012: 7). This ignores the obvious fact that so many struggling developing countries, from Venezuela to Bangladesh, are highly concentrated in a few commodity industries. They go on to suggest that the answer relies in the residual factor (once again) of poorly functioning institutions, although they do not test the effect of industrial policy separately from institutional strength, or whether the latter is sufficient. Similar to growth equations, the findings of the large-n studies suggest that countries with strong institutions are going to have successful economies – hardly a revelation.

Within Latin America, there are few signs of bolder thinking. Some CEPAL economists, namely Mario Cimoli and Jorge Katz, have long argued for the need to support technological industries through horizontal measures. In a 2002 report, they examined the relative distribution of manufacturing output by subsector for Argentina, Brazil, Chile, Colombia, and Mexico between 1970 and 1996. For metalworking industry and labour-intensive traditional industries, they found significant declines over this period. Increases in transport equipment manufacture occurred in some of the countries, but declined in others. The most significant increases, across the board, were in foodstuffs, beverages and tobacco and in natural resource processing industries, which also grew to constitute between 42 and 47% of all manufacturing in these countries. Only Mexico showed no growth in this category at 46% (Cimoli and Katz 2002: 25). The authors identified market failures (such as lack of competition); entitlement failures (such as weak health systems); learning and knowledge-creation failures; and a lack of coordination synergies as the underlying problems of Latin American economic performance (Cimoli, et al. 2003: 48), a diagnosis comfortably compatible with Rodrik and the World Bank.

Hausmann and Rodrik (2006) hint at the possibility of picking winners, but never explain how to do this, instead falling back on the principle of (limited) market failure. They suggest that the neoliberal arguments, that governments cannot substitute for decentralized market-based information, and suffer from incentives issues, do not hold up in all situations. Following Hausmann and Klinger (2006), they suggest that industrial policy choices can be metaphorically viewed as a forest of potential economic activities, with each state being a monkey on a tree. As the monkey can swing on a vine from tree to tree, countries can move most easily to adjacent areas to the products and services that they already produce. Using a large-n empirical study, they map out the production space to show that most countries have production profiles of similar products. This is a neat way of hedging bets by saying that states sometimes succeed and sometimes fail, but that general guidelines about how to improve success should preserve the doctrine of the optimality of markets, and comparative advantage.

Thus, their conclusion remains, unsurprisingly, muddled: 'what will work in specific settings must remain highly uncertain .... An open-minded, experimental approach, together with a penchant for evaluation to ascertain what is working and what is not, is more likely to produce structural transformation than an approach that relies on first principles or best-practice blueprints imported from elsewhere' (Hausmann and Klinger 2006: 38). Devlin and Moguillansky echo our conclusion that that the new industrial policy in Latin America is incoherent. 'In some cases (the new strategies) are only generic aspirational statements with little guidance on exactly what is to be done, how it is to be done, and who will do it. Some ... have so many priorities (that) there is no strategic prioritization at all, or even any hint of the sequencing of desirable actions' (2011: 238).

Three new economic strategy experiments emerge in Latin America

Within this context, the region was ripe for industrial policy lite experiments by the 1990s. Latin America, which had undergone democratic transitions in the 1980s–1990s, and was suffering from the neglect of distributional issues under the military regimes and the neoliberal reform programmes, was open to new ideas by aspiring politicians seeking to mark themselves as progenitors of a new era. At the same time, the rapid growth and control of inflation in a few model countries, particularly Chile, gave elements of the Washington Consensus sticking power. Moreover, the apparent failure of socialist ideas throughout the world, highlighted by the fall of the Berlin Wall in 1989, made a return to a central planning model, with which an active industrial policy was associated, unthinkable.

At the same time, with the return of democracy, distributional issues naturally became more pressing as new voices were openly heard. Moreover, the more activist and distribution-oriented policies of the European Union in the 1990s inspired renewed confidence that growth and distribution could work together. As the Chinese economy began to create a commodity boom and growth improved in LA, the urgency of addressing distributional issues increased, leading, for example, to protests in Argentina, Chile, and Brazil, and ongoing conflict in Paraguay.

This context could have led to an active industrial policy. Reinforcing Prebisch's analysis, the resource curse perspective re-emerged in the 1990s (Auty 1995; Karl 1997), which suggested that corruption and concentration of income could be related to over-reliance on a few commodities. These studies tended to focus on mineral exports because of the spectacular boom in oil prices, but similar arguments can be made for agricultural concentration, bearing in mind concentration in land ownership. High technology and capital–labour ratios, and limited spillover effects, along with Dutch disease effects are just a few of the plausible reasons why dependence on mineral exports could be problematic. Leamer et al. (1999) find that natural resource abundance, and particularly tropical agriculture, tends to soak up capital in a country, retarding the development of manufacturing. In the process, human capital (and therefore, income distribution) becomes under-developed as agriculture and mining are less labour-intensive. Other authors find that natural resources are correlated with lower growth, exports, and human capital (i.e., Chami Batista 2004; Blanco and Grier 2012). They therefore find a significant correlation between natural resource abundance and higher income inequality. More concerning still is the observation that concentration of mineral incomes seems to go with corruption (Kolstad and Søreide 2009).

However, by the 2000s, a response came from international institutions seeking to refute the resource curse, which pointed to exceptional countries such as New Zealand that achieved development largely on an agriculturally-based economy using specialized knowledge (Farinelli 2012). Collier and Venables (2011) reinforced the World Bank position, suggesting that natural resources (their focus is on mining) can be a very positive source of economic growth if the government takes an active role in exploration, taxation, property rights enforcement, and creating a funding mechanism to reduce the Dutch disease and save for busts. Other large-n studies found a positive relationship between natural resources, growth, and exports (Stijins 2006). International development organizations generally supported the mining industry. For example, on the World Bank website, the following statement is made, 'Ample evidence exists that countries that adopt modern mining legislation and offer an enabling environment can attract private sector investment …. This, in turn, contributes to increased tax revenues, export earnings, employment opportunities, infrastructure development especially in rural areas, and transfer of technology to the host countries', as long as 'good governance' accompanies it (World Bank 2013). The 'as long as' is never really defined or operationalized.

Thus, the post-neoliberal proponents via industrial policy lite see comparative advantage as an unavoidable truth (i.e., Wood and Berge 1997), and argue that industrial policy should be focused on developing new relatively abundant commodities, or complementary products where advantage is present. Protection is a dead-end as it leads to uncompetitive industries. Instead, regional economists focus on improving education, or human and productive capital, which is the other key differentiating factor (along with institutions) between Latin America and the successful resource exporters (US, Canada, and Australia) (Maloney et al. 2002). The diversification of Chile into new agricultural areas such as wine is a perfect example. If there are development problems, as noted, these are generally assigned to 'weak institutions', particularly property rights, which, if corrected, mean that resource abundance would be an advantage, as has occurred in the historical development of Australia, Canada, and the United States.

From this backdrop we can start to trace the outlines of three new models which combine different elements of both market forces and an attempt to address distributional issues in substantial fashion. The three general strategies are reflected in the democratic politics of each country, though naturally there are differences on a national level. In one set of countries, namely Mexico, Chile, Colombia, Peru, Paraguay and El Salvador, centrist and right-wing governments took power on a platform of conservative economic management, promising economic growth through neoliberal economic policies. These governments have embraced the comparative advantage argument that natural resources can be a vehicle for growth. They have aggressively signed free trade pacts, sought out foreign investment through promises of secure contracts, and shied away from large scale re-distributional programs, and generally aligned themselves with the US economy. There is a great deal of differentiation across the countries.

For example, in Mexico, the rightist National Action Party (PAN) government and the new conservative wing of the Institutional Revolutionary Party (PRI) have moved cautiously towards privatization of the energy sector, while in Colombia, the state-owned oil company, ECOPETROL, was allowed greater autonomy and to issue public stock shares. This is not to say that there have been no efforts at diversification, rather that, as in the case of Mexico or El Salvador's *maquiladora* (labour-intensive manufacturing assembly operations), or Chile's fresh fruit and fish industries, they come from the policies embedded in industrial policy lite, or market-friendly policies. They have primarily had as their basis a clearly identifiable comparative advantage based on natural resource abundance, and a goal of export promotion. In short, redistribution is largely expected to come from growth, led by the natural resource sectors, but lifting up the rest of the economy *en route*.

In the second set of countries, the state has gone in the opposite direction – instead of the state retrenching, it has become pro-active in seizing larger segments of the economy for the purpose of redistribution and the reduction of poverty and inequality. These 'Bolivarian' countries follow the example of President Hugo Chávez's Venezuelan revolution of the late 1990s and his efforts to develop a new brand of socialism in the region, uniting like-minded leftist countries into a common trade pact, the Bolivarian Alliance for the Peoples of Our America (ALBA), including Cuba, Venezuela, Ecuador, Nicaragua, and Bolivia. These governments rail against neoliberalism and seek to gain control over their natural, particularly mineral, resources. Redistribution also creates a new political base. There is an alignment between the military and the government, and a willingness to use the military (and to dominate the media) in the exercise of charismatic power. In many cases, policies have included expropriation and/or strict renegotiation of contracts with foreign mining companies under the threat of expropriation. This strategy can be categorized as primarily redistributive, with the expectation that growth will follow, naturally.

A third set of countries have sought a middle ground, ramping up social expenditures dramatically while still maintaining a high degree of liberalization in the economy. This group of countries includes Brazil, Argentina, Uruguay, and Costa Rica. The strategy is based on a 'social pact' between the productive sectors and the government which aims to maintain stable market business conditions and avoid expropriation in exchange for greater transfer payments to the government for pro-poor and pro-domestic industrial policies. These policies are often targeted at certain groups, such as the now famous conditional cash transfer programme that President Luiz Inácio 'Lula' da Silva popularized in Brazil. Like the second group of countries, this group was often led by strong charismatic populist leaders, such as Lula and Argentina's Néstor and Cristina Kirchner. Unlike the Bolivarian group, these countries have traditionally relied on agricultural commodity exports (although significant mining activity has developed recently in the cases of Brazil and Argentina).

Moreover, the leaders of these Southern Cone countries came from the reformed left, which had negotiated pacts with military dictatorships to assure smooth democratic transitions, perhaps leading to a more cautious approach. They have not been prone to expropriate natural resource companies, with the notable exception of Argentina's nationalization of its formerly privatized state oil company, YPF (Yacimientos Petrolíferous Fiscales), and therefore rely primarily on public expenditures to improve income distribution. At the same time, their approach towards industrial policy has on occasion been more pro-active than recommended by industrial policy lite, including a willingness to limit imports and foreign investment (such as restrictions on investment in Brazil's oil sector), and to seek to develop new industries where there is no clear current comparative advantage (such as Uruguay and Costa Rica's effort to develop high tech sectors). However, these industrial policy projects are more haphazard than indicating a long-term strategy for the structural transformation of the economy (Moreno-Brid and Paunovic 2008: 107).

It is, of course, difficult to categorize such a diverse set of national practices. Chile, for example, had many years of a left-centre government that attempted to improve distribution within the neoliberal model. Mexico also initiated a conditional cash transfer programme with national coverage, similar to Brazil's. In the next section, we summarise the highlights of our empirical examination into the outcomes of these three strategies.[2]

A preliminary evaluation of the three strategies

A common measure that economists use for liberalization is 'openness', calculated by the sum of the exports and imports divided by GDP. This measure gives us a clear sense of how important trade is for an economy, and thus is an indirect measure of its openness. Average openness increased every decade since 1980 for every country in Latin America. The net increases were lower for Peru and Venezuela, which shows that the choice of economic strategy regarding industrial policy does not correspond with the policy on trade liberalization. The Bolivarian countries, despite their anti-imperialist bent, did not reduce their dependence on trade.

Contrary to mainstream economic wisdom, many of the regional economies had negative or anaemic growth under neoliberalism, with the notable exception of Chile. It is hard to argue that stable institutions and property rights explained this growth, given rapid growth in Paraguay, one of the most corrupt countries in the world, and Colombia, with an ongoing guerrilla war. In contrast, Uruguay, one of the weaker performers on growth, has strong institutions and property rights. Furthermore, the redistributive policies of the Bolivarian countries did not cut their economic growth, though one can speculate that they may have reduced it.

There are no good international datasets for examining how different sectors develop in a country over time. The closest thing we have, that includes the ISI period, is a new dataset by CEPAL called BADECEL (Statistical Database on Foreign Trade). This database uses five general categories for exports in LA economies: agriculture, fishing, and hunting; food, beverages, and tobacco; intermediate goods; mining, including petroleum; metal/mechanical; and other, consumer non-durable goods. The intermediate category is problematic; after further investigation it appears to include mostly the finishing of raw materials, such as producing refined copper from ore or concentrate. However, in some cases, it also appears to include labour-intensive assembly (*maquiladora*) processes. Moreover, there is no category for services.

Nonetheless, by comparing the metal/mechanical sector to the agriculture, food and mining categories it is possible to see whether Latin America has been shifting its sectoral mix towards or away from manufacturing. For each country, I calculated 10 year averages, 1970–2010. We start with the neoliberal countries, for which export diversification should occur naturally through comparative advantage. For Chile, Colombia, and Peru we see increasing reliance on mining over time. For Paraguay, we see the growing importance of agriculture and food. In El Salvador, we see the continuing importance of agriculture and food up to the most recent decade. Subsequently, it appears that *maquilas* are increasingly important to the economy. Mexico is the one country in this group that shows significant growth in manufacturing, undoubtedly related to the benefits of manufacturing and assembly plants set up after the North American Free Trade Agreement (NAFTA) agreement in 1992.

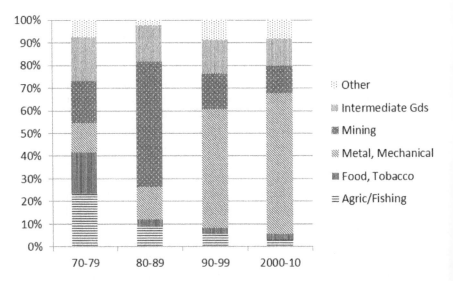

Figure 4.1 Mexico: export profile, 1970–2010

Source: Compiled by author from BADECEL (Base de Datos Estadísticos de Comercio Exterior).

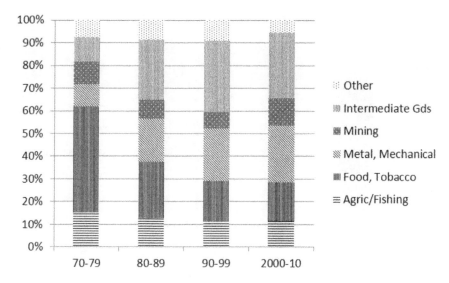

Figure 4.2 Brazil: export profile, 1970–2010

Source: Compiled by author from BADECEL (Base de Datos Estadísticos de Comercio Exterior).

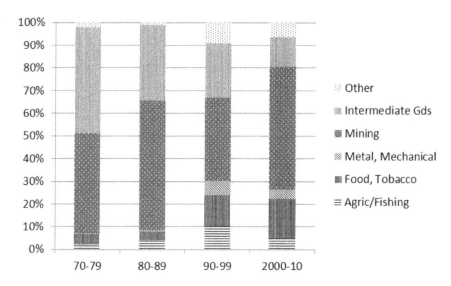

Figure 4.3 Bolivia: export profile, 1970–2010

Source: Compiled by author from BADECEL (Base de Datos Estadísticos de Comercio Exterior).

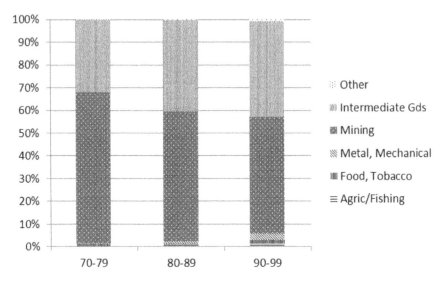

Figure 4.4 Venezuela: export profile, 1970–2010

Source: Compiled by author from BADECEL (Base de Datos Estadísticos de Comercio Exterior).

The Boliviarian countries, Bolivia, Ecuador and Venezuela, have all become remarkably focused on mining production. Ecuador continues to have a sizeable agricultural sector, however its relative importance has decreased over time. The Bolivarian strategy, despite its claims about resource nationalism and industrialization, clearly ignores the benefits of diversification.

For the countries that have followed industrial policies oriented towards diversification, the results are mixed. Argentina and Uruguay both continue to rely heavily on agriculture and food production. Argentina's mining sector has become more important, and there is a slight increase in manufacturing over time.

For Brazil and Costa Rica, who pursued the most active industrial policies in the group, there are clear signs of growth in manufacturing over time. Brazil's mining sector has become more important in line with its recent success in offshore petroleum development. Costa Rica's sectoral mix changed dramatically, in sync with the decision to attract IT (Information Technology) manufacturing in the 1990s.

It is apparent that LA is about the same or in some cases, even more, focused on primary product production in 2010 as compared to 1970. Only Brazil, Costa Rica, and Mexico show clear signs of shifting their sectoral mix towards manufacturing. Yet, only Costa Rica experienced above average growth during the period. If different types of strategies do not have a clear effect on economic growth or diversification, and diversification has no clear link with growth, do they affect distribution?

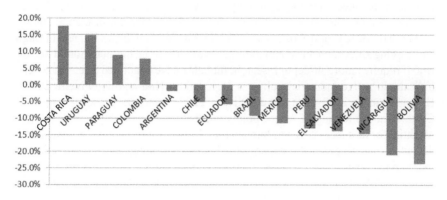

Figure 4.5 Change in the Gini coefficient, 1989–2012

Source: Author from CEPALSTAT.

Note: data for El Salvador, Nicaragua, and Peru date from 2001/2.

Examining distribution over time is even more problematic given the lack of attention to it by economists. Datasets and indicators are limited and problematic. UN-based indices such as the Human Development Index and its correlates show general improvements in reducing absolute poverty throughout the world, however because they include a wide variety of measures, it is difficult to trace progress over time. Moreover, most countries have different starting points, and we do not expect poverty to decline in linear fashion; as a country grows, it should be increasingly harder to make gains. The Gini coefficient is the most commonly used measure of income inequality. The higher the Gini is, the more unequal the distribution. Statistics for the region begin only in 1989.

We see alarming increases in inequality in Costa Rica and Uruguay, despite the fact that they have the strongest democratic institutions in the region, along with Chile. Chile's vaunted neoliberal (targeted) anti-poverty programmes may have reduced absolute poverty but they did little for relative distribution; small wonder, then, that the rightist coalition was defeated there in 2013. The Bolivarian countries clearly did the most to reduce relative inequality.

Conclusion

We have examined three general economic policy strategies, neoliberal, Bolivarian, and industrial policy lite, over the last three decades. What we found in terms of liberalization, economic growth, and distribution was that the general strategy does not seem to matter. Economic growth and absolute poverty reduction have been generally positive but volatile *throughout* the region. The only difference we found by strategy was in the Bolivarian countries where *relative* inequality declined after adoption of aggressive policies to capture and redistribute mining rent. The other result of note was the development of manufacturing in Mexico, Brazil, and Costa Rica. While Mexico can be explained through outsourcing of American manufacturing, particularly in the automotive sector, Brazil requires more in-depth research, though I have examined a few cases that indicate an active industrial policy is responsible (Hira and de Oliveira 2007c; Hira and Pineau 2010; Hira and de Oliveira 2009). Sánchez-Ancochea's study of Costa Rica's emerging IT sector points out that state leadership was absolutely essential for its success: 'it was bureaucratic leadership and not the private-sector demands that triggered the expansion of social spending and the attraction of more dynamic foreign investors that were behind the emergence of the new sectors' (2009: 62). These successful exceptions clearly demonstrate the inadequacy of industrial policy lite strategies.

Moreover, industrial policy is not just about exports, or the types of macroeconomic measures most economists use to measure success. What we lack is a way to measure the quality of the jobs that are created. Because of the way they measure success, economists ignore the distribution of wages in a sector, such as petroleum, where a few people command very large salaries. Similarly, while growing the economy through agriculture is important, the type of agriculture also matters – family farms distinguish Costa Rica's history and quality of life from the large farms that dominate El Salvador's coffee production. In sum, different industries have different characteristics, from distribution of wages, to spillovers and linkages to other industries to employment creation. More importantly, different industrial policies and instruments have different distributional effects.

The problem regarding equity is much deeper. Mainstream economists such as Acemoglu et al. (2001) trace inequality to colonial origins of institutional capture, particularly exclusion and lack of property rights, or to the speed of institutional modernization (Coatsworth 2008), neglecting agency and politics. Recent analysis points to the great concentration of family-based ownership in domestic private markets in Latin America (Schneider 2009). States are thereby captured by these private groups, and unable to create stable and pro-active institutions or engage in long-term investments, such as education and health care or economic diversification. This is reflected in a continuing weak ability to manage fiscal policy, including raising adequate tax revenues (Schrank 2009), thus creating a vicious cycle of economic concentration. Such a view potentially supports more drastic action towards redistribution as exemplified by the Bolivarian group, but it should also include economic diversification.

What is missing is a theory behind the factors that lead to a successful industrial policy. Such a theory could be developed by comparing successes and failures within the historical and geographic context and adapting them to it. The set of successful cases that I have examined over the past decade suggest that the following are necessary factors. First and foremost, the injection of market-type discipline in the form of performance targets. Second, understanding the timing of industry cycles and windows of opportunities. Third, it needs a match between *potential* policies, industries, and local resources and talent. Fourth, it needs integration between the financial and productive systems. Finally, it requires a well-developed and long-term strategic orientation, which includes knowledge transfer, development and diffusion in a partnership between researchers, autonomous and independent policymakers, and industry (Hira 2007b, 2012, 2014).

Notes

1 These authors also state that liberalization has led to 'good jobs' (De Ferranti, Perry and Lederman 2001: 2)
2 Contact author for detailed tables upon which this analysis is based.

References

Acemoglu, D., Johnson, S., and Robinson, S. (2001). The colonial origins of comparative development: An empirical investigation. *American Economic Review*, 91 (5), pp. 1369–401.
Auty, R.M. (1995). Industrial policy, sectoral maturation, and postwar economic growth in Brazil: The resource curse thesis. *Economic Geography*, 71 (3), pp. 257–72.
BADECEL (2015). Base de Datos Estadísticos de Comercio Exterior. Santiago: Economic Comission for Latin America and the Caribbean. Available from: http://interwp.cepal. org/badecel/index.html. [Accessed: 5 July 2015].
Bianchi, P., and Labory, S. (2011). *Industrial Policy after the Crisis: Seizing the Future.* Northampton, MA: Edward Elgar.
Blanco, L., and Grier, R. (2012). Natural resource dependence and the accumulation of physical and human capital in Latin America. *Resources Policy*, 37, pp. 281–95.
CEPALSTAT (2015). Databases and statistical publications. Santiago: Economic Commission for Latin America and the Caribbean. Available from: http://estadisticas. cepal.org/cepalstat/WEB_CEPALSTAT/Portada.asp?idioma=i. [Accessed: 5 July 2015].
Chami Batista, J. (2004). Latin American export specialization in resource-based products: Implications for growth. *The Developing Economies*, 42 (3), pp. 337–70.
Chong, A., and Zanforlin, L. (2004). Inward-looking policies, institutions, autocrats, and economic growth in Latin America: An empirical exploration. *Public Choice*, 121, pp. 335–61.
Cimoli, M., and Katz, J. (2002). Structural reforms, technological gaps and economic development: A Latin American perspective. Serie desarrollo productivo, No. 129. Santiago: CEPAL.
Cimoli, M., Correa, N., Katz, J., and Studart, R. (2003). Institutional requirements for market-led development in Latin America. Serie informes y estudios especiales No. 11. Santiago: CEPAL.
Coatsworth, J. H. (2008). Inequality, institutions and economic growth in Latin America. *Journal of Latin American Studies*, 40, pp. 141–69.
Collier, P., and Venables, A.J. (eds.) (2011). *Plundered Nations? Successes and Failures in Natural Resource Extraction.* NY: Palgrave Macmillan.
Devlin, R., and Moguillansky, G. (2011). *Breeding Latin American Tigers: Operational Principles for Rehabilitating Industrial Policies in the Region.* Herndon, VA: World Bank.

De Ferranti, D., Perry, G., and Lederman, D. (2001). *From Natural Resources to the Knowledge Economy: Trade and Job Quality.* Washington: World Bank.

Evans, P.B. (1979). *Dependent Development: the Alliance of Multinational, State, and Local Capital in Brazil.* Princeton: Princeton U. Press.

Farinelli, F. (2012). *Natural Resources, Innovation and Export Growth: The Wine Industry in Chile and Argentina.* Ph.D. dissertation (Economic and Policy Studies on Innovation and Technical Change). Maastricht University.

Hira, A. (1998). *Ideas and Economic Policy in Latin America: Regional, National, and Organizational Case Studies,* Westport: Greenwood.

Hira, A. (2003). Regulatory games states play: Managing globalization through sectoral policy. In M. Griffin Cohen and S. McBride (eds.) *Global Turbulence: Social Activists' and State Responses to Globalization,* London: Ashgate, pp. 41–58.

Hira, A. (2007a). Reassessing ISI and neoliberalism in historical context, *Revista de Economia Politica.* (Brazil), 27(3), pp. 345–56.

Hira, A. (2007b). *The New Path: An East Asian Model For Latin American Success,* Burlington: Ashgate.

Hira, A. (2011). Structural adjustment in Latin America: From crisis to ambiguity. In Jovanović, M.N. (ed.). *International Handbook on the Economics of Integration, Volume I.* Northamption, MA: Edward Elgar, pp. 443–56.

Hira, A. (ed.). (2012). States and high tech: Cases from the wireless sector. *International Journal of Technology and Globalization,* 6 (1/2).

Hira, A. (ed.). (2014). Mapping out the triple helix: How institutional coordination for competitiveness is achieved in the global wine industry, special edition, *Prometheus,* 31 (4).

Hira, A., and Pineau, O. (2010). Turning Privatization Upside Down: Petrobras as an example of successful state capitalism. *Canadian Journal of Latin American and Caribbean Studies,* 35 (69), pp. 231–61.

Hira, A., and de Oliveira, L.G. (2007c). Take off and crash: Lessons from the diverging fates of the Brazilian and Argentine aircraft industries, *Competition and Change,* 11(4), pp. 329–47.

Hira, A., and de Oliveira, L.G. (2009). No substitute for oil? How Brazil developed its ethanol industry. *Energy Policy,* 37 (6), pp. 2450–6.

Hausmann, R., and Klinger, B. (2006). Structural transformation and patterns of comparative advantage in the product space. CID Working Paper No. 128 (Aug.) Boston: Harvard University.

Hausmann, R., and Rodrik, D. (2006). Doomed to choose: Industrial policy as a predicament. Conference paper, Blue Sky seminar. Boston: Harvard University, Center for International Development, Sept. 9.

Hausmann, R., Rodrik, D., and Velasco, A. (2008). Growth diagnostics. In Serra, N., and Stiglitz, J. (eds.). *The Washington Consensus Reconsidered: Towards a New Global Governance.* NY: Oxford University Press, pp. 324–55.

Kolstad, I., and Søreide, T. (2009). Corruption in natural resource management: Implications for policy makers. *Resources Policy.* 34, pp. 214–26.

Karl, T.L. (1997). *The Paradox of Plenty: Oil Booms and Petro-States.* Berkeley: University of California Press.

Krugman, P. (2014). The stimulus tragedy. *The New York Times.* Feb. 20, found at: http://www.nytimes.com/2014/02/21/opinion/krugman-the-stimulus-tragedy.html?_r=0. [Accessed: June 2014].

Kuchiki, A., and Tsuji, M. (2010). *From Agglomeration to Innovation: Upgrading Industrial Clusters in Emerging Economies*. NY: Palgrave Macmillan and IDE/JETRO.

Leamer, E.E., Rodrigues, H.M, and Schott, P. (1999). Does natural resource abundance increase Latin American inequality? *Journal of Development Economics*, 59, pp. 3–42.

Lederman, D., and Maloney, W. (2012). *Does What You Export Matter: In Search of Empirical Guidance for Industrial Policies*. Latin American Development Forum. Herndon, VA: World Bank.

Levy, J.D. (2006). The state after statism: From market direction to market support. In Levy, J.D. (ed.). *The State after Statism: New State Activities in the Age of Liberalization*, Cambridge, MA: Harvard U. Press, pp. 367–94.

Maloney, W.F., Manzano, O., and Warner, A. (2002). Missed opportunities: Innovation and resource-based growth in Latin America. *Economía*, 3(1), pp.111–67.

Moreno-Brid, J.C., and Paunovic, I. (2008). What is new and what is left of the economic policies of the new left governments of Latin America? *International Journal of Political Economy*, 37 (3), pp. 82–108.

North, D. (1981). *Structure and Change in Economic History*. NY: W.W. Norton & Co.

Prebisch, R. (1950). *The Economic Development of Latin America and Its Principal Problems*. NY: UN.

Rodrik, D. (2006a). Industrial development: Stylized facts and policies. JFK School of Government. Boston: Harvard University, Mimeo.

Rodrik, D. (2006b). Goodbye Washington consensus, Hello Washington confusion? A review of the World Bank's economic growth in the 1990s: Learning from a decade of reform. *Journal of Economic Literature*, 64, pp. 973–87.

Schneider, B.R., (2009). Hierarchical market economies and varieties of capitalism in Latin America. *Journal of Latin American Studies*, 41, pp. 553–75.

Sánchez-Ancochea, D. (2009). State, firms and the process of industrial upgrading: Latin America's variety of capitalism and the Costa Rican experience. *Economy and Society*, 38, pp. 62–86.

Schamis, H.E. (2002). *Re-forming the State: The Politics of Privatization in Latin America and Europe*. Ann Arbor: The University of Michigan Press.

Schrank, A. (2009). Understanding Latin American political economy: Varieties of capitalism or fiscal sociology? *Economy and Society*, 38 (1), pp. 53–61.

Stijins, J-P. (2006). Natural resources abundance and human capital accumulation. *World Development*, 34 (6), pp. 1060–83.

Thorp, R. (1998). *Progress, Poverty and Exclusion: An Economic History of Latin America in the 20th Century*. Washington: The Inter-American Development Bank.

Wade, R. (1990). *Governing the Market: Economic Theory and the Role of Government in East Asian Industrialization*. Princeton: Princeton University Press.

Wade, R. (2013). Return of industrial policy? *International Review of Applied Economics*, 26 (2), pp. 223–9.

Warwick, K. (2013). Beyond industrial policy. *OECD Science, Technology and Industry Policy Papers*, No.2. Paris: OECD.

Williamson, J. (1989). *What Washington Means by Policy Reform*. In Williamson, J. (ed.). *Latin American Readjustment: How Much has Happened*. Washington: Institute for International Economics, pp. 7–38.

Williamson, J. (2008). A short history of the Washington consensus. In Serra, N., and Stiglitz, J. (eds.). *The Washington Consensus Reconsidered: Towards a New Global Governance*. NY: Oxford University Press, pp. 14–30.

Wood, A., and Berge, K. (1997). Exporting manufactures: Human resources, natural resources, and trade policy. *The Journal of Development Studies*, 34 (1), pp. 35–59.

World Bank. (1993). *The East Asian Miracle: Economic Growth and Public Policy*. Washington: World Bank.

World Bank (2013). Mining: Sector results profile. Available from: http://www.worldbank.org/en/results/2013/04/14/mining-results-profile [Accessed: 14 January 2014].

World Bank (n.d.). Doing business [online] Available from: http://www.doingbusiness.org/reports. [Accessed: June 2014].

5   The regional context for Latin American resource nationalism

Pablo Heidrich

Introduction

The return of resource nationalism to Latin America at the beginning of the twenty-first century has been nested in a series of surprising and comprehensive regional trends that few external observers could have predicted. Firstly, the neoliberal economic policies and conservative political regimes of the 1990s have been replaced in most countries by leftist and populist governments with more state interventionist economic policies than those of the recent past (Flores-Macías 2010). Secondly, close relations with the United States and its hemispheric plans for free trade have been displaced by several regionalist initiatives such as the Union of South American Nations (UNASUR) and Community of Latin American States (CELAC), as well as antagonist alliances such as Bolivarian Alliance for the Peoples of Our America (ALBA), all of which are quite supportive of resource nationalism (Riggirozzi 2012). Thirdly, rapidly growing prices for mining, energy and agricultural commodities have created a much closer relationship with China and the rest of Asia, while simultaneously decreasing the importance of trade relationships with the United States and Europe (Gallagher and Porzecanski 2009). These higher commodity prices have created a policy environment whereby exports have continued to grow, current accounts have improved, and levels of external indebtedness have fallen, inducing a wholesome reversal of the 1990s regional thirst for financial capital and direct investment. By the late 2000s and early 2010s, Latin America has instead mutated to a much more circumspect if not sometimes hostile treatment of foreign capital, while openly discussing more participation of state agencies in regulation, production and investment (Dabene 2012; Hornbeck 2014).

Some of the sources of these region-wide changes are domestically grounded, such as the widespread (but not complete) turn to left-of-centre politics, and the consequent change in the character of regional integration, dialogue and cooperation. Others are externally generated, such as the dramatic rise of China as an economic superpower, accompanied by the continued resurgence of Russia (prior to the 2014 sanctions), and sustained growth from India and most of South East Asia. These trends are accentuated by the contrasting troubles, since 2008, in the United States and the European Union, beset by financial crises and subsequently slow recoveries. The combination effects not only drove commodity prices to unprecedented heights between 2003 and 2008, but also induced great volatility between 2008 and 2015; all while modifying the global geography of economic growth, trade and investment in an apparently long-term manner (ECLAC 2013).

This chapter elaborates on these domestically-originated as well as externally-produced but equally regionally-felt dynamics to provide, through their interaction, a macro-explicatory context for resource nationalism in Latin America. For this purpose, resource nationalism is understood as the following combinations of policies: increased state apportionment of profits from extractive industries; heightened regulation to better integrate production processes with national economies; and state influence in or a determination of directions of trade of natural resources. Other chapters in this volume explore the different ways in which these policies have been created, rationalized, implemented and executed to varying extents in particular Latin American countries. The obvious conclusion is that while externally-driven and regionally-produced trends have favoured this type of policies of resource nationalism during the last decade and a half, national practices and policies have varied substantially within these contours.

Domestic sources of change: Latin American politics

Let us begin with the domestically-driven processes that, across the region, have transformed the way natural resources are governed and related industries are regulated. The election of Hugo Chávez as president of Venezuela (1998), later followed up by the elections of 'Lula' da Silva in Brazil (2002) and Néstor Kirchner in Argentina (2003), represented an enormous, and in retrospect, defining challenge from left and populist politics to the neoliberal status quo that had governed the region since the early 1990s. The wave continued through the 2000s with another dozen countries electing left-of-centre presidents.[1] By 2014, of the 19 countries in Latin America, there were only two with openly neoliberal governments in South America (Paraguay and Colombia) and three in Central America (Guatemala, Honduras, Panama).

The governance of natural resources, particularly the regulation and ownership of extractive industries, already figured prominently in several of the transitions to left-of-centre rule in the region during the late 1990s and early 2000s, prior to the later period of high international commodity prices. Hugo Chávez focused, during his first successful electoral campaign in 1998, on how the state-owned oil company of Venezuela (PDVSA) was run by an oligarchy that favoured the entry of foreign capital on overly advantageous terms, and also invested heavily in the United States and Europe instead of doing so domestically. Lula da Silva emphasized in his 2002 campaign how Fernando Cardoso's government had fumbled the privatization of electricity production, the entry of private capital in Petrobras as well as the sale of Companhia Vale do Rio Dolce, which resulted in the increased energy prices and electricity blackouts the country suffered in early 2000s, as well as a decrease in royalties and mining production (Kingstone 2004). Evo Morales led the popular uprisings in Bolivia during the early 2000s against the neoliberal administration of Sánchez de Losada, campaigning against the export of gas to Chile and United States, and more generally against the privatization policies in the resource sector (Webber 2010). In 2006, when Morales became president of Bolivia, one of his first actions was to nationalize the oil and gas industries, followed subsequently by the main mining projects. Other examples include Ricardo Lagos who, during the 2000 Chilean election campaign, argued for higher mining royalties to differentiate himself from his right-wing opponent, and more recently, Ollanta Humala who argued for obligatory and state-mandated royalty payments in both of his Peruvian presidential campaigns, in 2006 and 2011.

Therefore, the turn to the left in Latin America has, from the very beginning, included an explicit critique and reform agenda with regards to natural resource policy, this time towards more state regulation and participation in its profits. It is interesting to note that the earliest attacks of left candidates on the extractive industries' neoliberal status quo, such as those in Venezuela (1998), Chile (2000) and Brazil (2002), predated the global commodities boom. In fact, international prices were very low in those years, in some cases, at extraordinarily low levels, such as oil at $US 8 per barrel in 1998 and copper at $US 0.8 per pound. This implies that domestic dissatisfaction with neoliberal reforms from the 1990s had already bred discontent, and thus leftist candidates' critique, before the opportunity to bring in significantly more fiscal resources started to figure as an attractive option.

External sources of change for the regional context

Several authors have claimed that the turn to the left in Latin American politics and its recourse to policies widely labelled as resource nationalism would have not been possible without the great increases in commodity prices that took place between 2003 and 2012 (Flores-Macías 2010; Rosales 2013; Hornbeck 2014). In that period, prices for oil, gas, minerals and agricultural commodities such as soybeans, corn and coffee, grew between 300% and 1,000%, greatly improving the terms of trade for Latin American countries that were significant commodity exporters (Giordano et al. 2015). This aspect is covered in detail in Chapter 2 of this book but it is necessary to underline here what it has meant for the region in terms of trade, investment and credit partners.

The improvement in terms of trade facilitated increases in the current account without having to continue to try politically difficult improvements in international competitiveness, a crucial rationale for the structural adjustment plans several countries had been undertaking during the 1980s and 1990s under IMF-World Bank tutelage (Argentina, Mexico, Peru, Uruguay), and a few on their own (Brazil, Colombia, Chile) (Weyland 2009). It also pushed economic growth via increased domestic and foreign direct investment, which in turn improved fiscal finances and reduced the short-term levels of external indebtedness.[2] The political spaces opened up for different sorts of policymaking by this change cannot be underestimated. Governments, regardless of ideologies and electoral pressures, now did have more room to experiment, modify or correct policies inherited from the previous period of unfavourable terms of trade, debt crisis and conditional lending from international financial institutions.

That improvement in terms of trade is shown most clearly in Table 5.1, which depicts the composition of Latin American exports until 2013. Total exports have tripled (305%) in size, roughly in line with trends in world trade, but what has changed most significantly is the composition of those flows. The rows in Table 5.1 are ordered by how much each category of goods has changed in this period, showing that while manufactures have trailed the total growth trend by as much as half (151.3%), commodities from extractive industries such as gold, copper, iron, oil and gas have grown at much higher rates (between 350.3% and 765.7%). This process is even more notable as the amounts of commodities exported have not grown faster than those of manufactured goods, but the income received for

Table 5.1 Latin America: exports to the world, 2000–2013 (in current $US millions)

Types of Goods (UN SITC V.4 Classification)	2000	2005	2008	2011	2013	% Change 2000-2013
Miscellaneous manufactures (textiles, footwear, furniture, etc.)	38,486	49,314	53,887	54,837	59,775	155.32
Machinery and transport equipment	122,773	160,620	221,801	253,948	296,349	241.38
Manufactured goods (paper, pulp, steel, manufactures)	42,381	74,634	110,723	120,665	106,576	251.47
Total all products	**363,570**	**585,163**	**908,740**	**1,106,028**	**1,109,714**	**305.23**
Beverages and tobacco	4,721	7,418	10,956	12,894	14,515	307.44
Chemicals (plastics, fertilizers, etc.)	16,802	29,399	49,288	58,716	55,846	332.37
Mineral fuels (gas, oil, coal, etc.)	63,828	122,671	216,214	248,282	223,629	350.36
Food (fruits, cereals, coffee, sugar)	43,389	72,291	117,378	157,980	162,398	374.28
Animal and vegetable oils (soybeans)	2,619	5,695	12,718	12,372	10,184	388.73
Crude materials (oilseeds, copper, iron ore, paper)	23,359	51,938	92,122	144,294	140,508	601.51
Precious commodities (gold, silver)	5,207	11,136	23,581	41,884	39,879	765.77

Source: Elaborated by author with UNCTAD Statistics. Accessed on 20 May 2015. Goods in parenthesis are examples of the most traded from the region. Totals do not match those of Table 2 and 3 because non-specified goods are not counted here.

the former has increased much faster. That pattern accelerated between 2005 and 2011, followed by a deceleration that has continued into 2014–2015 (Giordano et al. 2015).

Nonetheless, the table clearly shows that the growth of Latin American exports for the 2000–2011 period is chiefly explained by the growth of extractive industry exports instead of manufacturing goods, with the latter group only slowly recovering since 2012. This decomposition analysis gives special significance to governance policies of natural resources in Latin America, since those industries became, during that first decade of the 2000s, ever more important drivers of the region's export growth. As a corollary, counterbalancing or compensatory policies to support manufacturing became more necessary over time given the evident loss of competitiveness they are enduring (Rosales and Kuwayama 2012). This underlines that another relevant rationale to tax and regulate extractive industries more actively, is the use of the surplus or supplier relations from these enclaves to support local industry.

A complementary perspective on this phenomenon of the 'primarization' in Latin American exports is seen in the growth dynamics of different countries from the region. Table 5.2 lists several countries ordered by their relative export growth in the same period of 2000 to 2013, as compared to the region as a whole. Bolivia, Peru, Ecuador and Brazil, all with significant extractive industries, have led the region in terms of export growth. Paraguay, the exception, has strongly specialized in the export of energy (hydroelectricity) to Brazil and Argentina, and soybeans. In contrast, the countries that have underperformed the regional export growth average are El Salvador, Dominican Republic, Costa Rica, Mexico and Honduras, which specialize in *maquila* type of export manufacturing for the United States market. The exception is Venezuela, which due to a combination of mismanagement of its national oil company and an extensive programme of energy subsidies for several countries in the region, has not expanded its commercial exports as much as it could have done otherwise (Trinkunas 2014). Again, it is interesting to note the deceleration in export growth between 2011 and 2013 for several of the most important mineral and energy exporters, such as Chile, Peru, Venezuela and Brazil.

In combination with these increases in the prices of commodities and the growth of exports of those goods, there has been a significant modification in the geography of destinations for Latin American sales. China and East Asia, more generally, have become much more relevant for the region, just as the United States has declined rapidly in importance, while the European Union has barely maintained its position. Table 5.3 shows the relative importance of each trading partner for Latin America as a whole. China, as noted by multiple authors since the mid-2000s, has grown as a market from a mere 3.5% of total exports to a whopping 26.2% in 2013. In contrast, the United States has declined from being the destination of half (49.4%) of all Latin American exports to just 36%. A different process had already happened to the European Union, which declined as a destination for Latin America very significantly in the 1990s, when it went from 25% to 12.1% in 2001. And in the 2000s, in spite of having remained the largest

Table 5.2 National versus regional export performance in Latin America, 2000–2013 (in current $US millions)

	2000	2005	2008	2011	2013	% Change 2000- 2013	Country Growth / Regional Growth
Bolivia	1,246	2,791	6,527	8,332	11,496	922.58	3.01
Peru	6,955	17,368	31,019	46,268	41,783	600.76	1.96
Paraguay	2,329	3,352	7,798	12,639	13,605	584.16	1.91
Ecuador	5,057	10,468	19,461	23,082	25,789	510.00	1.67
Brazil	55,086	118,308	197,942	256,000	242,000	439.32	1.43
Colombia	13,760	21,730	38,534	58,322	59,992	436.00	1.42
Uruguay	2,384	3,774	7,095	9,274	10,284	431.40	1.41
Chile	19,210	41,267	66,259	81,438	76,684	399.19	1.30
South America	**193,392**	**357,002**	**611,591**	**761,238**	**746,064**	**385.78**	**1.26**
Guatemala	3,085	5,459	7,846	10,519	10,190	330.31	1.08
Argentina	26,341	40,387	70,019	84,051	83,026	315.20	1.03
TOTAL	**361,961**	**569,103**	**884,359**	**1,093,081**	**1,108,465**	**306.24**	**1**
Panama	5,839	7,375	10,323	16,926	17,505	299.81	0.98
Venezuela	33,529	55,716	95,021	92,811	89,532	267.03	0.87
Honduras	3,343	5,048	6,347	7,977	7,833	234.29	0.77
Central America	**208,369**	**270,142**	**365,848**	**439,835**	**479,853**	**230.29**	**0.75**
Mexico	166,396	214,633	291,886	350,000	381,000	228.97	0.75
Costa Rica	5,813	7,099	9,555	10,383	11,506	197.93	0.65
Dominican Rep.	5,737	6,145	6,748	8,492	9,662	168.42	0.55
El Salvador	2,963	3,465	4,703	5,401	4,897	165.25	0.54

Source: Elaborated by author with UNCTAD statistics, accessed on 20 May 2015.

foreign investor in the region, trade flows have not reflected any change. In the last decade the EU was the destination of 12% of Latin American exports, decreasing markedly in the worst of its own regional crisis and then recovering to its previous level of 13.1%.

The sum of these three tables show that the trade growth of Latin America has therefore been mostly from South America, concentrated in extractive commodities and agricultural goods, and increasingly oriented towards China. While these three dynamics are already well known, only once they are observed together their combined power truly comes alive. In other words, Latin America's relationship with the world has changed and grown because its Southern half started to trade more minerals, oilseeds and energy with China and the rest of Asia. Everything else has either not changed since the 1990s or progressed much more slowly.

And that is what matters as a context for resource nationalism in Latin America because this change in the configuration of external economic relations implies a

Table 5.3 Total Latin American exports by main destination, 2001–2013 (in current $US millions)

	2001		2005		2008		2011		2013	
China	12,600	3.5%	39,865	7.01%	134,877	15.25%	221,678	20.28%	289,000	26.20%
United States	179,000	49.40%	254,678	44.75%	372,164	42.10%	361,432	33.07%	401,065	36.01%
European Union	43,790	12.10%	71,908	12.63%	110,123	12.45%	102,006	9.34%	145,000	13.10%
Total	**361,961**	**100%**	**569,103**	**100%**	**884,359**	**100%**	**1,093,081**	**100%**	**1,108,465**	**100%**

Source: Elaborated by author with UNCTAD Statistics. Accessed on 20 May 2015.

very significant mismatch between the nationality of the production capital, North American and European, and the nationality of the buyer, China and East Asia. That is the structural departure from previous historical Latin America commodity booms, where the investors and buyers were one and the same country (United Kingdom for Argentina, Chile, Peru, Brazil; United States for Mexico, Central America, Colombia) (Bulmer-Thomas 1994). And it is in this difference of nationality between the investors and the buyer where the political space for resource nationalism flourishes. In other words, Latin American host countries can take actions to increase their share of the rent from companies based in Western countries without jeopardizing access to their export markets in East Asia.

Besides this policy space opened up by global economic rivalries between East Asia and the North Atlantic, the character of China, main purchaser of Latin American natural resources, cannot be represented here as solely a passive buyer. Instead, it is one that has, with increased activism, sought to secure the supply of commodity imports its economy requires now and will require later via active economic and political diplomacy (Jenkins 2008; Slipak 2014). To achieve this end China has deployed its growing financial might in the region, further enabling commodity exporters to exercise their chosen policy mix of resource nationalism. Summarizing that relationship: Gallagher et al. (2012) indicate that China has played this role of financing partner in the region by providing over US$75 billion in loans since 2002 until 2012.

That generosity has been concentrated in oil exporters such as Venezuela and Ecuador, with important loan commitments to Argentina and Brazil, providers of oilseeds and iron ore to China (Gallagher et al. 2012: 4–6). The character of the loans is evidently more political than commercial as the largest loans have been to support regimes that have leftist politics (Venezuela and Ecuador), but which are relatively unimportant providers of oil for China (Jenkins 2012, estimated their combined market-share of Chinese oil imports at 3%). In contrast, governments with left-of-centre politics such as those in Brazil and Argentina, which are very significant providers of soybeans (50% combined) and iron ore (25%) to China, have received smaller loans in relation to the size of their economies (Jenkins 2012). Nonetheless, Chinese lending in these countries has focused not on supporting state deficits as in Venezuela and Ecuador, but on underpinning the expansion of extractive exports, such as hydrocarbons, iron ore and soybeans, as well as the infrastructure required to export them, such as seaports and railroads (Jenkins 2012: 10–13). Slipak (2014) finds this axis of Chinese investment also correlated with the incipient foreign direct investment made by Chinese multinationals, which is heavily concentrated in the petroleum sector in these two countries.

The sum of that new dynamism generated by higher commodity prices, the changing geography of trade and the rising role of China as both a political funder and an entrepreneurial investor (albeit in different places), has created a positive context where Latin American countries with extractive industries can exercise different latitudes of resource nationalism. The ability to carry out this strategy depends, of course, on a variety of factors, including each country's geography and the relative weight of that sector in the overall of the economy. Pre-existing institutional capacity, electoral mandates, and ideological inclinations of the governments in office matter as well, providing the enthusiasm or lack thereof to follow this route of stronger state control or ownership of extractive industries.

New trends in Latin American regionalism

Once the transition to left-of-centre or populist regimes was in place and the global economic context had altered the region's trade and investment flows to the benefit of commodity exporters in South America, it became clear that a corollary of these two trends was the modification of regional and hemispheric relations.

First in line was the conclusion of the unsuccessful negotiations to create a hemispheric trading group, the Free Trade Area of the Americas (FTAA) with Latin America, the Caribbean, United States and Canada. This process, begun in the heyday of neoliberalism in the mid-1990s, came to a screeching halt at the 2004 Monterrey Summit of the Americas and was given its last rites at the 2005 Mar del Plata Summit (Cooper and Heine 2009). Nothing substantive inside these negotiations merited such change of fortunes except that enough opposition against the project had accumulated from Lula's Brazil, Kirchner's Argentina, and Chávez's Venezuela to stop them (Tussie 2011). These left-of-centre leaders, strengthened with mandates to moderate or reverse market reforms at home, and riding on growing popularity as their economies improved, had no qualms about opposing the United States, and Canada's desire to conclude this hemispheric free trade deal.

One of the issues that impacted natural resource management, and also mobilized strong opposition in Brazil, Argentina and Venezuela, was the FTAA's vision for foreign direct investment. This sought to extend the North American Free Trade Agreement (NAFTA) model on FDI to the entire hemisphere, which enshrined the right of foreign investors to access binding international arbitration (Gomez-Mera and Barrett 2010). Given the rise of commodity prices since 2002, Latin American countries reassessed the convenience of signing such costly clauses because they would have precluded policy options in regards to natural resources. Since the rest of the FTAA agreement did not significantly improve their access to North American markets, while new commodity markets across the world (particularly in Asia) were proving increasingly profitable, the costs of signing the treaty became politically unsustainable (Russell and Tokatlian 2011).

Maintaining the same presidentialist tack used by neoliberal leaders in the 1990s to rapidly build open-regionalism and a possible free trade treaty with the United States – and consequently the same political accountability deficit – most South American countries in the 2000s have tried instead a 'post-hegemonic' regionalism anchored on their common trading advantages and ideas (Legler 2013).[3] While some of these new projects, such as the CSN (South American Community of Nations) and UNASUR (Union of South American Nations) developed out of jockeying for position within the FTAA bargaining process, such as the Brazil-initiated ALCSA (South American Free Trade Area), another – ALBA – was a clear break in direction and method from the previous tendency towards open-regionalism (Serbin 2014).

At that 2005 Mar del Plata Summit of the Americas, President Chávez proposed to his Latin American and Caribbean peers a new type of agreement: the *Alternativa Bolivariana para los Pueblos de Nuestra América* (ALBA), which had already begun as a bilateral cooperation treaty with Cuba (Diamint 2014). ALBA's idea was – and is still today – to create a regional initiative where its member states would trade goods and services either commercially or (preferably) by barter, in order to complement one another. Unlike other trade groupings, ALBA's design has the state and not private enterprises as main trading parties, and its explicit goal is to focus these exchanges in sectors that will directly improve the social and economic wellbeing of their populations, particularly its poorer classes (Altmann 2009). In practical terms, ALBA has developed in a hub and spoke pattern where Venezuela, the hub, trades its oil and oil-related technology for medical services, agricultural goods, food, mechanical spare-parts, and other consumer goods, as it had been doing with Cuba since 2002 (Giacalone 2015). While no one signed up for ALBA at 2005 Summit, three Latin American countries have done so since: Bolivia (2006), Nicaragua (2007) and Ecuador (2009). Additionally, six small island nations from the Caribbean also joined, given their dependence on a related Venezuelan regional initiative, Petrocaribe, which is analysed in the next section.

A different manner of leveraging natural resources abundance into further opportunities for resource-based development was undertaken by Brazil, while keeping track of the key interests of its necessary allies in Mercosur and the Andean Pact (Briceno Ruiz and Hoffmann, 2015). Using the basis it had established in the 1990s with ALCSA, Brazil split the trade from the integration agenda in 2004, creating for the latter purpose the South American Community of Nations (CSN) (Riggirozzi 2012). By bringing together Mercosur and Andean Pact in this non-trade initiative, Brazil focused it on the creation of a South-America-wide transportation and energy network of projects that would physically integrate the sub-continent with a series of roads, dams, railroads and seaports designed to facilitate the export of hydrocarbons, mining and agricultural commodities (Garzón Pereira 2014). The project, named IIRSA (Initiative for the Integration of the Regional Infrastructure of South America), was to be funded by a mix of private and state investment, but planned by governments (Carciofi 2012). This, in comparison to the previous model of open-regionalism, gave a much stronger role to the state, domestically, and by extension, in the region (Palestini Céspedes and Agostinis 2014). Additionally, state funding was provided by the BNDES, which is Brazil's national development bank and several of the largest projects concluded thus far or in construction were given to Brazilian construction firms (Burges 2007).

Natural resources and Latin American regionalist initiatives

Besides the macro trends of Latin American regionalism and its changing directions, a number of natural resource-centred initiatives and processes have redrawn the contours of resource nationalism in the region. Some have been cooperative, such as Petrocaribe and the regional expansion of Petrobras, but others have shown how national interests and policies can stop and reverse regional cooperation in extractive industries, as in the case of Argentina and Chile.

The most ambitious link in the extractivist renaissance of South America during the 2000s was the Gasoducto del Sur or 'Hugoducto', proposed by Hugo Chávez at the 2005 summit of the CSN, which would have brought Venezuelan crude to Brazil and the Southern Cone (Serbin, 2014). That initiative did not progress for several reasons, some technical (length of the pipeline, natural barriers, Venezuelan oil requiring different processing) and others, political (Brazil would not support it). But another initiative from Venezuela, Petrocaribe, did progress and between 2005 and 2014, gained 16 members, mostly among the smaller states of the Caribbean, as well as four Latin American countries (Cuba, Dominican Republic, Honduras and Nicaragua). Unlike ALBA, which implied political alignment with Chávez's version of socialism, Petrocaribe has been an energy-specific treaty that provides members with access to Venezuelan oil and refined products at a discounted price, with long-term financing and the possibility of paying in kind (barter). The resulting fiscal surplus for importing countries is to be invested in social programmes, emulating those done in Venezuela with Cuban assistance, and in strengthening the energy sector. However, only US$150 million had been invested by all the Petrocaribe countries by 2013, out of $13bn accrued in benefits (Scotiabank 2014: 2).

Venezuelan largesse to export its politics in the Caribbean and to Central America has contrasted with the accident-prone expansion of Petrobras, the Brazilian energy giant. Since the late 1990s and early 2000s, this firm undertook a process of internationalization whereby it bought other South American energy companies and bid for opportunities to developed privatized oil and gas reserves (Sohr 2010). This was done in a crucial period of low energy prices at the end of the neoliberal period, allowing Petrobras to obtain assets at bargain prices (Sennes and Narciso 2009). However, when the political winds changed, it faced a series of challenges. First came Evo Morales, who nationalized gas reserves in Bolivia in 2005; and then Néstor Kirchner, who maintained the freeze on gas and oil prices in Argentina, eventually forbidding their export in 2006. In both cases, resource nationalist measures affected the most valuable foreign assets of Petrobras, creating difficulties for the Lula da Silva government in Brazil (Burges 2015). After those incidents, Petrobras focused its expansion beyond South America and within Brazil itself, as explained by Nem Singh and Massi in this volume.

While Brazilian energy investments were damaged by the resource nationalist measures of other South American leaders, they did not face the complete undoing of other energy initiatives from the neoliberal period. In the 1990s, Argentina and Chile, both under centre-right governments, had promoted foreign investment in seven different pipelines that would feed energy-poor Chile with Argentine gas (Gadano 2013). When the Kirchner and Fernández administrations were unable to satisfy domestic gas demand in Argentina, they simply reduced and later prohibited gas exports to Chile, then responsible for over 40% of the electricity of that country. In spite of numerous protests from Santiago, the Argentine government effectively shut down this market-driven energy initiative to feed domestic demand at subsidized prices (Mares and Martin 2012). The multinational companies producing the energy, those owning the pipelines and those with advance purchases were left with enormous losses.

Conclusions

The combination of a favourable external context of high commodity prices and a changed internal political panorama in much of Latin America created a region-wide trend towards resource nationalism. While the shift to the left in several governments during the 2000s implied a stronger state voice in how natural resources were to be extracted and commercialized, social pressures for increased public spending and the opportunities presented by high prices combined to maintain a momentum in this policy direction.

This changed regional environment was reflected in turn in the character and content of the regional integration schemes in Latin America, which separated the trade agenda from the physical and political integration agendas. Furthermore, the drive for free trade at a hemispheric scale has been extinguished even if some of the Andean and Central American nations have continued to sign bilateral free trade agreements with the United States, the European Union and some East Asian countries. Even in some of those cases, the goal is to attract even more foreign investment to accelerate the extractive economy (Carranza 2014).

Natural resource industries have, by the potential benefits they can bring by themselves, structured new patterns of economic cooperation and, sometimes, conflict in the region, as the cases of Petrocaribe, Petrobras and the Argentina–Chile gas dispute underscore. These do not constitute a trend in themselves but they are, however, important markers of the re-configurative power of the extractivist boom and resource nationalism in the relations among Latin American countries in this early part of the twenty-first century.

Notes

1 Daniel Ortega was elected in Nicaragua, Fernando Lugo in Paraguay, Tabaré Vázquez in Uruguay (2005), Mauricio Funes in El Salvador (2009), Ricardo Lagos in Chile (2000), Evo Morales in Bolivia (2006) and Ollanta Humala in Peru (2010).

2 A significant illustration in this regard was the early repayment of IMF loans by the Lula and later, Kirchner administrations in 2005 and 2007, respectively. In both instances, both governments explained the gesture as facilitating their ability to enact alternative policies.

3 Post-hegemonic regionalism is the term used by Riggirozzi and Tussie (2012: 12) to characterize regional initiatives in Latin America since the beginning of the 21st century, defined as 'regional structures characterized by hybrid practices as a result of partial displacement of dominant forms of US-led neo-liberal governance, and in the acknowledgment of other political forms of organization and management of regional (common) goods'.

Bibliography

Altmann, J. (2009). El ALBA, Petrocaribe y Centroamérica: ¿intereses comunes? *Nueva Sociedad*, 219, pp. 45–59.

Briceño-Ruiz, J. and Ribeiro Hoffmann, A. (2015). Post-hegemonic regionalism, UNASUR, and the reconfiguration of regional cooperation in South America, *Canadian Journal of Latin American and Caribbean Studies*, 40(1), pp. 48–62.

Bulmer-Thomas, V. (1994) *The Economic History of Latin America Since Independence.* Cambridge: Cambridge University Press.

Burges, S. (2007). Building a global southern coalition: The competing approaches of Brazil's Lula and Venezuela's Chávez. *Third World Quarterly*, 28(7), pp. 1343–58.

Burges, S. (2015). Revisiting consensual hegemony: Brazilian regional leadership in question. *International Politics*. 52(2), pp. 193–207.

Carciofi, R. (2012). Cooperation for the provision of regional public goods: The IIRSA case. In Riggirozzi, P. and Tussie, D. (eds.) *The Rise of Post-Hegemonic Regionalism. The Case of Latin America.* United Nations Series on Regionalism. Springer Verlag, pp. 65–81.

Carranza, M. (2014). Resilient or declining? Latin American regional economic blocs in the postneoliberal era. *Latin American Politics and Society*, 56(3), pp. 163–72.

Cooper, A. and Heine, J. (eds.). (2009). *Which Way Latin America? Hemispheric Politics Meets Globalization.* United Nations University Press.

Dabene, O. (2012). Consistency and resilience through cycles of repoliticization. In Riggirozzi, P. and Tussie, D. (eds.). *The Rise of Post-Hegemonic Regionalism. The Case of Latin America.* United Nations Series on Regionalism. Springer Verlag, pp. 41–64.

Diamint, R. (2014). Regionalism and South American orientation: UNASUR and ALBA. *Revista CIDOB d'Afers Internacionals*, 101, pp. 55–79.

ECLAC (2013). *Foreign Direct Investment in Latin America and the Caribbean.* Santiago: ECLAC.

Flores-Macías, G. (2010). Statist vs. pro-market: Explaining leftist governments' economic policies in Latin America. *Comparative Politics*, 42(4), pp. 413–33.

Gadano, N. (2013). YPF y el petroleo latinoamericano. *Nueva Sociedad*, 244, pp.113–20.

Gallagher, K. and Porzecanski, R. (2009). *China and the Latin America Commodities Boom: A Critical Assessment.* Working Paper 6. Political Economy Research Institute. University of Massachusetts – Amherst.

Gallagher, K., Irwin, A. and Koleski, K. (2012). *The New Banks in Town: Chinese Finance in Latin America.* Washington, DC: Inter-American Dialogue.

Garzón Pereira, J.F. (2014). Hierarchical regional orders: An analytical framework, *Journal of Policy Modeling*. 36(1), pp. 26–46.

Giacalone, R. (2015). Latin American answers to mega-regional projects: Options and limits. In Joaquín Roy (ed.). *A New Atlantic Community: The European Union, the US and Latin America.* Miami: University of Miami European Union Centre, pp. 175–88.

Giordano, P., Michalczewsky, K. and Ramos, P. (2015). *Latin American Trade Trend Estimates. Update 1st Quarter 2015.* Washington, DC: Inter-American Development Bank.

Gomez-Mera, L. and Barrett, B. (2010). The political economy of preferential trade agreements: Latin America and beyond. *Latin American Politics and Society*, 54(1), pp. 181–98.

Hornbeck, J. (2014). *US-Latin America Trade and Investment in the 21st Century: What's next for Deepening Integration?* Washington, DC: Inter-American Dialogue.

Jacome, F. (2011). *Petrocaribe: The Current Phase of Venezuela's Oil Diplomacy in the Caribbean.* Working Paper 40. Bogota: Friedrich Ebert Stiftung.

Jenkins, R. (2008). *China's Global Growth and Latin American Exports*. Research Paper 2008/104. Helsinki: UNU-WIDER.

Jenkins, R. (2012). Latin America and China—a new dependency? *Third World Quarterly*, 33(7), pp. 1337–58.

Kingstone, P. (2004) *Critical Issues in Brazil's Energy Sector. The Long (And Uncertain) March to Energy Privatization in Brazil*. Working Paper 12. Institute for Public Policy, Rice University.

Legler, T. (2013). Post-hegemonic regionalism and sovereignty in Latin America: Optimists, sceptics, and an emerging research agenda. *Contexto Internacional*, 35(2), pp. 325–52.

Mares, D. and Martin, J. (2012). Regional energy integration in Latin America: Lessons from Chile's experience with natural gas. *Third World Quarterly*, 33(1), pp. 55–70.

Palestini Céspedes, S. and Agostinis, G. (2014). *Constructing Regionalism in South America: The Cases Of Transport Infrastructure And Energy Within UNASUR*. Robert Schuman Centre for Advanced Studies. Global Governance Programme. Florence, Italy: European University Institute.

Riggirozzi, P. and Tussie, D. (2012). *The Rise of Post-Hegemonic Regionalism. The Case of Latin America*. United Nations Series on Regionalism. Springer Verlag.

Riggirozzi, P. (2012). Reconstructing Regionalism: What does development have to do with It? In Riggirozzi, P. & Tussie, D. (eds.). *The Rise of Post-Hegemonic Regionalism. The Case of Latin America*. United Nations Series on Regionalism. Springer Verlag, pp. 17–40.

Rosales, A. (2013). Going underground: The political economy of the 'left turn' in South America. *Third World Quarterly*, 34(8), pp. 1443–57.

Rosales, O. and Kuwayama, M. (2012). *China and Latin America and the Caribbean. Building a Strategic Economic and Trade Relationship*. Santiago: CEPAL.

Russell, R. and Tokatlian, J. (2011). Asserting Latin America's new strategic options toward the United States. *Latin American Politics and Society*, 53(4), pp. 127–46.

Scotiabank (2014). Special Report on Petrocaribe. Global Economics Research Office. Toronto, Canada. Available from: http://www.gbm.scotiabank.com/English/bns_econ/isr140904.pdf. [Accessed: 20 June 2015].

Sennes, R. and Narciso, T. (2009). Brazil as an international energy player. In Rainard, L. and Martinez-Diaz, L. (eds.). *Brazil as an Economic Superpower? Understanding Brazil's Changing Role in the Global Economy*. Washington, DC: Brookings.

Serbin, A. (2014). Regionalismo y soberanía nacional en América Latina: los nuevos desafíos. *Nueva Sociedad* 252, pp. 70–86.

Slipak, A. (2014). América Latina y China: ¿cooperación Sur-Sur o «Consenso de Beijing»? *Nueva Sociedad* 250, pp. 27–42.

Sohr, R. (2010). Energía y seguridad en Sudamérica: más allá de las materias primas. *Nueva Sociedad* 204, pp. 150–59.

Trinkunas, H. (2014). *Changing Energy Dynamics in the Western Hemisphere: Impacts on Central America and the Caribbean*. Latin America Initiative Policy Brief. Washington DC: Brookings Institution.

Tussie, D. (2011). Hemispheric relations: Budding contests in the dawn of a new era. In Mace, G., Cooper, A. and Shaw, T. (eds.) *Inter-American Cooperation at a Crossroads*. New York: Palgrave MacMillan, pp. 23–42.

UNCTAD. (2015). *International Trade Statistical Database*. United Nations Conference on Trade and Development. Geneva. Accessed on June 20, 2015 at: http://unctadstat.unctad.org/wds/ReportFolders/reportFolders.aspx?sRF_ActivePath=p,15912&sRF_Expanded=,p,15912.

Webber, J. (2010). Carlos Mesa, Evo Morales, and a divided Bolivia (2003–2005). *Latin American Perspectives*, 37(3), pp. 51–70.

Weyland, K. (2009). The rise of Latin America's two lefts: Insights from rentier state theory. *Comparative Politics*, 41(2), pp. 145–64.

6 Natural resource nationalisms and the Compensatory State in progressive South America

Eduardo Gudynas

Introduction

Latin America has witnessed repeated debates and policy initiatives on the issue of the national control of natural resources. This is understandable considering the region's distinct experience with past export booms, in which states were incapable of controlling them, or adequately benefiting from the revue obtained. Of course, some political positions also rejected nationalization. In this respect, we are confronted with a long and complicated history that includes a diverse set of cases that range from the first attempts to assert national control over oil in Argentina under Hipólito Yrigoyen in the 1920s; the nationalization implemented by President Lázaro Cárdenas in Mexico in 1938; efforts to build state-owned companies in the mining sector, such as Companhia Vale do Rio Doce, created in 1942 by President Getúlio Vargas; to the nationalization of Chilean copper mining in 1971 under Salvador Allende.

In the last few years, even though we have seen a return to resource nationalism, it has occurred under very different circumstances than in the past. This chapter examines the current situation, paying particular attention to the governments identified as progressive or belonging to the new left in South America. Beyond their distinctive characteristics, all of these governments have embarked upon styles of development, in which *extractivisms* have become an essential component. This has generated a particular type of state, which here we characterize as *compensatory*. The chapter examines the nature of this state and some of its principal policy expressions.

The return of resource nationalism

At least since the middle of the 1990s, distinct narratives on natural resource nationalism have emerged, which played an important role in the political transformation that occurred in several South American countries when a new left replaced conservative governments. This shift included Hugo Chávez in Venezuela, and his gradual adoption of a 'Bolivarian' strategy; the Movement to Socialism (MAS), led by Evo Morales in Bolivia; Rafael Correa and his National Alliance (AP) in Ecuador; the Worker's Party (PT) administration and its allies in Brazil, with Presidents 'Lula' de Silva and Dilma Rousseff; the transformation of classical Peronism in Argentina under the presidencies of Néstor Kirchner and later his wife, Cristina Fernández; and the Broad Front (FA) in Uruguay with Tabaré Vázquez and José 'Pepe' Mujica. Without a doubt, this is a diverse set of administrations, but for the purposes of this analysis it must be emphasized that all of them self-identify as part of the same political perspective, and share great similarities in comparison to conservative governments, as found in Colombia or Peru (for more information on the left turn see Moreira et al. 2008; and Philip and Panizza 2011). In this chapter, we refer to these administrations as *progressive* (a label used by these governments themselves, and which helps to differentiate them from their origins in the traditional left).

These governments rejected the idea that development is just a by-product of market capitalism, arguing instead that it is a process unto itself, which should be oriented towards improving people's quality of life and reducing poverty, and that the state should have an important role in this process. Their strategies have been labelled *neo-developmentalist*, and understood as corresponding to the duties of a developmental state (referring, at least in part, to the debate at the end of the 1970s represented by Cardoso and Faletto 1979; also see Schneider 1999; Sicsú et al. 2007).

The developmental approaches pursued between the 1950s and the 1970s were very popular in Latin America. They focused on industrialization (including import substitution industrialization) at a time when dependence on *extractivisms* and primary exports was understood as symptom of backwardness (see also Sikkink 1991). The stance of the modern-day progressives questions that perspective, both in discourse and in practice. On the one hand, they defend the intensification of extraction and exportation of commodities such as hydrocarbons, minerals and agricultural goods as indispensable 'engines' of development. This corresponds with what has been called extractivist strategies (in the sense of Gudynas, 2015). On the other hand, although these governments have programmes that aim at industrialization, they have not always been successful, and a significant part of the concrete measures taken remain focused on the primary sector.

While in the past it was understood that countries should aim to eliminate their dependency on the extractive sectors, currently the progressive lines of thinking defend this option and emphasize that the state should play a leading role in it. In the past, the objective was to strengthen industrialization, but, today, efficiency in the export of commodities is promoted (that which separates this approach from Asian versions of the nationalist developmental state; see Johnson 1999). A conceptual shift is occurring in Latin America's ideas about its own industrialization, which are moving away from those defended by the Economic Commission for Latin America and the Caribbean, and are accepting the region's role as a provider of primary resources (see CEPAL and UNASUR 2013).

Within this framework, governments in the region have debated, proposed or pushed forward particular varieties of this type of development. In terms of examples, we point to the following:

- Neo-developmentalism in Brazil (*neodesenvolvimento*), widely promoted by the economist L.C. Bresser-Pereira (for example, Bresser-Pereira 2011; Sicsú et al. 2007);

- National and popular development in Argentina (known as the 'nac & pot' strategy), which is based on government practices more than academic theories;
- Various references to a 'socialism of the 21st century', especially in Venezuela;
- Andean-Amazonian communitarianism, which is contemporarily capitalist, but which aims to re-orient itself as a form of socialism or communism, along the lines of propositions made by the Vice-President of Bolivia, Álvaro García Linera (for example, García Linera 2015);
- Socialist biorepublicanism of *buen vivir* (living well), promoted by intellectuals working in the Ecuadoran government (i.e., Ramírez 2010).

In almost all of these strategies, natural resources are understood to be the property of the people, the nation, or the state – and the state acts as the governor, administrator and authority responsible for managing them, and taking advantage of their developmental potential. The sentiment behind these ideas was expressed in a speech by Hugo Chávez, President of Venezuela, at the 141st OPEC Ministerial in Caracas, when he asserted that, 'Never, was there a drop of oil for the people of Venezuela, instead oil has always been sucked up by the *criollo* oligarchy and by the American empire. Now, oil belongs to the Venezuelan people, and it will be used for justice, for equality, and for the development of our people – this is the truth' (MPPPM and PDVSA 2006).

Of course, these ideas are racked by various tensions. For example, what do we understand by 'people' or 'nation', what measures will the state use to manage these resources, and how effective will the state be in promoting its version of development? Furthermore, in Bolivia and Ecuador, which are now recognised as 'plurinational' states, natural resources could be the property of a specific indigenous nation. It is important to keep in mind these two levels, especially since there are already cases of resource nationalism by indigenous peoples who oppose foreign actors, the government, and other groups within the same country. In these cases, we see conflicts over what is meant by 'national' in multi-ethnic societies.

The enormous importance attributed to natural resources occurred in a very particular context of high prices for many primary commodities, high demand for these resources from consuming nations, and inflows of foreign direct investment. This generated an important increase in commodity exports from the region, and the arrival of new investors.

This context allowed almost all of the Latin American countries to register solid levels of economic growth, and even meant that many passed through the financial-economic crisis of 2007–2008 without major problems. Imports also took off, as did public consumption, particularly among the popular sectors, who gained access to household appliances, cars, motorcycles, etc., thanks to cheaper goods, new sources of imports, and lines of personal credit. In parallel, every one of these countries strengthened social assistance programmes for the poorest segments of society, in particular, by using conditional cash transfers (CCTs). Poverty declined from the high levels registered in 1990s, estimated at 48% of the population, to 26% in 2014. Links between factors such as economic and political stability, the reduction of poverty, and the increase in consumption, explain the widespread perception of advancement and increased wellbeing.

In any case, as previously discussed, a wide range of practices exists among progressive governments, from those that exercise more intensive controls, including expropriations and nationalizations (such as Venezuela), to heterodox practices (Argentina's intervention in markets for certain goods and capital flows), and finally, more moderate approaches (Brazil and Uruguay).

All of these governments, without exception, defend extractivisms. They promote the intensification of activities in sectors that already have projects under way, and also encourage expansion into to new sectors. Moving beyond their diverse theoretical positions and slogans (from twenty-first century Bolivarian socialism to conventional neo-developmentalism in Brazil), in practice, all agree on a resource nationalism that should be in the hands of the state.

The simplest formulation of this position is expressed in direct state control, for example, through state-owned companies. This practice has been repeatedly used in the petroleum sector in Argentina, Bolivia, Ecuador, and Venezuela. In other cases, the state controls using indirect methods (as with Petrobras in Brazil). In mining, the situation is much more diversified. The largest state presence in mining is found in Bolivia (especially through COMIBOL, and more recently with state-owned companies in gold and lithium). In Brazil, the Vale Corporation is formally private, but the state retains enormous influence through federal financing and as a shareholder, via some unions' pension funds. Most other countries promote mining through private enterprise. In the agribusiness sector private business activity also predominates, and state intervention is much more limited (with the exception of Argentina, which taxes the export of grains).

There are various ways to capture surplus (note that in my theoretical work on extractivisms, the concept of surplus is used as an umbrella category that includes surplus value created by labour and also rents from renewable and non-renewable resources; see the discussion in Gudynas 2015: 209–30). Royalties and taxes have been substantially increased in the petroleum sector, including through direct taxation such as the Direct Hydrocarbons Tax (IDH) in Bolivia. In comparison, taxes on mining projects are much lower, and even less on export agriculture.

Justifications for this resource nationalism and the role of the state in it are varied. Often, allusions are made to national identity or patriotic pride, but also to concrete problems such as the need to finance the social programmes that fight poverty. These arguments are easily articulated with broader discourses that assert national sovereignty against the imperialism of governments and transnational corporations from the Northern hemisphere, including, on occasion, in opposition to capitalism.

It is very common that a nationalist extractivism is considered indispensable for capturing part of the profits from these exports, and therefore to finance the state, and especially its social programmes to reduce poverty. Since a reduction of poverty has been achieved in many of these countries, this argument holds a lot of weight. It also serves to reinforce a distinct identity in South American progressivism, as compared to previous governments that were committed to more conservative strategies. Thus, resource nationalism offers an explanation that is also a source of legitimacy: it is necessary to incentivize mining, oil extraction, and agribusiness exports, in order to finance the reduction of poverty and assure development.

In any case, it is important to note that beyond the nationalist rhetoric there has been a return of private investors, even in the oil sector. In Bolivia, Ecuador, and Venezuela, state companies have signed agreements with transnational corporations, under the so-called 'migrations' to service contracts and joint ventures, etc. States grant exemptions and make agreements in exchange for exploration, and also flexibilize social and environmental regulations. This is a complicated and often contradictory process, which goes beyond the scope of this chapter, but which nevertheless reflects the nature of the new progressive extractivism (for further discussion, see Gudynas 2015).

The recourse to resource nationalism as a means to assert national independence in the face of globalization, or to combat 'imperialism', also confronts many practical problems. This is because extractivisms are activities based on exporting to international markets and, therefore, are only possible if governments accept the rules and institutions of globalization. It is necessary to comply with the norms of the World Trade Organization (WTO), and accept the mechanisms that govern exports, and meet the institutional requirements for capital flows, and so on. The export of natural resources is embedded within the value-chains of global capitalism. For example, beyond the rhetoric and good intentions, the crude produced by Ecuador or Venezuela, in one way or another, ends up being managed by global corporations and likely refined in the United States.

These and other examples are useful to show that a rigorous examination of the concrete practices of development reveal strong tensions, and even contradictions, between the discourse of a nationalism over natural resources and the real practices of progressive governments. The aspiration for resource nationalism creates demands on the state, but this same state, which must extract and commercialize these natural resources, falls into all kinds of contradictions.

State contradictions under progressivism

In states with progressive administrations and a resource nationalist discourse, we observe situations that are characterized by at least three different aspects: contradictions, equilibria, and compensations. The first refers to the fact that states are under intense contradictory pressures between promoting and liberalizing capitalist processes, and attempting to regulate these dynamics and iron out their most negative aspects. The second refers to the challenge of achieving an equilibrium between the concessions offered to, and the limitation imposed upon, capital. The latter are, of course, necessary to avoiding a crisis, or extremes of one kind or another; as well as being key to sustaining the state and the progressive political actors embedded in those administrations. The third alludes to the overwhelming importance of economic compensation within this dynamic, which is used to reduce the level of social conflict and maintain electoral support. These elements appear to be intimately interconnected, but here they will be analysed separately to facilitate the explanation.

South America's progressivisms acknowledge that economic growth is indispensable for development, but differ from conservative or neoliberal administrations in so far as they believe that the state should intervene in this process. Therefore, the state protects and supports the dynamics of contemporary capitalism, such as promoting exports, accepting the rules of the global governance of international trade, and attracting investors, etc. Without a doubt, one of the clearest examples of this stance is the great importance that they have attributed to extractivisms, which is none other than a variety of capitalism that rests on the appropriation and globalization of natural resources. In other words, this is a state that yields to capital, abstains from intervention when it puts the accumulation process at risk, but promotes accumulation when necessary (behaviour which is, in part, similar to Offe's (1984) description of the welfare state in the advanced capitalist economies).

But on the other hand, this same state tries to control the market, and intervenes to capture part of the surplus, and to reduce some negative effects through the use of social assistance programmes. A good example of these methods is the IDH tax on oil in Bolivia. These interventions are an important source of legitimacy for progressivism, making it distinct from previous conservative administrations, and permitting the identification of itself as part of the left. In other words, it is a state that also restrains capital. Furthermore, the manner in which the state realizes its insertion in the global economy with calls to increase exports, improve competitiveness, and attract investments, renders it more dependent on the international environment, conditions set by investors, and the governance of the international financial economy.

This results in a state always caught between contradictions and tensions: to promote economic growth, and to regulate the market; to accept the conditions set by foreign investors, and to attend to the demands of local citizens; and to sell natural resources on global markets, but to question the capitalist system.

These tensions are very evident in the region's extractivisms, where there are many examples of the protection and promotion of extractive ventures and their exports. With regards to the promotion of capital, the direct assistance to productive sectors and companies that occurred in Brazil under the Lula da Silva administration is noteworthy (see essays in HB 2012). The support for capitalist dynamics in general, and certain corporations in particular, were widely backed by unions and party militants. Significant financing was granted to exporting companies and to support the transnationalization of a small group of large corporations, known as the 'champions', such as JBS FriBoi in cattle and meats, Odebrecht in construction, and Vale in mining. A massive programme of agricultural subsidies was also undertaken that disproportionately favoured export-oriented agribusiness.

Other cases demonstrate that capital is favoured through special benefits and protection. This includes the agreements on fiscal stability made with large investors, in which the state promises not to increase taxes, or if they do, they will compensate the affected party. (This measure originated with conservative governments, but it continues to be applied by progressive governments, as shown by the Mujica administration's policy towards a large cellulose plant in Uruguay.) These countries have also granted fiscal benefits (for example, in Bolivia, to promote the exploration of new hydrocarbon deposits), arranged territorial concessions (as in Ecuador, for the purpose of encouraging large-scale mining), subsidized inputs (especially energy or water; Bolivia offered cheap natural gas to investors), and constructed infrastructure (roads, bridges, or ports built for investors).

The progressive state also acts in the opposite sense, intervening in the market and imposing obligations on capital. In terms of extractivisms, the most important measures are those that allow for the appropriation and commercialization of resources, be it through controls, taxes, or state-owned companies, in order to increase the capture of economic rent and expand social programmes.

An example of this approach is the strengthening of state oil companies (as happened with PDVSA in Venezuela, YPFB in Bolivia, and more recently YPF in Argentina). The strengthening of state-owned companies has been more limited in the mining sector (the most important case is COMIBOL in Bolivia), and almost non-existent in the case of agribusiness. High royalties or taxes were imposed on the oil sector in Bolivia, Ecuador, and Venezuela, yet a similar effort was not made in the mining or agribusiness sectors. In mining, progressive states have generally opted to attract investors and increase revenue collection by encouraging the expansion of exports rather than by raising taxes. In the agribusiness sector, only Argentina has placed a tariff on the export of grains. In Paraguay, a proposal to tax soy exports failed, and in other progressive countries governments have continued to use conventional taxes, expecting to increase governmental revenue through growth in exports.

These as well as other measures attempt to capture the economic surpluses associated with the export of natural resources. The nationalist discourse recalls that, in the past, under neoliberal administrations economic wealth was monopolized by foreign companies, and in consequence, the alternative is that the state should capture the benefits of this surplus. But, as already indicated, there is a big difference between the rhetoric of those plans, the programmes that embody them, and what the governments really do. All of this is very clear in the case of oil extraction, where even if the ownership of the resource and the wells belong formally to a state-owned company, and are therefore 'nationally-owned', in many cases the government has partnered with transnational corporations that control the operations, transport and commercialization of the oil.

The state must also intervene in reducing and appeasing the civil resistance and conflict that are unleashed by its measures to encourage investment and exports. This is evident in South America's extractivisms where open-pit large-scale mining projects and the arrival of oil companies in the Amazon have fomented intense social conflict. Since this social resistance puts the viability of such investments at risk, the state has deployed various measures to control it, such as lowering legal standards on social and environmental norms, reducing controls and law enforcement, limiting NGO activity by criminalizing civil protests, and in some cases, using police or military force. In other words, the state itself, is actively reducing, weakening or impeding the mobilization of civil society.

Under this dynamic, which alternatively supports and restricts capital, the sources of legitimacy for the state's development strategies have changed. The state defends extractivisms as necessary for growth, legitimizing a vision of development that is essentially economic, and indispensable for financing its poverty reduction programmes. In this way, compensations such as social programmes are of fundamental importance, above all for their symbolic and legitimating value, associated with a certain kind of extractivist development. However, the state can only intervene up until a certain point because if too many conditions and regulations are introduced, many extractive projects become unviable (at least under current conditions).

In this context, the state must achieve a balance between the concessions it makes to capital and its regulatory measures; between advancing export-driven extractivisms, and cushioning its social impacts, and so on. A good number of the instruments that permit the management of these tensions have a limited efficacy (for example, the police or military cannot be overused for repression). This explains why compensations, particularly those that are economic, are becoming more important. They are able to alleviate many problems, and also provide political cover for state decisions. In this way, the illusion of a benevolent capitalism is sustained: the state maintains a nationalist discourse, and is able to provide economic compensations, but only as long as these compensations do not interfere with the fundamental economic processes.

One can see that these are very delicate balance points, which are very difficult to achieve, and because the impacts of extractivism persist, and corporate demands are renewed, these equilibria must be continuously re-constructed. They are dynamic, yet unstable and risky equilibria, largely because a significant part of the revenue depends upon the price and demand for primary exports, which are not controlled by these governments. At the same time, once a balance is struck it limits even more the developmental options of the state. In order for the situation to remain viable, the capitalist mode (and extractivisms) must be further entrenched, which will create new social and environmental impacts that will require new compensations.

A Compensatory State

It is argued here, that the progressive state, under these particular conditions, namely the repeated construction of an equilibrium, is required to constantly resort to all kinds of compensations. The resulting condition is called a Compensatory State. This term puts the accent on the fact that the state, which has not renounced its economic development strategies and remains functional for capitalism, also attempts to confront its most controversial and negative effects through compensations in the market sphere. This characterization fits within the perspective of earlier analyses by Bunker (1985) on the dynamics between the state and social groups using resources and territories in Brazil, and Coronil (2002), on the popular belief in a 'magical state' based on the ecological riches of Venezuela.

The Compensatory State has a developmentalist vocation, as already discussed, which is based on economic growth, but mediated by market interventions, support to certain industries, and the promotion of infrastructure, among other elements. These ideas about development are much more conventional than expounded in public discourse, due to the central role given to the export of primary materials. The interventions in the market, and compensations are very important, and in fact have contributed to a reduction in poverty, but they cannot put the 'engines' of development at risk. Although capitalism is harshly criticized in countries, the progressive state is not promoting radical change to the basic structures and dynamics that sustain economic growth. President Correa bluntly recognised this state of affairs: 'We have not been able to drastically change the model of accumulation. Basically, we are doing things better with the same model of accumulation, before changing it, because it is not our intention to harm the rich, but it is our intention to have a more just and equal society' (*El Telégrafo*, 15 January, 2012). Therefore, the measures that are possible are those that allow the rough and negative edges of this development to be smoothed, and this occurs, in particular, through the use of compensatory economic measures.

Even the most radical projects, such as the promotion of the 'plurinational' state in Bolivia by the Movement towards Socialism (MAS), are still based on the classical institutions of the state, which have all the virtues and defects that are well known in South America. And this, in turn, is functional for both extractivisms and conventional ideas of development.

The compensatory measures are varied and are applied on multiple fronts. First, attention should be drawn to the promotion of popular consumption, which is focused on access to consumer goods such as household appliances, cars, motorcycles, and other electronic goods. The consumerist bias is clear, and it is presented as a source of wellbeing that the state has supported in various ways (as was illustrated above). Surprisingly, it is the state that promotes the idea of a wellbeing that can be bought in the hundreds of new malls that have been inaugurated across the entire continent.

Secondly, social assistance programmes that provide money have become very important for the poorest families. These instruments existed under previous conservative and neoliberal governments, but the progressives have improved and enlarged them. The most well-known are conditional cash transfers, which offer monthly payments to fathers or mothers heading families, and demand in exchange that their children go regularly to medical clinics and attend school. These types of mechanisms include *Bolsa Familia* (Family Basket) in Brazil, which has the largest coverage by number (reaching 14 million families in 2014), and the *Bono de Desarrollo Humano* (Human Development Bond) in Ecuador, which has the highest coverage by proportion of the population (reaching almost 45% of the population) (Gudynas 2015).

Thirdly, the state acts by providing other forms of direct assistance, such as financial support to municipalities or subnational governments, and funds for civil society organizations, unions, and federations that organize peasants, indigenous peoples and students, etc. For example, the Bolivian IDH provides funds for a diverse set of causes such as those mentioned above, even including university scholarships. There are also examples of progressive governments that concretize these compensatory measures by granting housing, health centres, soccer stadiums, tractors, or boat motors, etc. Finally, the state also acts to pressure, or even require, some companies to provide compensations directly to local communities.

It must be underlined, that by these and other means, the Compensatory State generates a process through which the idea of justice shrinks to mean distributive economic justice. Once this has taken root, it is further reduced to what is called in Spanish *asistencialismo* – charitable handouts.

Other dimensions of justice, such as those that refer to the quality of life, education, housing, or civil rights, remain secondary or are limited. In consequence, all of the emphasis is placed on economic compensation. This is very evident in the region's extractivisms, where the state supports these projects but relies on the intensive use of compensations in order to realize them. A rhetorical statement such as 'your community will be contaminated or destroyed, but you will be compensated with money', applies in many cases. Important social sectors support this bargain, some by conviction, but others in order to receive direct economic compensation. At the same time, governments have learned to use such compensations discretionally, to support some groups, and to punish others by taking those benefits away. This reinforces, once again, the role of state as a compensator.

This dynamic also reinforces the notion that the negative social impacts of development and poverty can be compensated, and that this can be achieved through monetary means. The attribution of economic value reinforces the dominance of this concept over other forms of value, and deepens the commodification of social life and Nature. It is important to underline the profound impact that this has had, since this expansion of commodification was one of the consequences of Latin America's neoliberalisms that the progressives had promised to reverse. But, against expectations, the progressives, by means of the Compensatory State, have further expanded this commodification, even if it follows a different trajectory.

While the appropriation of surplus is important for the Compensatory State, it is important to clarify that, in the case of South American progressivism, the concept of a rentier state does not apply. In a strict sense, the rentier state has been identified as an authoritarian or totalitarian regime with a strong patrimonial tendency (Omeje 2008). In these contexts, local elites capture the largest share of the available rents for personal gain (for themselves, their families, or their allies), while linked to transnational extractivisms, and do not apply significant redistribution schemes. In contrast, the progressive Compensatory States meet the formal requirements of democracy, have rolled out redistributive mechanisms with wide coverage, and have worked to strengthen the state in other areas.

The Compensatory State is also distinct from the neoliberal state, which characterized Latin America in the 1980s and 1990s. Even if it is accepted that in some countries and in some sectors, progressive reforms were limited, they still expressed intentions, institutional fixes and political discourses that were very different from the neoliberals. This does not prevent us from recognizing that the current Compensatory States were implanted on top of structures, organizations, and institutional modes of action that were substantially influenced by prior neoliberal reforms.

The South American situation also differs greatly from classical ideas on the *welfare state*. In the European examples, the state was integrated into a capitalist development that simultaneously maintained various mechanisms of social protection, appropriate coverage in education and health, low levels of poverty, and a human rights framework, including third generation human rights. However, in the Compensatory State welfare rests on economic handouts (*asistencialismo*) and consumerism, while the rights framework was rarely strengthened. On the contrary, there are South American examples of the state limiting or violating rights in order to maintain its development strategy.

Facing contradictions and oppositions

A few ideas should be considered regarding the methods used by the Compensatory State to manage the political and citizen interactions that occur in the context of the contradictions and equilibria that characterize it. The analysis that follows is partially inspired by the ideas of Offe (1984), and Jessop (2002), and some of its conclusions can be found in Gudynas (2012).

Firstly, one can suppose that an autonomous, effective, and capable state should ensure its actions are both objective and independent, and use similar criteria to accept or deny concessions made to capital. Examples of such actions could include fiscal benefits granted to investors that do not depend upon friendships or seek to leverage economic benefits for the governing party; or environmental impact assessments that are scientifically rigorous and independent. However, there is overwhelming evidence that in Latin America these are not the prevailing conditions.

Examples of this include the manipulation of environmental impact assessments in Brazil that led to the approval of megaprojects like the Belo Monte dam, or the new legal framework for large-scale mining in Uruguay, which was designed for a specific foreign investor (including a new taxation regime, flexibilization of environmental standards, and the concession of a seaport, etc.).

Secondly, there are situations in which the state cannot impose regulations that are supposedly neutral or objective, and therefore capitulates, in one way or another, to political and economic pressures, or to its own interests in appeasing corporate demands or realizing electoral objectives. In renouncing its independence and neutrality, the state encourages political conflict.

South American progressivisms, in many cases, respond to the demands made by their most numerous or best organized bases of support. For example, in Bolivia, the Morales administration is unresponsive to peasants and indigenous people, but usually accepts the demands of mining cooperatives or urban federations (such as the powerful federation of cooperative miners FENCOMIN, or the Federation of Neighbourhood Associations of El Alto – FEJUVE). But also they bend before the economically powerful: in order to promote exploration in Bolivia, the government granted fiscal benefits, and more recently, access to protected areas (thus, the state renounced its own mandate to conserve biodiversity and protect indigenous peoples), to oil companies.

Thirdly, another dynamic to deal with these contradictions and oppositions occurs when the state discretionally chooses the actors that it will recognize as partners on development issues. Progressivism was very successful in terms of using political leadership to address important sectors of society who were politically marginalized, especially indigenous people and the popular sectors. However, it also successfully excluded those who decried the social and environmental impacts of development as it really occurred. For this reason, when states make reference to 'national' management of natural resources, they support certain actors such as unions or peasant federations in some cases, while in other situations, they distance themselves from other citizen organizations, and sometimes even harass them.

Without a doubt when a resource nationalist approach is pursued, the state needs the broad support of its citizens to legitimate its role as administrator of those resources in the name of the entire nation. But if some of these same social actors reject its practices, the foundation of the state's legitimacy crumbles. The Compensatory State, in order to maintain these equilibria, recognizes only some actors as being within the 'nation' or the 'people', while ignoring, isolating, or even attacking others. A significant problem in the management of natural resources is that a good part of the current opposition comes from groups of citizens that are small in number, such as peasant or indigenous communities. These groups are unable to exercise much political pressure, have little electoral clout, and tend to be neglected by the urban centres. For these reasons, there are few political costs to the state by silencing their demands, or even, in some cases, repressing them. In this respect, the Compensatory State reinforces a style of hyper-presidential and delegative democracy (following O'Donnell 1994).

Fourthly, the state insists on boosting the symbolic value of its compensatory measures as the best and most effective solutions to problems of development. Beyond the quantity of money that is actually transferred to social programmes, instruments such as conditional cash transfers to the poorest are used as a political justification for actions such as invading indigenous territories to permit oil exploitation. In fact, expenditures on cash transfers represents less than 1% of GDP in Argentina, Bolivia, Brazil, and Uruguay, and is only 1.2% in Ecuador. In turn, the state rejects the critiques that are made by civil society groups, peasants, or indigenous groups and suggests that they are hindering the fight against poverty and economic growth. This creates a perverse cycle of argumentation, which asserts that the plans to fight against poverty require financing from new extractive projects, and since these will generate new social impacts, more compensatory measures will be required. This symbolic expansion of the role of the state hides the fact that other dimensions of justice are being curtailed at the same time, such as social and political rights, quality of life, or environmental conservation.

Unsolved tensions under a commodified nationalism

The resurgence of resource nationalism in South America took place under very particular national, continental, and global circumstances. On the one hand, the arrival of new left governments marked an important political change in many countries. On the other hand, commodity prices and the demand for these commodities were very high, which resulted in massive inflows of foreign investment and impressive increases in exports. Under this particular conjuncture, it was possible to try out a new kind of resource nationalism that was inscribed within a developmentalism that attempted to achieve a type of benevolent capitalism. Most of those governments enjoyed increased revenues that permitted innovations. The state took on an important and functional role for this type of development, although it focussed on economic objectives and neglected to strengthen important dimensions of social and environmental justice. In consequence, compensatory measures assumed a central role, which led in turn to the development of the Compensatory State.

This is a condition that has important and diverse social support. Its base of legitimacy includes partisan political groups, unions, certain business actors, and many actors among the 'popular' sectors. The inclusion of the popular sectors is particularly understandable considering that resource nationalism has increased the level of national autonomy and sovereignty, reinvigorated feelings of national pride, and has permitted the reduction of poverty and an increase in consumption. But this condition is also questioned by those groups that suffer from the social and environmental impacts of this type of development, especially indigenous peoples, peasants, and other social sectors with limited access to democracy and justice. Looking beyond these criticisms, it is notable that the Compensatory State has been able to maintain itself in equilibrium, in some cases for more than ten years.

The establishment of the Compensatory State has not resolved all of the problems related to what is meant by the 'national' in resource nationalism. Certain kinds of statism have prevailed as a result of its claims to be custodian, manager, and the sole representative of diverse nationalities. And it is precisely the creation of a Compensatory State that is necessary to sustain these kinds of positions. But this also creates huge tensions, particularly when there are peoples that want to participate more directly in the benefits of exploiting natural resources, and these same peoples are capable of rejecting extractive activities within their territory. In Bolivia in particular, the constitutional recognition of 'plurinationality' could empower every indigenous community to claim the right to manage resources located within its territory and negotiate directly with companies and investors, bypassing the central state. For this reason, the Bolivian government, while valorizing the indigenous contribution to the nation, has repeatedly limited the powers that threaten the government's monopoly over the management of natural resources. This is another contradiction: where a state claims to be plurinational, yet acts in practice to suppress that diversity.

Consequently, we find ourselves confronted with a nationalist discourse on natural resources that has expanded the economy and reduced poverty, but has simultaneously triggered serious problems. On the one hand, it is associated with development practices that over-exploit or destroy these resources (evident in the severe impacts of extractivisms, see Gudynas 2015). Thus, it is a nationalism that does not allow space for allegations of contamination or losses in biodiversity, and is incapable of preserving these resources that are said to belong to everyone. The state uses nationalism to justify its race to extract and sell to the global market the largest possible quantity of resources in the shortest possible timeframe.

On the other hand, this nationalism is part of developmental strategies that believe the negative effects are compensable, and in this way contributes to the commodification of social life and Nature. Nationalism is converted into a statism that is in charge of providing compensation using stunted visions of justice that overemphasize the value of money. Through this logic, the state commodifies many aspects of society and portrays social struggles as disputes over the division of profits, denying that they could be over justice or the meaning of development itself.

The Compensatory State is democratic, but it neither contributes to improving its quality (the radicalization of democracy was a promise of the progressive left), nor deepens political, social, economic, or cultural rights. The state takes on a role as the provider of charity, benevolence, and compassion. Politics shrinks because many disputes are based around actors that are only interested in benefiting from some type of compensation scheme, and non-utilitarian forms of understanding Nature are replaced by the search for environmental goods and services.

This commodification of social life is accepted by many sectors of society, and as a result they follow development strategies that come with serious impacts, contenting themselves with the compensation that is paid. But this should not prevent us from recognizing the negative consequences of this view, or the lack of political leadership that aims for a change of course. The progressivism that governs in South America is certainly more nationalistic, but finds itself unable to advance the promise of the left from which it originated: to prevent the commodification of social life.

Bibliography

Bresser-Pereira, L.C. (2011). From old to new developmentalism in Latin America. In Ocampo, J.A. (ed.), *Handbook of Latin American Economics*. New York: Oxford University Press.

Bunker, S.G. (1985). *Underdeveloping the Amazon. Extraction, unequal exchange, and the Failure of the Modern State*. Chicago: University Chicago Press.

Cardoso, F.H. and Faletto, E. (1979). *Dependency and Development in Latin America*. Berkeley: University California Press.

CEPAL and UNASUR (2013). *Recursos naturales en UNASUR. Situación y tendencias para una agenda de desarrollo regional.* Santiago: CEPAL and UNASUR.

Coronil, F. (2002). *El Estado mágico. Naturaleza, dinero y modernidad en Venezuela.* Caracas: Nueva Sociedad.

El Telégrafo (2012). El desafío de Rafael Correa, 15 January, 2012. Quito: Ecuador. Available from: http://www.telegrafo.com.ec/noticias/informacion-general/item/el-desafio-de-rafael-correa.html). [Accessed: 12 July 2015].

García Linera, A. (2015). *Socialismo comunitario del Vivir Bien.* La Paz: Vicepresidencia Estado Plurinacional Bolivia.

Gudynas, E. (2012). Estado compensador y nuevos extractivismos. Las ambivalencias del progresismo sudamericano. *Nueva Sociedad* 237: 128–46.

Gudynas, E. (2015). *Extractivismos. Ecología, economía y política de un modo de entender el desarrollo y la Naturaleza.* Cochabamba: CEDIB.

HB (Heinrich Böll Foundation) (2012). *Um campeão visto de perto. Uma análise do modelo de desenvolvimento Brasileiro.* Rio de Janeiro: H. Böll Foundation.

Jessop, B. (2002) *The Future of the Capitalist State.* Cambridge: Polity.

Johnson, C. (1999) The developmental state: odyssey of a concept. In Woo-Cumings, M. (ed.). *The Developmental State.* Ithaca: Cornell University Press.

Moreira, C., Raus, D. and Gómez Leyton, J.C. (eds.). (2008). *La nueva política en América Latina. Ruptura y continuidades.* Montevideo: FLACSO Uruguay, Universidad Arcis and Universidad de Lanús.

MPPPM (MINISTERIO DEL PODER POPULAR DE PETRÓLEO Y Minería) and PDVSA (2006). Palabras del Presidente de la República Bolivariana de Venezuela Hugo Chávez, en la Iinstalación de la 141ª, Reunión Extraordinaria de la Conferencia Ministerial de la Organización de Países Exportadores de Petróleo (OPEP), Caracas, 1 de Junio de 2006. Caracas: Bolivarian Republic of Venezuela [Online.] Available from: http://www.pdvsa.com/index.php?tpl=interface.sp/design/readmenuprinc.tpl. html&newsid_obj_id=4814&newsid_temas=314 [Accessed: 12 July 2015].

O'Donnell, G. (1994) Delegative democracy. *Journal of Democracy* 5(1), pp. 55–69.

Offe, C. (1984) *Contradictions of the Welfare State.* Cambridge: MIT Press.

Omeje, K. (2008) Extractive economies and conflicts in the global south: re-engaging rentier theory and politics. In Omahe, K. (ed.). *Extractive Economies and Conflicts in the Global South.* Hampshire: Ashgate.

Philip, G. and Panizza, F. (2011) *The Triumph of Politics. The Return of the Left in Venezuela, Bolivia and Ecuador.* Cambridge: Polity.

Ramírez, R. (2010) Socialismo del sumak kawsay o biosocialismo republicano, In: *Los nuevos retos de América Latina. Socialismo y sumak kawsay.* Quito: SENPLADES.

Schneider, B.R. (1999) The Desarrollista State in Brazil and Mexico, In: Woo-Cumings, M. (ed.) *The Developmental State.* Ithaca: Cornell University Press.

Sicsú, J., De Paula, L.F. and Michel, R. (2007). Por que novo-desenvolvimentismo? *Revista Economia Política* 27 (4): 507–524.

Sikkink, K. (1991) *Ideas and Institutions. Developmentalism in Brazil and Argentina.* Ithaca: Cornell University Press.

PART II

From limited to radical resource nationalism

The country-cases

7 The liberal rarity of South America

Oil and mining policy reform in Colombia in the 2000s[1]

Carlos Caballero Argáez
and Sebastián Bitar

Introduction

Colombia produces minerals and oil, but it is not a mining or petroleum-rich economy. With a complex geology that is quite distinct from neighbouring Venezuela, extracting, refining and transporting petroleum is much more costly in Colombia than in other countries of the region.

Petroleum was discovered in Colombia at the beginning of the twentieth century. However, the exploitation and exportation of this resource was only made possible thanks to foreign direct investment (FDI). Colombia began to export coal in large quantities in the 1980s, despite the identification of large deposits in the middle of the nineteenth century. Nickel production and export was centred on a single large project, *Cerromatoso*, located in the north of the country, where, since the 1970s, the concession had been held by a foreign corporation, BHP Billiton. Gold, the principal mineral export of the colonial era, continued to be exploited by both national and foreign companies, as well as by small-scale and artisanal miners. Despite the importance of mining and hydrocarbons for national GDP (8% in 2012), in relative terms, Colombia is not an economy that is rich in these resources, and due to a low capacity to mobilize investment, has not been able to assure the development of the oil and mining sectors by either the state or national capital. Thus, in recent years, it has been necessary for Colombia to attract private investment, both national and foreign, to develop the sector and generate income for the central and subnational governments.

While Venezuela, Brazil, Mexico and Ecuador are among the top twenty countries with the largest proven oil reserves in the world, as Figure 7.1 demonstrates, Colombia is ranked 35th, with reserves of 2.2 billion barrels, only 0.8% of Venezuela's (Central Intelligence Agency 2014b). Oil production in Colombia in 2012 was 969,000 barrels/day (bpd). In comparison, Venezuela, Mexico and Brazil produced an average of 2.7 million bpd in the same year (Central Intelligence Agency 2014a). In this regard, Colombia cannot be considered a petroleum-rich economy. On the other hand, while Colombia is a significant exporter of coal, with a total production of 89 million tonnes in 2012, this figure is relatively small compared to production in China (3549 Mt), the United States (953 Mt), or India (595 Mt) (World Coal Association 2014).

This chapter provides an overview of the principal milestones in the history of mining and petroleum in Colombia, with the objective of understanding the government's position towards foreign investment in these sectors. In the case of petroleum, we concentrate on the evolution of the Empresa Colombiana de Petróleos (ECOPETROL) and foreign direct investment (FDI) in the country. In the case of mining, we concentrate on the association contract signed between the Colombian state and Exxon to exploit the coal deposit *El Cerrejón Zona Norte*. We also examine the impact of reforms to the institutional and regulatory regime for the management of petroleum and mining resources.

We argue that Colombia has not experienced energy and resource nationalism at a comparable level to other countries of the region due to the low capacity of the state to develop these sectors in the absence of private and foreign investment. At the same time, the government of Colombia recognizes the importance of revenue from oil and mining, without which it would suffer serious fiscal short-falls and balance of payments disequilibria. Consequently, the state has sought to offer guarantees and advantages to foreign investors with the objective of maintaining exports and revenue flows.

We argue that ECOPETROL could not develop the oil sector in the country as a public company without private investment. Before the 2003 reform, ECOPETROL's ability to make major investments in oil exploration was limited for three main reasons. Firstly, due to its inclusion in national accounts, ECOPETROL had no capacity for independent borrowing. Borrowing money from capital markets to increase exploration meant increasing Colombia's international debt, and that was not permitted by the central government. Secondly, ECOPETROL did not have the technical capacity to engage in major exploration projects. The company had neither the human resources nor the technology that foreign companies enjoyed, and which made them more efficient and profitable. Thirdly, the national state, ECOPETROL's only owner until the reform, did not leave sufficient money in the company for investment and growth. Instead, the government sought to extract the maximum possible rent from the company to maintain or increase public spending.

The general trend from 1974 to 2003 reveals that the policy followed by different governments of Colombia looked to promote private investment in circumstances in which oil production and reserves were low; and to tighten those conditions when important discoveries were made.

In 1974, one year after the Organization of Petroleum Exporting Countries (OPEC) asserted their power and international oil prices increased, Colombia adopted the 'association contract'. At the time, Colombia imported oil and the concessions previously granted to foreign oil companies had not resulted in an increase of exploration activity in the country. The new contract established a 50/50% partnership between the state and the oil company in a concession area (less the 20% royalty payment), but the exploration risk was entirely borne by the private partner. With the discovery of the *Caño Limón* field near the border with Venezuela in 1983, the Barco Administration (1986–1990) tightened the conditions on private investors and,

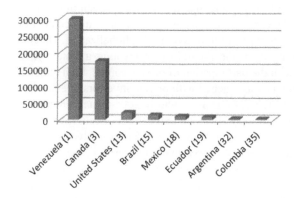

Figure 7.1 Proven oil reserves, Colombia (millions of barrels).

Source: Central Intelligence Agency (2014b). The numbers in parentheses indicate the world ranking of the country in terms of proven reserves. Compiled by the authors.

notwithstanding the discovery of the *Cusiana-Cupiagua* fields in 1989, incentives for private investment were reduced and exploration activity declined dramatically.

At the beginning of the 1990s conditions were liberalized and by 1998/99 the decision was taken to attract foreign investment and to avoid losing self-sufficiency in oil. However, even though important changes were made to reduce the government take and the royalties on the sector, these policies were not enough to guarantee the arrival of new foreign investment, given the international context in which Colombia's competitors also liberalized swiftly.

Private investment in Colombia and the founding of the state oil company

Colombia has a long tradition of honouring contracts with foreign investors. The most notable case in the twentieth century was the oil exploitation contract for the *De Mares* concession, which was granted in the first half of the century to the Tropical Oil Company, a subsidiary of Standard Oil Company of New Jersey (ESSO).

In 1905, the Colombian government granted a concession to exploit petroleum to Roberto de Mares, who later ceded his rights to the Tropical Oil Company in August 1919. The operation was approved on June 1921 through a resolution that established that the concession would last thirty years from the date at which exploitation activities commenced – 25 August 1921. However, this wording, which failed to define 'commencement of exploitation', led to a lengthy legal struggle of over twenty years between Tropical Oil and the Colombian state (Santiago 1986: 24–6). In April 1941, the government notified the Tropical Oil Company that the concession would expire on 25 August 1946. This notice was rejected by the company, and as a result, the government decided to send the issue to the Supreme Court. The final judgment of the Court was handed down in September 1944 and established that the concession would expire on 25 August 1951 (Caballero and Amaya 2011: 76).

The government conformed to the ruling and subsequently began the process of studying what to do with the concession at its termination date, in a context of significant union and political mobilization in favour of nationalization. Diverse options were explored, among them the possibility of creating a state-owned enterprise and of operating with the participation of private capital, both national and foreign. When no agreement was reached with private investors, the government decided to constitute ECOPETROL as a wholly state-owned enterprise. Tropical Oil was required to turn over all its equipment and assets used in the operation of the *De Mares* concession on 25 August 1951, at twelve midnight. One of the articles of the governmental decree that gave birth to the company established that it had the right to associate with private capital in the future (Ministerio de Minas y Energía 1986: 475; Caballero y Amaya 2011: 63–5).

At midnight on the 25 August 1951, in a festive atmosphere, the *De Mares* concession was transferred to ECOPETROL (Caballero y Amaya 2011: 82). At the hand-over ceremony, the president of the International Petroleum Co. of Toronto, a subsidiary of Standard Oil, who represented the outgoing foreign investor, declared that Colombia had met the terms of the *De Mares* concession and made the following statement:

> As far as I am aware, this is the first time in the history of the oil industry that such an important property, developed by private capital under concession, returns to state-ownership due to the legal expiration of the concession period as specified in the original contract.
>
> (Santiago 1986: 112)

In turn, the Colombian minister responsible for mines and petroleum responded that strictly respecting Colombia's commitments was of world-wide importance, since it avoided 'misguided nationalism', political crises, and internal commotion, and allowed the state to take over the resource and create the Empresa Colombiana de Petróleos in a 'pacific and legal way' (Santiago 1986: 113). In this regard, the history of the *De Mares* concession and the creation of ECOPETROL clearly demonstrate the pragmatism of Colombian leaders with regard to foreign investment, as well as the distinctiveness of the Colombian approach to petroleum policy, in comparison to other countries in Latin America.

From the concession model, to association contracts, and back again

Until 1974, Colombia used a concession regime for investors, who were principally foreign. However, the likelihood of finding oil in Colombia was low. In fact, outside the *De Mares* concession, few significant petroleum discoveries were made over a fifty-year period (Segovia 2011: 462).

The relationship between exploratory wells and commercially viable discoveries was only 13 to 1 until 1969 (Segovia 2011: 462). Nonetheless, the perception endured that Colombia should have large oil fields, due to its proximity to

Venezuela, and foreign companies were accused of freezing their activities in concession areas, given that the contracts envisioned little state oversight to encourage effective exploration activities. However, the reality was different, as low international prices at the time made it unattractive to invest in exploration given the reduced likelihood of discovering a commercially viable reserve. At the end of the sixties, Colombia's oil reserves were very low, and together with a lack of foreign exchange, the capacity to import fuels was effectively zero. This situation led the government of the day to send a law to Congress (Law 20 of 1969), which stipulated that the state would prioritize the delivery of areas with potential to ECOPETROL, which could explore 'directly, or in association with public or private capital, either national or foreign' (Segovia 2011: 466).

This was the genesis of the association contracts, which were formalized in October of 1974, and established that hydrocarbon exploration in Colombia was to be exclusively controlled by ECOPETROL. The state-owned enterprise could pursue this goal 'directly, or by means of association contracts, service delivery, or of any nature, different from a concession, used by natural or legal persons, either national or foreign' (Segovia 2011: 476). Principally, this meant a contract between ECOPETROL and a private company, by which the latter committed to explore and exploit hydrocarbons in a specific and clearly delimited area of the Colombian territory, during a period of six years. If ECOPETROL determined that a sufficient volume of petroleum had been discovered, it would assume half of the cost of the exploratory wells that became commercially viable, and would receive 50% of the product after royalties had been paid to the state (royalties were set at 20%). Consequently, the risk of exploration was entirely assumed by the private contracting company.

In 1973, a fundamental political change in the oil industry occurred when OPEC reduced global supply and sharply increased oil prices. One of the consequences in the early 1970s was that international oil companies found themselves under pressure to cede part of their oil rents to the national governments of those countries where they operated. Bargaining power shifted from the large multinational companies to the producing countries.

In the 1980s, the association contracts began to bear fruit. The US company Occidental Petroleum (Oxy) discovered the *Caño-Limón* deposit in the Llanos Orientales region, and requested its commercialization in 1983. With the contribution of *Caño-Limón* crude, Colombia became once again self-sufficient in petroleum, a status which it had lost twenty years earlier, and began exporting oil in December 1985 (Segovia 2011: 486–7).

The *Caño-Limón* discovery, which is predicted to produce close to 1.4 billion barrels during its lifetime (and which has produced more than 1 billion at the time of writing) also inflamed nationalist sentiment in the country. Political leaders, the oil industry union (la Unión Sindical Obrera – USO), and public opinion, embraced the belief that the country was rich in petroleum, and consequently, should demand more from the association contracts. The first changes to contract clauses occurred in November 1989 in what is known as the 'stepped' production model. The participation of ECOPETROL continued to be 50% of the output, but it started to increase when production rose above 60 million barrels, attaining 70% when output exceeded 150 million barrels.

In 1993 a series of interconnected deposits were discovered in *Cusiana*, *Cusiana Sur* and *Cupiagua*, in the piedmont region of the *Llanos Orientales* by British Petroleum (UK), Total (France) and Triton (Australia).[2] The discovery was estimated at 2.2 billion barrel equivalents, as the deposit contained both crude and gas. However, it was a high-cost deposit to exploit, due to the geological characteristics of the piedmont: the hydrocarbons were located at 'five or six km below the surface, twice as deep as in *Caño-Limón* and five times deeper than the *De Mares* concession in Barrancabermeja' (Segovia 2011: 495).

These factors, combined with the financial weakness of ECOPETROL, and the increase in guerilla activity in the exploration zone, led the Colombian government to introduce the so-called 'R Factor', which calculated the production value taking into account income and spending of the associated company during the length of the contract (López et al. 2012: 27). The R Factor required that 'if the production of a contract exceeded 60 million barrel equivalents, the scale affecting the portion of the petroleum available to the associated partner would not be applied until the partner had recuperated his investment'(Segovia 2011: 501). This benefited investors by lessening the risk of not recuperating their initial investment, and reduced the government take in cases where that threshold was not surpassed.

The international oil industry was not enthusiastic about the new contract terms and as a result there was a marked decline in the number of wells drilled in the second half of the 1990s, in comparison to the first. Furthermore, the incumbent government prioritized the monetary transfers to the Treasury from ECOPETROL, rather than investing in the state-owned firm.

By the end of the twentieth century, the conditions for foreign investment in hydrocarbons were not favourable.[3] For this reason, some multinational mining companies ceded their contracts to other companies already operating in Colombia; such was the case with Texaco in 1995, and Exxon between 1995 and 2000. In addition, half way through this latter year, the *Cusiana* and *Cupiagua* oil fields reached their peak level of production, declining rapidly afterwards. In this context, the government began to favour the associated companies, offering them the possibility of reducing the participation of ECOPETROL to 30% in the development of new discoveries and using a more favourable formula to calculate the 'R Factor'. Simultaneously a new royalty regime was designed to promote production in small oil fields, and the fixed royalty of 20% was eliminated. Instead, the new royalty was variable and could oscillate between 8 and 25% depending on the production volume of the oil field.

In 2002, it was evident that the model of association contracts had lost legitimacy and attractiveness to foreign investors. The international petroleum industry had undergone profound changes and Colombia lagged behind, running the risk of once again losing self-sufficiency in oil production in the first decade of the twenty-first century. This reality opened the way for the 2003 institutional reform.

The petroleum reform of 2003

Colombia returned to the concession model with the 2003 reform. In 2003 two kinds of concession contracts were introduced: An exploration and production (E&P) contract and the technical evaluation contract (TEA) (Benavides 2001: 541). The former is limited to six years and can be renewed for four more; the latter is two years, renewable for two. Royalties were reformed to be flexible, starting at 8% for wells producing 5,000 barrels per day and increasing to 20% for production between 400,000 and 600,000 barrels per day, and to 25% above that level (see Table 7.1).

In addition, in July 2003, the National Hydrocarbon Agency (ANH) was created in order to manage Colombia's subsoil hydrocarbon wealth. The institutional reform in the oil sector in Colombia was undertaken by Presidential Decree, with the previous authorization of the National Congress (Decree No 1760 of 2003). This Decree established that the Ministry of Mines and Energy would have the responsibility for hydrocarbons policy making, the ANH would independently manage the concessions and auction oil and natural gas resources to energy companies, which no longer had to associate with ECOPETROL.

Table 7.1 The ECOPETROL reform

The effects of the ECOPETROL reform on the petroleum sector	
Government take	In 2011 the Government take was 43%
Concession contracts for exploration and exploitation	Duration: 6 years, extendible for 4 years more Evaluation period: 1 to 2 years The company has the right to exploit discoveries and keep profits after payment of royalties
Royalties	Calculated according to the volume of production, by Thousands Barrels of Oil Equivalent per Day (TBOED) • 8% between 0–5 TBOED and escalating progressively up to 125 • 20% between 125–400 TBOED and escalating progressively up to 600 • 25% over 600 TBOED • Windfall Royalties: are paid when the accumulated production exceeds 5 million barrels, and the price of petroleum exceeds a base reference price.
Revenue to the Colombian government from the petroleum sector	Distribution of profits from ECOPETROL via dividends National Taxes • (2013) 25% Income tax • 9% Income tax for CREE (Contribución Empresarial para la Equidad) • 3% VAT and assessment on financial transactions of 0.4% (4x1.000) Local Taxes Industry and trade property tax, among others Revenue that the state receives from corporate income tax (for this sector) rose from 0.5% of GDP in 2002 to 1% of GDP in 2007. Profits from ECOPETROL increased along the same lines.

Source: Benavides (2011); López, Montes, Garavito, and Collazos (2013); Rincón, Lozano, and Ramos (2008). Table compiled by the authors.

Historically, ECOPETROL had been in a conflict of interest between its regulatory and producing role. Before 2003, ECOPETROL was not only the state's oil company, but it also had the authority to regulate the oil sector, design the country's petroleum policy, and manage all contracts with private foreign or domestic investors. The reform stripped ECOPETROL of all these functions and gave them to the ANH, a new proper regulatory body which did not participate in the oil market. As a result, ECOPETROL today competes on a level playing field with private companies (national or foreign) for contracts issued by the ANH.

With the creation of ANH, ECOPETROL had to change. In order for this company to compete with private companies, grow and indebt itself, it had to be taken out of the national budget, and run according to corporate principles. In 2007 ECOPETROL went public with a share offering to national and foreign investors, which reduced the ownership stake of the state from 100% to 88.5%. This change was made possible by legislation that allowed the company to reduce state ownership to 80%. Beginning in September 2008, shares of ECOPETROL were listed on New York Stock Exchange.

The reform occurred without crisis or violent protest. As one expert noted:

> The spirit of the times was different than during the great international nationalizations. ... The coalition of interests that could have opposed the change found no echo, and in practice was limited to the company's union, the reaction of which was anticipated and neutralized.
>
> (Benavides 2011: 541)

The reform of 2003 was highly successful. In 2002 Colombia produced 578,000 barrels/day, while in 2013 it had attained slightly more than a million barrels/day. It not only allowed for an increase in production and exports of oil during a period of high international oil prices, but also an increase in foreign investment in the oil sector in Colombia (see Figure 7.2). The reform also prepared the country for a period of low international prices – since the government's take is smaller than under the association contracts, the oil companies can still receive positive returns on their investments.

Coal: 'A good deal to quit a bad business!'

From the middle of the nineteenth century, it was known that large deposits of thermal coal exited on the La Guajira peninsula in the north of Colombia. Although these deposits were shallow and located close to the Caribbean Sea, their exploitation and exportation required large investments, particularly in transportation and specialized port infrastructure. For this reason, it was only in the 1970s, as a result of increases in the international price of petroleum, that multinational corporations began to show interest in alternative sources of energy, including coal, and turned their gaze to countries with substantial reserves.

In the first half of the 1970s, the Colombian government held negotiations with a foreign company, Peabody Coal Company, to develop the Guajira deposits,

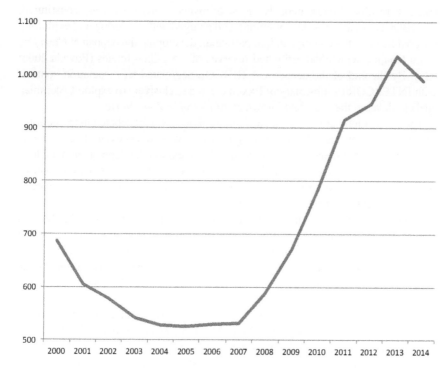

Figure 7.2 Average annual oil production in Colombia (1000s barrels/day).

Source: Agencia Nacional de hidrocarburos (ANH) (2014). Compiled by the authors.

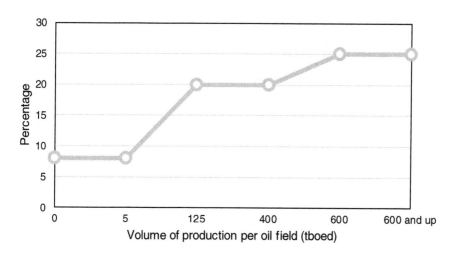

Figure 7.3 Royalty percentages according to production levels.

Compiled by the authors.

without results. Simultaneously, a state-owned enterprise was constituted, CARBOCOL (Carbones de Colombia), and charged with exploring and exploiting the coal fields in the country, and, in particular, developing the deposit at *Cerrejón*, in La Guajira, which had estimated reserves of 3.5 billion tonnes (Poveda 2005: 623). By the end of the decade CARBOCOL negotiated an association contract with INTERCOR (a subsidiary of Exxon created exclusively to exploit Colombian coal) to develop the coal field known as *El Cerrejón Zona Norte*.

The association between the state and Exxon was widely debated in the political sphere; some members of Congress argued that it was not necessary to collaborate with a multinational energy company in order to exploit the deposit. Nonetheless, the government's position won the day, which was that an association contract was preferable because of the size of the deposits and the lack of experience in Colombia regarding how to develop it.

Both companies participated equally in the contract, and INTERCOR was designated as the project operator. The value of the initial investment was US $3,360 million, of which, the Colombian state was responsible for US $1,680 million, obtained in loans through private international banks. The project began to operate in 1984, in the depths of the debt crisis in Latin America. As a result, Colombia became a net exporter of coal.

When the contract was signed in 1979, it was projected that coal prices would rise to US $250/tonne by the year 2000. These prices never materialized, but the investment continued. For this reason the project also produced important losses for the state, which had guaranteed the debt taken by CARBOCOL from private international banks, and which had to be paid annually.

In the early 1990s, the government began considering the possibility of selling its participation in the project. This approach gathered steam under subsequent administrations, which gradually designed the terms and steps necessary for realizing the sale. These steps included opening the railway and port facilities to third party producers of coal located near the central and southern part of the mine (and which were not included in the CARBOCOL-Exxon association contract), and extending the original production agreement with Exxon until 2034. It was a unique case in Colombia of 'continuity and coherence between administrations and their ministers' (Caballero 2007: 315).

The sale of the state's participation in the venture, which only recuperated US $560 million of the total investment, opened a national political debate that extended to the National Congress, and involved investigations by the institutions responsible for fiscal and administrative oversight and control. The reality, however, was that the international price of coal was, at the moment of the transaction, only US $28/tonne. This was far from the World Bank projections that had been used as the basis of the original investment decision.[4]

In addition, the project was unable to expand due to the lack of resources available from the state, which further doomed the project to continued economic losses. By selling the state's ownership stake to private foreign investors with experience and technology in coal extraction, it was expected that the state would receive more taxes and royalties. For this reason, the government of the day

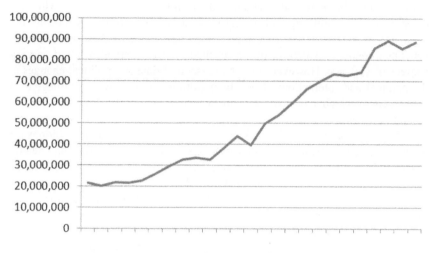

Figure 7.4 Coal production in Colombia (tonnes).

Source: Sistema de Información Minero Colombiano (SIMCO) (2014). Information compiled by the authors.

considered that it had made 'a good deal to quit a bad business!' (Caballero 2007: 313). The figures bear out this decision, as coal production from *El Cerrejón Zona Norte* increased substantially after the sale, rising to 40 million tonnes, and Colombia's overall production to 90 million tonnes in 2010 (see Figure 7.4). At the time of writing of this chapter, coal is currently the second most important Colombian export after oil.

Why does Colombia seek to attract and respect foreign investment?

A country with oil, but not an oil-rich country

The relative scarcity of large hydrocarbon and mineral reserves in Colombia has determined the state's policy for exploiting these natural resources. In significant part, this explains the absence of energy nationalism, although there has been a recurrent political debate about the control of these resources throughout the history of the country. In the 1920s, for example, a powerful oil workers' union was created (USO), which advocated for the exploitation of petroleum by the state instead of by multinational oil companies. This union continues to exist, albeit with reduced power, despite the structural changes to the institutional role of the state in the hydrocarbon sector.

From a historical perspective, two cultures have existed in ECOPETROL: one corresponds to a capitalist, internationalist, and pro-democratic view, which is represented by the shareholders and the administration of the company; while the other is socialist, anti-imperialist, and pro-state ownership, represented by the union (Urrutia 2011: 273). In the past, the coexistence of these two cultures generated conflicts, which, at times, resulted in strikes, stoppages and varying degrees of violence. However, with the passage of time and political changes at the national and international level, both cultures have shown some degree of convergence, which has made the management of industrial relations in the company easier.

Before the creation of ECOPETROL, the union demanded better conditions for workers, in terms of wages and improvements in housing, education, and health. In the 1970s and 1980s, the union was politically active, following the communist strategy of pursing 'all forms of fighting'. However in this century, despite a strike in 2004, the relationship between the administration of the company and the union has been better and cordial.

As was indicated at the beginning of this chapter, in comparison to Venezuela, Mexico, Ecuador and Brazil, Colombia has not found large reserves of petroleum. The country has reserves that will last for only seven years of production given increasing rates of exports and domestic consumption of fuels. Furthermore, the likelihood of finding more petroleum in Colombia today is low – about one in 10 exploration wells. For this reason, exploration in Colombia is considered a high-risk business. In the second half of 2014 the international price of oil decreased from US $115 to US $45, making it even less attractive for foreign companies to explore in Colombia.

Despite these problems, petroleum and its derivatives remain, in the second decade of the twenty-first century, the principal export of Colombia: representing 56% of the total value of sales abroad. In fiscal terms, taxes and dividends generated by ECOPETROL, and royalties, constitute 20% of the current income of the country. Coal exports account for 11% of the total. In this respect, Colombia is very dependent on hydrocarbon and coal in its current account balance (trade and investment).

The history of the management of energy resources in Colombia clearly signals that the country has not had the economic, administrative or technological capacity to take on, by itself, exploration and exploitation projects in hydrocarbons. It has always needed the contributions of foreign capital, and for this reason has sought to attract FDI by offering advantageous conditions in comparison to other areas of the world. When Colombia did not offer such incentives, due to the belief that the geology of the country was similar to Venezuela's, foreign companies did not have the incentives to conduct oil exploration and production suffered.

ECOPETROL never had, since its creation in 1951 until the reform of 2003, the financial strength to invest in oil exploration, due in part to the fact that as a state-owned enterprise its net earnings and financial debt were treated as part of the consolidated national accounts of the government. In this context, the government sought to maximize transfers from the company to the national Treasury in order to cover the ongoing expenses of the state, and never assigned sufficient financial resources to investment in exploration. When ECOPETROL drilled wells in some prospective areas, this implied significant investments that ran the risk of failure. In this regard it was preferable for these same operations to be done by foreign partners, either through concession or association contracts.

The development of coal shares some similarities with hydrocarbons. One very important similarity is that the exploitation of large-scale mines required massive investments in transportation infrastructure and machinery, which could not be undertaken by the state because of their size, and due to the prioritization of public spending in favour of social projects. Furthermore, when the state tried to partner with the multinational Exxon to develop the *El Cerrejón Zona Norte* mine it had to take on foreign debt, which, given the volatility of international coal prices, led to large economic losses for the country and to the sale of its stake in the joint venture in 2000.

As was explained above, the reform of 2003 created the ANH to manage hydrocarbon resources (oil and gas), and contracts with both national and foreign oil companies – functions previously performed by ECOPETROL. With the reform, ECOPETROL was released from the constraints of the national accounts, and acquired the financial autonomy which permitted it to invest in exploration and exploitation projects.

Nonetheless, both the ANH and ECOPETROL face critical challenges. The ANH must maintain attractive conditions to incentivize national and foreign firms to invest in oil exploration, which is particularly important due to the low levels of proven reserves in the country. This objective is crucial for the Colombian macro-economy: if there is a failure to locate new reserves, the country will not only face a balance of payments crisis, but also a fiscal crisis for governments at the national and subnational levels.

ECOPETROL, in turn, must establish a structure of corporate governance that gives the company autonomy and independence from its principal shareholder – the state. Autonomy is needed to ensure both efficient management and the investments that are necessary to survive in the long run as a company. The problem is that with 88.5% of the company's capital in state hands, and with only limited representation of the minority private shareholders on the board of directors, the national government is frequently tempted to extract financial resources from the company to meet the needs of the Treasury. Such a situation could lead to an increase in company debt, without making the needed investments in oil exploration.

Investor confidence

One of the principal objectives of the Álvaro Uribe Vélez (2002–2010) and Juan Manuel Santos (2010–2018) administrations has been to increase investment in the country by creating attractive conditions for private investment, both national and foreign. During the Uribe government, investment increased from 13 to 28% of GDP (Bernal-León 2014). Even during the crisis of 2008–9, international markets remained open for the purchase of ECOPETROL and Colombian public debt. Various elements have contributed to the success of Colombia in encouraging investment, such as responsible fiscal policy, a floating exchange rate, and the independence of the Central Bank (Junguito 2009). In addition, the Uribe government granted tax breaks, signed tax stability agreements, created free trade zones, and gave other benefits in exchange for large investments (Galán 2006). Uribe constantly reiterated his commitment to an economic model that was friendly to investment, and criticized the nationalizations that had occurred in other countries of the region (Dinero 2009).

At the same time, improvements in the security situation in Colombia facilitated the arrival of foreign direct investment. The principal pillar of the Uribe administration was to establish public security after the state had been displaced from large areas of the country by the FARC (Revolutionary Armed Forces of

Table 7.2 Regulation of FDI in the mining sector, Colombia

Regulation of foreign investment in the mining sector	
Legislation	Mining Code, 2001
Type of contract	Concession
General characteristics	Minerals of any class (ground or underground) belong to the state, regardless of land ownership, including the presence of indigenous groups; Some zones may be declared indigenous or afro-descendent mining zones, conferring special rights on those communities; Extraction is forbidden in areas that are environmentally protected, or which do not have adequate security conditions; Foreign and national firms are to be treated equally.
Concession period	Up to thirty years, with exploration rights for three years
Legal stability	Alterations to the mining regime are not to be applied retroactively to concessions already granted: Royalties paid on production cannot be increased; There will be stability in the regulatory framework governing operations.
Royalties	Coal (by volume of annual extraction) • 10% when greater than 3 million tonnes • 5% when less than 3 million tonnes Copper and Iron • 5% of the mine-head value of the product extracted Gold and Silver • 4% of the mine-head value of the product extracted • 6% on alluvial gold Platinum • 5% of the mine-head value of the product extracted Salts • 12% of the mine-head value of the product extracted
Payroll	Companies should privilege national workers and inputs. The majority of the payroll should be composed by Colombian workers: • 70% of specialized workers • 80% of unskilled workers

Source: Departamento Nacional de Planeación (DNP), 2007. Table compiled by the authors.

Colombia) and paramilitary groups. Attacks on oil infrastructure had been common for decades. Nonetheless, Colombia managed to reverse this deterioration of public security and provide better conditions for investment as a result of the professionalization of the armed forces and the renewed presence of the state in peripheral areas, in part thanks to a military assistance package from the United States.[5]

Although its principal objective was the struggle against drug production and trafficking, part of the US military and economic support to Colombia aimed, specifically, to protect American investments in the petroleum sector. On February 5th, 2002, the Bush government announced that it would allocate an additional US $98 million to Plan Colombia for the protection of the *Caño Limón-Coveñas* pipeline which was partially owned and operated by Occidental Petroleum. Between 2002 and 2003, a programme was established to locate 70 US military personnel in Arauca in order to train 2,000 troops from the XVIII Brigade of the Colombian army for the protection of the pipeline (Dunning and Wirpsa 2004).

In this regard, the attraction of foreign investment by means of fiscal incentives and guarantees of security continues to be a priority for the current government of Colombia in 2015.

Mineral and energy rents in Colombia

The Colombian state has traditionally taken a rentier approach to ECOPETROL. Before the reform of 2003, the state managed oil policy with the intention of maximizing its revenue and financing public spending (Benavides 2011). Following the reform, the state let companies make all decisions about production, investment and exports (Goodwin 2009: 9), and allowed private companies, both national and foreign, to exploit petroleum resources without the participation of the state-owned enterprise. With this change, the state ceased controlling the planning and profits of the sector. Nonetheless, through taxes and royalties, private companies continued contributing to both state revenue and an important share of public spending.

Figure 7.5 shows that revenue to the state from ECOPETROL increased six times between 2003 and 2013. Although the government is no longer the owner of 100% of the capital of the company, total state revenue increased to US $18 billion. This includes transfers to the central government as well as royalties paid to subnational governments.

The largest beneficiary of the rents generated by ECOPETROL is the central government, which receives 88.5% of its dividends, as well as national taxes (income, wealth, value-added, and others). Dividends originating from ECOPETROL and managed by the central government have increased from US $375 million in 2003 to US $7,059 million in 2013. With regards to income tax, government receipts have increased from US$ 187 million in 2003 to US$ 3,657 million in 2013. Total national government income from ECOPETROL increased six times in ten years: growing from US $1,969 million in 2003 to US $18,059 million in 2013.

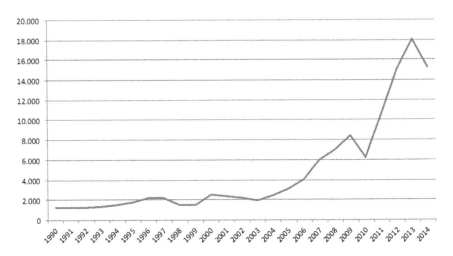

Figure 7.5 Total transfers from ECOPETROL to the Colombian state ($US millions).

Source: ECOPETROL (2012–2015) and Benavides (2011). Compiled by the authors.

Figure 7.6 shows the evolution of the importance of the financial resource transfers from ECOPETROL within the total revenue of the central government. In 2013, total revenue was close to US $64 billion, of which US $10.9 came from ECOPETROL. This means that the oil company generated 17.1% of the revenue

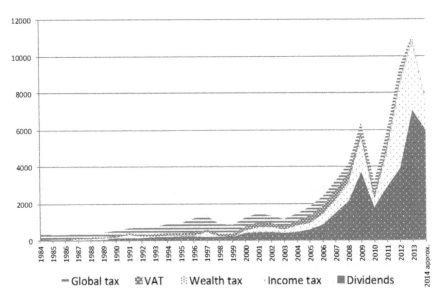

Figure 7.6 Central government income originating from ECOPETROL ($US millions).

Source: ECOPETROL (2012–2015) and Benavides (2011). Compiled by the authors.

appropriated by the central government. Consequently, it is evident that public spending in Colombia is highly dependent on the petroleum sector. This is cause for concern in so far as international prices have fallen, known oil reserves are low, and there is little expectation of new discoveries.

If the sustainability of revenue derived from petroleum is questionable, it should also be noted that the mining sector is growing in Colombia thanks to foreign direct investment. Consequently, state revenues from royalties and taxes on this sector have also become important sources of public sector financing, as well as having a positive impact on the balance of payments (through exports and capital inflows).

Conclusion

While episodes of oil nationalism did certainly take place during the twentieth century, and were reflected in union mobilization and political debates, these facts did not give rise to the adoption of policies that threatened foreign investment in the sector, as occurred in other countries of the region. The use of 'association contracts' between state and private companies was a political solution that went half-way, and which did facilitate exploration for hydrocarbons in Colombia, although the arrangement eventually outgrew its usefulness.

Currently, with only seven years of petroleum reserves remaining, and given the importance of hydrocarbons to state coffers, Colombia is at risk of an energy and economic crisis. It is clear that the sustained growth of Colombian GDP depends at present on the mining and energy sector. Without an increased commitment to exploration which yields new deposits, the Colombian economy is at serious risk of slowing economic growth in the near future. Signs of economic hardship were already appearing in 2015, due to the recent fall of oil prices.

On the other hand, fiscal fragility generated by the scarcity of petroleum may require that the government increase taxes, reduce public spending, and cut social programmes and subsidies. Due to projections of declining revenue from ECOPETROL, in 2015 the national government responded by increasing other taxes (Portafolio 2014). Higher taxes and reduced spending may induce a worsening of the economic crisis, while reduced social expenditures might stimulate social unrest in the future. The reduction in the revenue of the central government from ECOPETROL (estimated for 2016 at Col $20.0 billion; US $7,300 million in July 2015), has demonstrated to the government the need for a new tax reform, in order to increase revenue from the income tax paid by individuals or an increase in the VAT. For this purpose the government created a commission of experts that should present its recommendations of reforming the tax code in 2016.

Colombia must attract private investment, both national and foreign, to petroleum exploration, as well as strengthen ECOPETROL's capacity to invest. In the last two rounds of contract auctions in 2014, the ANH opened 95 areas to petroleum exploration, but only received 27 offers, which were accepted. Foreign and national investors are no longer responding to the incentives offered by Colombia, and instead, are looking at the Mexican market, as well as other counties with greater prospects and fewer environmental, social and security restrictions. In the mining sector similar problems and restrictions exist, in addition to the particular challenge of illegal mining and environmental damage.

Although it would not be popular with Colombians, this serious situation may require a further reduction of the government take, as well as a re-evaluation of the processes already established for environmental licencing and consultations with local communities, as well as prioritizing the physical defence of oil wells and pipelines.

Notes

1 This project was made possible thanks to the research assistance of Lucía Forero, Paula Mora, and Christian Medina, and generous funding from the Universidad de los Andes. We also thank Pedro Nel Ospina for his useful comments on previous versions of this document, and Marcela Villa for her rigorous editing.
2 This discovery was made within the *Santiago de las Atalayas* concession contract, between ECOPETROL and these foreign firms. It took the companies eleven years to explore this area, in part to delay paying fees to ECOPETROL, with which they were in extended bargaining over that period.
3 According to Barrios and Cárdenas (2003), the *government take* was 58.71% between 1974 and 1989, and rose to 58.79% in the 'stepped' production model, then fell to 47.8% in 2000 under the progressive model. (Barrios and Cárdenas 2003: 52).
4 Shortly after concluding the sale of the state's ownership stake, Exxon also sold its share of the enterprise to the same group of investors (a Swiss-Australian consortium), although the value of the latter transaction is not publicly known.
5 For a discussion of the re-establishment of public security in Colombia, see Feldmann (2012).

Bibliography

Agencia Nacional De Hidrocarburos (ANH). (2014). *Cifras y estadísticas* Bogotá: Government of Colombia. Available from: http://www.anh.gov.co/ANH-en-Datos/Paginas/Cifras-y-Estad%C3%ADsticas.aspx [Accessed: 22 August 2014].

Banco De La República. Balance fiscal del Gobierno Nacional Central. Estadísticas - Finanzas públicas. Available from: http://www.banrep.gov.co/es/series-estadisticas/see_finanzas_publi.htm [Accessed: 22 August 2014].

Barrios, A. and Cárdenas, J.C. (2005). ¿Es atractiva la contratación petrolera para la inversión privada en Colombia? Bogotá, CID.

Benavides, J. (ed.) (2011a). *Ecopetrol – Energía limpia para el futuro, 60 años*. Series and figures [CD-ROM]. Bogotá: Villegas.

Benavides, J. (2011b). De los contratos de asociación a los contratos de concesión en Colombia: La perspectiva económica. In Benavides, J. (ed.). *Ecopetrol – Energía limpia para el futuro, 60 años*. Bogotá: Villegas, p. 517–49.

Bernal-León, A.J. (2014). Sobre la confianza inversionista. *La República*. [Online], 24th February. Available from http://www.larepublica.co/sobre-la-confianza-inversionista_115631.

Caballero, C. (2007). *Memorias incompletas: crónica del despertar del siglo XXI en Colombia*. Bogotá: Grupo Editorial Norma.

Caballero, C., and Amaya, A. (2011). La Fundación de ECOPETROL o el pragmatismo de la clase dirigente colombiana. In Benavides, J. (ed.). *Ecopetrol – Energía limpia para el futuro, 60 años*. Bogotá: Villegas, p. 63–102.

Central Intelligence Agency (CIA). (2014a). *The World Factbook: Country Comparison: Crude Oil – Production*. [Online] Available from https://www.cia.gov/library/publications/the-world-factbook/rankorder/2244rank.html [Accessed: 20 August 2014].

Central Intelligence Agency (CIA). (2014b). *The World Factbook: Country Comparison: Crude Oil – Proved Reserves*. [Online] Available from: https://www.cia.gov/library/publications/the-world-factbook/rankorder/2244rank.html [Accessed: 20 August 2014].

Colombia. Departamento Nacional De Planeación (DNP). (2007). *Actualización de la cartilla 'Las regalías en Colombia'*. Available from http://www.simco.gov.co/simco/documentos/Regalias/ACT_cartilla_regalias.pdf. [Accessed: 8 June 2015].

Dinero. (2009). Que la crisis económica no deteriore la confianza inversionista: Uribe. *Dinero*. [Online] September 30. Available from: http://www.dinero.com/economia/articulo/que-crisis-economica-no-deteriore-confianza-inversionista-uribe/84340 [Accessed: 8 June 2015].

Dunning, T., and Wirpsa, L. (2004). Oil and the political economy of conflict in Colombia and beyond: A linkages approach. *Geopolitics*, 9(1), pp. 81–108.

ECOPETROL (2015). *Reporte Integrado de Gestión Sostenible 2014*. Available from: http://www.ecopetrol.com.co/documentos/Reporte_integrado_Ecopetrol_2014.pdf. [Accessed: 22 July 2015].

ECOPETROL (2014). *Reporte Integrado de Gestión Sostenible 2013*. Available from: http://www.ecopetrol.com.co/especiales/informe2013/pdf/ecopetrol_2013.pdf. [Accessed: 22 July 2015].

ECOPETROL (2013). *Reporte Integrado de Gestión Sostenible 2012*. Available from: http://www.ecopetrol.com.co/documentos/Reporte_Integrado_de_Gestion_Sostenible_2012%20%28V1%29.pdf. [Accessed: 22 July 2015].

ECOPETROL (2012). *Reporte Integrado de Gestión Sostenible 2011*. Available from: http://www.ecopetrol.com.co/especiales/ReporteGestion2012/pdf/ri2011.pdf. [Accessed: 22 July 2015].

Feldmann, A. (2012). Measuring the Colombian 'success' story. [Online] *Revista De Ciencia Política (Santiago)*. 32, 3, p. 739–752. http://www.scielo.cl/scielo.php?script=sci_arttext&pid=S0718-090X2012000300014 [Accessed: 8 June 2015]

Galán, D. (2006). Los contratos de estabilidad jurídica: un estímulo a la inversión extranjera en Colombia. *Estudios Gerenciales*, 22 (101), pp. 111–23.

Goodwin, N., Harris, J., Nelson, J., Roach, B., and Torras, M. (2009). *Macroeconomics in context*. Milton Park: Routledge.

Junguito, R. (2009). La confianza inversionista, *Portafolio*. [Online] 11 de agosto. Available from: http://www.portafolio.co/columnistas/la-confianza-inversionista [Accessed: 8 June 2015].

López, E., Montes, E., Garavito, A., and Collazos, M.M. (2013). Relaciones intersectoriales e importancia en la economía nacional. *Borradores de Economía, Banco de la república*, 748, p. 58. Available from: http://www.banrep.gov.co/sites/default/files/publicaciones/archivos/be_748.pdf. [Accessed: 8 June 2015].

Ministerio de Minas y Energía. (1986). *Código de Petróleos y Recopilación de las Normas que lo Adicionan*. Ministerio de Minas y Energía. Bogotá.

Portafolio. (2014). Estudian nuevos impuestos por baja de ingresos petroleros, *Portafolio*. [Online] July 18. Available from: http://www.portafolio.co/economia/impuestos-caida-ingresos-petroleros. [Accessed: 8 June 2015].

Poveda, G. (2005). *Historia económica de Colombia en el siglo XX*. Medellín: Universidad Pontificia Bolivariana.

Rincón, H., Lozano, I., and Ramos, J. (2008). Rentas petroleras, subsidios e impuestos a los combustibles en Colombia: ¿Qué ocurrió durante el choque reciente de precios?. *Borradores de economía, Banco de la República*, 541, pp. 23. Available from: http://www.banrep.gov.co/sites/default/files/publicaciones/pdfs/borra541.pdf. [Accessed: 8 June 2015].

Santiago, M.Á. (1986). *Crónica de la Concesión de Mares*. Bogotá: Empresa Colombiana de Petróleos.

Segovia, R. (2011). Auge y legado del Contrato de Asociación. In Benavides, J. (ed.). *Ecopetrol – Energía limpia para el futuro, 60 años*. Bogotá: Villegas, pp. 462–513.

Colombia. Sistema De Información Colombianno (SIMCO). (2014). Histórico de Producción de Carbón Anual. Bogotá: Republic of Colombia. Available from http://www.upme.gov.co/generadorconsultas/Consulta_Series.aspx?idModulo=4&tipoSerie=121&grupo=368&Fechainicial=01/01/1940&Fechafinal=31/12/2014. [Accessed: 21 August, 2014].

Urrutia, M. (2011). El reto de las relaciones industriales en Ecopetrol. In Benavides, J. (ed.). *Ecopetrol – Energia Limpia para el futuro, 60 años*. Bogotá: Villegas, pp. 273–314.

World Coal Foundation (WCA). (2014). Coal Statisctics. Available from http://www.worldcoal.org/resources/coal-statistics/. [Accessed: 20 August 2014].

8 Mexico's new wave of market reforms and its extractive industries

Juan Carlos Moreno-Brid
and Alicia Puyana[1]

It is impossible to understand the Mexican economy without a proper account of the pivotal role played by mining in the colonial period, and even during the nation-building process from the nineteenth century up until the first half of the twentieth century. Throughout that period, mining accounted for a major share of exports and investment, and was the key to political power. A visit to downtown Mexico City or to Taxco, Guanajuato, or Zacatecas – old cities that developed during the colonial and post-colonial times – offers a glimpse of the vast wealth accumulated by Spaniards and *criollos* as a result of the exploitation of New Spain's mineral resources, and the labour of its enslaved indigenous people. Furthermore, and speaking to the central theme of this collection, Spanish imperial power, to an important extent, was built fiscally on 'El Quinto Real' (The Royal Fifth); the 20% levy charged in kind on all gold and silver extracted from its American colonies.

Subsequently, extractive industries lost ground in Mexico's exports and output for a brief period in the second half of the twentieth century. In 1976 this situation changed, when the Mexican government announced the discovery of vast oil reserves in *Cantarell*.[2] The newly discovered oil resources allowed the government to launch an ambitious industrialization programme financed, in significant part, by loans from the international banking community that used the oil deposits as implicit collateral.

This moment, when the external constraint on Mexico's economic growth was apparently lifted, was, paradoxically, a key step in the country's journey to a critical, and ultimately ill-fated, fiscal dependence on oil. By 1980, oil accounted for 67% of Mexico's total exports and contributed 78% of public sector revenues, as well as serving as collateral for a growing spiral of foreign debt. Not surprisingly, the country's main macro-economic variables – GDP growth, exchange rate, exports, the balance of payments, and most importantly, fiscal sustainability – were increasingly linked to the fortunes of the price of oil in world markets (Cámara de Diputados 2015).

The oil boom ended abruptly in 1982, triggering Mexico's sovereign default and a balance-of-payments crisis. In response, President De la Madrid (1982–88) launched a series of ambitious reforms to open Mexico's domestic markets and to reduce state intervention in the economy. The aim was to promote market forces, private investment, and non-oil exports as the new engines of growth. The rationale was that protectionism and excessive state intervention in the economy had undermined stability, caused a deterioration in competitiveness, and cut the potential for growth (Moreno-Brid and Ros 2009).

These reforms turned Mexico into one of most open large economies in the world, transforming its productive and trade structure by the beginning of the twenty-first century. Exports jumped from 6% of GDP in 1980, to 10% in the early 1990s, and more than 30% in the 2000s. Their composition also changed, with the share of oil in exports collapsing from 80% in 1982, to 9.2% by 2000, while manufactured exports expanded to 91%. Since then, energy exports have risen again due to the commodity boom, accounting for 17% in 2008, but declining afterwards to 10.8% in 2014 as the price-hike lost momentum after 2009. Mining, in contrast, remained a relatively insignificant contribution to Mexico's total exports. In 2000, it accounted for just 0.23%, in 2008 for 0.66%, and in 2014, 1.27%.

Paralleling the trade figures, by 2000 the oil industry's share of nominal GDP was 4.1% and the mining industry's share was 0.5%. In 2008, at the very peak of the commodity boom, the corresponding shares were 7.9% and 0.7%. By 2014 the oil industry accounted for 5.3% and mining for only 1.1% (Moreno-Brid 2015). In both sectors, their direct contribution to employment was also relatively small. Clearly Mexico is not, and has not been for decades, an extractive economy in the classical understanding of the term.

The success of market reforms in transforming Mexico's trade and productive structure during the 1990s and consolidating a low inflation path was, however, not accompanied by a major reduction in the contribution of oil revenues to public sector income. In fact, on fiscal matters these reforms were myopic and made matters worse. They only cut the deficit by slashing expenditure, mainly public investment, and closing or privatizing public firms, and not by raising revenues, thus keeping tax reforms off the agenda. Mexico went from a fiscal deficit of 15% of GDP in 1982 to a surplus in 1991–94. Since then, the fiscal deficit has never exceeded 3% of GDP (Moreno-Brid and Ros 2009).

However, up until 2014, oil-related income accounted for 30% or more of Mexico's total fiscal revenue. This oil dependence is partly explained by the fact that the Mexican state, through its oil company Petróleos Mexicanos (PEMEX), has a monopoly on oil extraction and refining as well as on the sale of gasoline, diesel and other fuels. But it also embodies a long-standing fiscal pact marked by the incapacity (or unwillingness) of the government to implement any significant fiscal reform given the ruling classes' systematic opposition to paying taxes. Not surprisingly, all non-oil extractive activities – characterized in Mexico by the virtual absence of public enterprises – have been far from heavily taxed.

In contrast to this experience, during the recent commodity boom (2003–08), mineral and energy-rich countries in South America implemented regulatory and fiscal changes to increase the government's take of the surplus from extractive activities. In Mexico, the Peña Nieto administration (2012–18) has only recently put forward an ambitious package of market reforms that includes an initiative to open all of PEMEX's activities to the private sector and a motion to increase taxes and concession payments on mining activities. These new reforms, approved by Congress in 2013–14, are another step in the market liberalization path initiated by De la Madrid in 1986 to push back the state in favour of the market (Grupo Nuevo Curso de Desarrollo 2013, 2015).

At face value, these initiatives have two other short-term objectives. Firstly, the oil-sector reform seeks to halt or reverse the decline of oil production by ending PEMEX's monopoly and opening the industry to local and foreign investors and modern technology. It assumes that when the new entrants increase oil production they will significantly augment fiscal revenues, although they will not be taxed at the same 'expropriation' levels as PEMEX has been. Secondly, the mining-sector reform, as part of a larger fiscal package, is geared to capture for the state a higher share of mining rents from existing and future private investments, similar to reforms implemented much earlier in South America, in the midst of the commodity boom.

The rest of this chapter is organized as follows. Firstly, we review the key market reforms applied in Mexico in the wake of the oil and financial crisis of the first half of the 1980s, including the launch of the North American Free Trade Agreement (NAFTA). Secondly, the chapter examines the macro-economic performance of the Mexican economy up to 2012, and identifies key structural challenges that the Mexican economy faced and continues to face in its long-term rate of expansion. We conclude with an analysis of the new wave of market reforms launched by President Peña Nieto, with a particular emphasis on those aspects that affect the oil and mining industries.

Reforming the Mexican economy through market liberalization

From booms and busts to slow growth and an oil-dependent public sector

Trade liberalization was implemented in Mexico as part of the market reforms put in place in response to the acute crisis of the early 1980s. Its first stage was the unilateral elimination of trade barriers, and it concluded in 1993 with the signature of the North American Free Trade Agreement (NAFTA) between Mexico, the United States and Canada that reduced tariff and non-tariff barriers on commerce, capital flows and foreign investment within the sub-region. It should also be noted that in 1992 Mexico modified its Constitution to change the legal status of the *ejido* and allow these communal lands to be rented or sold.[3] This regulatory change was of great importance for the future expansion of mining activity. For the Mexican government, NAFTA was a key instrument in the consolidation of its new agenda for development, and provided a legally binding and internationally constraining anchor that would make trade liberalization irreversible (Moreno-Brid et al. 2005; Moreno-Brid and Ros 2009).[4]

The NAFTA negotiations touched on the deregulation of Mexico's oil sector. Energy subsidies to manufacturing became unacceptable under the treaty, and as a result, PEMEX stopped being the financial lynchpin of a broader industrialization strategy. Strict constraints were imposed on the state-owned enterprise's legal capacity to use its own funds to modernize or expand its physical capital. This restriction had the effect of gradually reducing its own investments in exploration, drilling, extraction, refining, and even R&D.

The path of slow growth cum fiscal fragility followed by Mexico during these years had important negative impacts on the oil industry, heightening its exhaustion and, in consequence, the vulnerability of the whole national economy. Indeed, after the oil bust of 1982, the government decided to strip PEMEX of its control over the use of oil revenues. Through a combination of taxes, rights, levies, rules and regulations, PEMEX had to channel virtually all its earnings to the Ministry of Finance. Moreover, since 2000, PEMEX's debt expanded significantly, but with virtually no impact on its investments. The special fiscal regime that governed PEMEX allowed the federal government to appropriate rent and use it to finance public expenditures in other activities. The government's decision to drastically restrain PEMEX's capacity for investment weakened its long-term viability.

As Figure 8.1 shows, oil production rose very rapidly in the 1970s, lost steam in 1981, and finally started to wane in 2005, when extraction from the *Cantarell* oil fields peaked. This decline has continued and, given the key role that oil

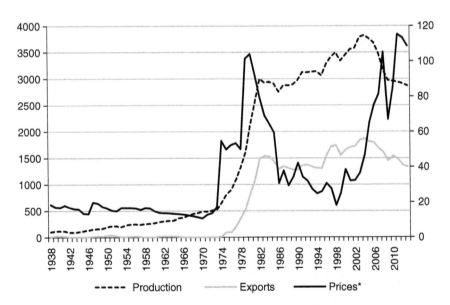

Figure 8.1 Mexico: oil production, exports and world prices, 1938–2014.

Source: Puyana, A. (2015).

Note: Production and exports measured in thousands of barrels per day (left axis); world prices measured in constant 2012 US dollars per barrel (right axis).

revenues play in public sector revenue, it has presented a medium-term challenge for the fiscal sustainability of the Mexican state.

Essentially, PEMEX became a cash-cow for the government beginning in the 1990s, channelling its revenues to the Ministry of Finance, where they were increasingly used to fund current expenditures. During this process, scant attention was paid to PEMEX's own long-term viability in the world market. Recall that in the 1990s legal reforms were undertaken to change Pemex's legal status: its monopoly on the commercialization of gas was broken; the international price of petroleum was introduced as the key reference for pricing in the domestic market; parts of the petrochemical industry were privatized; energy subsidies for industrial consumption were reduced; and private investment was allowed in electricity distribution, gas importation, and in the construction of gas pipelines (Puyana 2008). As Table 8.1 shows, between 1983 and the late 1990s, the Federal Government taxed away practically all of PEMEX's profits. In more recent years, the amount of taxes paid by PEMEX has vastly exceeded its profits, pushing its balance sheet deep into the red.

The United States has maintained that NAFTA required a common, integrated market of oil and gas to guarantee energy security for the three signatories. In contrast, Mexico has argued, until recently, for preserving the state's exclusive ownership of oil resources as the pillar for national security on energy matters. Historically, Mexico had always resisted pressures to liberalize its oil industry and had preserved PEMEX as a monopoly in all up-stream oil activities. Even when Mexico joined the Organization for Economic Cooperation and Development (OECD) in the 1990s, it refused to become a member of the International Energy Agency (IEA) due to its demands regarding energy sector privatization (Puyana 2006).

The Pacto por México and the new wave of market reforms

In his first day in office in 2013, President Peña Nieto and the leaders of three main political parties – the Institutional Revolutionary Party (PRI), the National Action Party (PAN) and the Party of the Democratic Revolution (PRD) – publicly launched the '*Pacto por México*'; a formal agreement to carry out a set of ambitious reforms in key areas of Mexico's economic, social and political life. This agreement set out a list of actions to be carried out during Peña Nieto's six year administration (2012–18) with, in its own words, a long-term perspective to secure a good standard of living for all Mexicans and guarantee their personal freedom and security (Mexico 2012).

The *Pacto* was a major, and mostly welcome, political act in Mexico. After twelve years or more with scant cooperation between the key political parties on any significant issue, it demonstrated that the three parties could agree to work together on a common agenda for long-term development. The agenda implied major reforms in controversial areas of economic policy. In practice, the *Pacto* was a success as major fiscal, financial, energy, telecommunications, and education reforms were put forward and approved in 2013–14 by Congress, as well as the corresponding secondary legislation (by-laws), and regulatory changes needed to implement them.[5] However, the agenda lost steam as differences among the

Table 8.1 Pemex: killing the golden goose? Taxing away PEMEX's profits and income

		1983	1985	1988	1990	1993	2000	2004	2008	2009	2010	2011	2012	2013**
Observed price Mexican oil US$/b	1	59.9	53.1	23.4	33.0	20.6	24.6	31.1	84.4	57.4	72.5	101.1	101.8	100.4
Programmed price Mexican oil US$/b	2	26.4	25.3	12.2	19.1	13.2	15.5	29.3	46.6	80.3	53.9	63.0	84.9	86.0
Difference in observed and programmed prices	3	33.4	27.8	11.1	13.9	7.4	9.1	1.8	37.8	-22.9	18.6	38.1	16.9	14.4
Total PEMEX income*	4	20.9	22.7	13.4	19.3	25.9	48.8	68.7	117.2	79.7	100.7	123.8	124.2	92.7
Pemex debt as % of assets	5	57.2	48.5	38.2	24.0	29.6	71.1	96.9	97.8	105.0	108.0	94.8	113.4	117.8
Pre taxes Pemex profits*	6	8.2	11.3	5.9	11.4	15.2	28.9	40.8	65.9	33.1	49.1	56.1	69.6	43.5
Federal Taxes on PEMEX*	7	8.2	11.3	5.8	9.7	13.6	30.6	41.5	68.0	40.0	51.4	69.6	68.1	50.9
Post taxes Pemex profits*	8	0.0	0.0	0.0	1.7	1.6	-1.7	-0.7	-2.1	-6.9	-2.3	-13.5	1.5	-7.4
Taxes as % of total Pemex income	9	39.4	49.7	43.4	50.5	52.8	62.7	60.4	58.1	50.2	51.0	56.2	54.8	54.9
Taxes as % of pretax Pemex profits	10	99.7	99.8	99.6	85.5	89.7	105.9	101.7	103.2	120.9	104.6	124.1	97.8	117.1

Source: Compiled by the authors, based on INEGI, 1993, 1987–92; Presidencia de la República, 2012, 2010, 2005; and PEMEX, various years.
Notes: *$US millions **provisional figures (estimated).

parties on some of the key reforms emerged and their positions became more polarized. In the early months of 2014, in the midst of negotiations over the Energy Reform, the PRD left the *Pacto*, although the reform was approved none-theless with the votes of the PRI and PAN. Not much later, the PAN, in the midst of an acrimonious political struggle over the selection of a new leader, also left the *Pacto*, rendering it moot by the second half of 2014.

But until it came apart, the *Pacto* had served the PRI's purpose: getting multi-party approval for the implementation of a new wave of market reforms. According to the government, it is expected that the reforms will boost the growth of the Mexican economy, in the near future, to an annual rate of 4%–5%, driven by revi-talized competitiveness based on lower energy costs, and a rebound in public, private, and foreign investment. For such an optimistic scenario to be realized, the reforms, particularly in the energy sector, will need to remove the binding constraints on Mexico's development path.

Mexico's new wave of structural reforms for extractive industries (2013–18)[6]

Oil and energy sector reforms

Currently, Mexico's energy sector faces several crucial challenges. Natural gas imports have soared over the past 15 years but inadequate expansion of the national pipeline system has resulted in supply bottlenecks. The consumption of energy, and gasoline in particular, is highly subsidized in a regressive and inefficient way. There are about two million people without access to electricity, located in small and remote rural villages. The Federal Electricity Commission (CFE), the public company responsible for electricity provision throughout the country, faces a number of important problems including financial difficulties, uncompetitive elec-tricity rates relative to major trading partners (USA and Canada), high energy losses, poor quality service, and a very low share of electricity produced through renewable resources. Potentially, Mexico has very large shale reserves, but extracting them is a challenge, and an adequate regulatory framework for this is not yet in place.

In terms of the oil industry, extraction and reserves have been declining for years in an institutional quagmire where, on the one hand, a set of constitutional laws limit foreign ownership and involvement in the exploration and exploitation of the nation's hydrocarbon resources, and on the other hand, PEMEX's own ability to explore, invest and develop operations has been tightly restricted by the government's appropriation of its profits, as well as by legal limits on its access to domestic or external financial resources. Consequently, for decades, PEMEX has confronted major difficulties in improving its productivity due to lack of investment, diminished research and development activities, and a powerful trade union reluctant to change.

It is not surprising then, that the 2013–14 *Pacto por México* paid special attention to the oil and energy sector. While reiterating its 'commitment that hydrocarbons remain the property of the nation', the government also announced its intention to transform PEMEX and CFE into so-called 'productive public enterprises' capable of operating in competitive environments (Mexico 2012). This has meant opening the door to private sector participation (both foreign and local) in most areas of the oil, gas and electricity industries, in which it had previously been prohibited. This opening commenced formally in December 2013 when the Energy and Oil Reforms were approved, followed by secondary legislation in 2014. In synthesis, the reform amended the three key articles of the Mexican Constitution related to energy industries.

1   Amendments to Article 25 introduced the concept of 'productive state enterprises' in strategic areas, seeking to strengthen these enterprises, improve efficiency, transparency and accountability and introducing the concept of sustainability in the development of energy industries. Congress stated that CFE and PEMEX would soon be expected to function in the (competitive) regime of 'productive state enterprises'.
2   Amendments to Article 27 referred to state ownership in natural resources. Private participation was to be allowed in the electricity industry. In oil, the state monopoly was ended, and PEMEX can (and must) enter into contracts with private companies, although it is recognized that '…hydrocarbons in the subsurface are the property of the nation'.
3   The amendment to Article 28 calls for the creation of the 'Mexican Petroleum Fund for Stabilization and Development', which will administer and distribute the resources generated from energy contracts.

The Peña Nieto government explicitly stated that this reform was an initial move to improve the competitiveness and efficiency of the energy sector. It is hoped that the legislation will allow the achievement of 100% reserve replacement rates in oil and gas. Another goal is to induce massive investment. All in all, official estimates pointed to an expected increase of 1% in GDP by 2018 and of around 2% by 2025. If realized, such growth would generate nearly 500,000 additional jobs in the next six years and a total increase of 2.5 million jobs by 2025.

The Mexican Petroleum Fund for Stabilization and Development (FMPED) will receive and administer all the non-tax revenues derived from oil licenses and production contracts. FMPED revenue will be disbursed according the following priorities: i) payments for contracts; ii) the Oil Revenues Stabilization Fund and the Fund for the Stabilization of the Revenue of Federal Entities; iii) the Hydrocarbons Extraction fund that finances research on hydrocarbons, energy sustainability, and on oil taxation; iv); transfer resources equivalent to a minimum of 4.7% of GDP to the Federal Treasury to finance the Federal Fiscal Budget; and v) allocate resources to long-term public savings accounts, including investment in financial assets.[7]

The government expects that additional benefits will include improved access to energy for the poorest sectors of society, more effort in research and development, as well as better access to new technologies. Whether and when these benefits will materialize is unclear, especially given the current market conditions characterized by the conspicuous fall in the international price of oil. In so far as it appears that lower oil prices are here to stay, some of the FDI and domestic investment in oil projects that were expected have been postponed or cancelled.

Fiscal and regulatory reforms on mining activities

To better assess the international impact of this reform, it should be noted that Mexico is today an important player in a number of global minerals and metals markets. Besides being the major producer of silver, it ranks among the top ten producers of gold, copper, cadmium, fluorite, celestite, lead, and zinc, among others. The commodity boom of 2000-08 witnessed an extraordinarily expansion of mining in Mexico, as in other mineral-rich countries in Latin America. The value of mineral exports practically trebled during these years, but not as quickly as oil, which increased its value nearly fourfold. Nonetheless, the recent international financial crisis (2009-10) cast a long shadow over the trade and economic activity of the country. In 2009, extractive industry activity shrank markedly; exports declined 26% in mining, and 40% in oil.

Increased economic activity in mining over the last fifteen years is also reflected in the number of concessions granted by the government for private-sector exploitation. That number peaked in 2007 with 2,423 concessions, covering a surface area of 8.4 million square hectares; before declining to 885 concessions and 1.1 million ha^2 in 2014 (Secretaría de Gobernación 2014). While 70% of the national territory has a geology favourable to mining, Diego Quintana (2014) and Paré (2013) estimate that, at most, 20% of Mexico's territory in under concession for private exploitation. Therefore, there is consensus that the mining industry in Mexico still has potential for strong growth.

In regulatory terms, the baseline for the recent reforms was the Mining Law of 1992, in which Mexico applied a combined regime of taxes and concession payments on non-oil extractive activities. These payments were determined in function of the area of the concession with no regard whatsoever for the value of its production. Table 8.2 shows the evolution of the income tax and concession payments collected from mining in 2003–14.

Thus, the amount collected by the Mexican authorities via such concessionary payments was independent of the movements of mineral prices. Such historical practice was in stark contrast with the recent experience of mineral-rich countries in South America, whose tax regulations were targeted to capture larger shares of the Ricardian rents generated in mining. As could be expected from their outdated design and the low income tax rate, Mexico captured, in contrast, an extremely low proportion of the rents generated in mining. Over the 2003–14 period, concession payments do not exceed 2% of the value of production. Nonetheless, collection through income taxes is much higher, and has oscillated between 9% and 18% of the value of production. As Table 8.3 shows, tax collection from extractive industries is still heavily concentrated on the oil industry, with mining contributing nearly 30 times less.

The fiscal reform approved in 2014 introduced significant changes in the income tax and concession payments applied to the mining industry. The aim was to enable the state to capture a larger share of the rent. The reform means that

Table 8.2 Mining: income taxes and concession rights relative to GDP, 2003–14

	Total Revenue	Income Tax/Mining GDP	Concession Rights/ Mining GDP
2003	12.7	11.8	0.9
2004	11.8	10.9	0.9
2005	17.1	16.3	0.7
2006	15.8	15.4	0.4
2007	16.7	16.2	0.5
2008	18.9	17.1	1.8
2009	20.4	18.5	1.9
2010	12.3	10.9	1.4
2011	10.1	8.7	1.3
2012	10.9	9.5	1.4
2013	14.8	12.8	2.0
2014*	18.9	17.8	1.1

Source: INEGI (various years) and SHCP (2015).

*Preliminary figures.

Table 8.3 Mexico: federal revenues by economic activity of origin, 2003–14

	Relative to GDP (%)				Composition (%)			
	Total	Non-oil	Oil	Mining	Total	Non-oil	Oil	Mining
2003	14.72	11.16	3.51	0.05	100	75.8	23.8	0.3
2004	14.61	10.03	4.52	0.06	100	68.7	31.0	0.4
2005	14.96	9.32	5.54	0.10	100	62.3	37.1	0.6
2006	14.79	9.13	5.54	0.12	100	61.7	37.5	0.8
2007	15.01	10.05	4.83	0.13	100	67.0	32.2	0.9
2008	10.48	9.19	1.14	0.14	100	87.7	10.9	1.4
2009	16.54	12.35	4.04	0.16	100	74.6	24.4	1.0
2010	15.66	10.70	4.83	0.13	100	68.3	30.8	0.9
2011	15.95	9.96	5.84	0.15	100	62.5	36.6	0.9
2012	15.69	9.62	5.91	0.16	100	61.3	37.6	1.0
2013	16.77	11.25	5.34	0.18	100	67.1	31.9	1.1
2014	16.94	12.15	4.58	0.21	100	71.7	27.0	1.2

Source: INEGI (various years) and SHCP (2015).

Note: Federal Government revenues, excluding public sector enterprises.

concession payments should now correspond, not to the magnitude of the land conceded, but instead to the value of production. The fundamental changes introduced in this reform are two taxes of 7.5% and 0.5%, applied respectively to metal mining and to precious metals. Both are levied on the gross value of production, and they are introduced on top of the standard income tax applied to all types of economic activity. In this sense they may be considered royalties. Small miners, with annual sales of no more than 50 million pesos, are exempt. Table 8.4 shows the impact of these changes on resource taxation rates in Mexico, as compared to other jurisdictions.

Table 8.4 Comparison of the Mexican mining tax regime to other jurisdictions

		Mexico prior to fiscal reform, 2013	Mexico after fiscal reform	Argentina	Brazil	Canada			Chile	Colombia	Peru
Income taxes	Min	30%	30%	35%	34%	25%	25%	25%	20%	33%	30%
	Max					31%	31%	31%			
Employee participation in profits		10%	10%								8%
EBITDA (Earnings Before Interest, Taxes, Depreciation, and Amortization)	Min	0.00%	7.50%	3%		2%					
Sales	Min	0.00%	0.50%		1%						1%
	Max				2%						
Profits before taxes	Min					13%	5%	16%		3%	
	Max						10%			12%	
Profit mining operation	Min								0%		1%
	Max								14%		12%
Average tax burden on mining taxes (% of sales)		1.20%	2.80%	1.20%	1.80%	2.90%	2.00%	3.70%	4.40%	2.20%	4.00%
Average tax burden including employee participation profits, income taxes and taxes and dividends (% tax profit)		38.30%	46.1%*	44.50%	39.00%	48.70%	46.30%	50.70%	45.90%	39.50%	47.60%

Source: SHCP (2015)

*Tax burden for minerals other than gold, silver and platinum.

The introduction of these changes is, however, somewhat paradoxical. They were presented as a long-needed tool to ensure that the state receives fair remuneration for the concession of mining rights. This would have been most useful and justifiable when international prices were on a rapidly ascending trend, as during the 2002–08 period. But the reform was introduced and approved in 2014 when the commodity boom was past its peak and already in the downswing (World Bank 2015). In sum, it is a small step in the right direction, but with the wrong timing. Too little, too late!

Unsurprisingly, mining firms have been vociferously opposed to the reform. They claim that their profitability will be severely affected. Certainly, after-tax profits will be lower. In our view, given that the previous regime was extremely light, the changes introduced in this reform are fair and most welcome from a fiscal viewpoint. In any case, as Table 8.4 shows, following the reform, the tax burden as a proportion of revenues in mining is not too high (2.8% versus the 1.2% pre-reform) and well within the range of that prevailing in comparable jurisdictions. This is true when taking into account the overall tax burden, which includes income tax, retained earnings, as well as profits distributed to workers.

Conclusions

Strictly speaking, Mexico is not an oil-economy or mineral-economy, even though it is an important exporter of oil and some minerals and metals. Nevertheless, Mexico's overall fiscal performance strongly depends on oil revenues. Mining, in contrast, has been a relatively insignificant source of fiscal revenues in Mexico. Mining policies have traditionally been, apparently, more motivated by the idea of trying to stimulate the development of the sector, whether by local or by foreign investors. The recently approved initiative to capture a larger, albeit, in our view, moderate share of mining rent by the state is desirable in principle. But unfortunately, its timing could have been much better. Its implementation in 2014–15, when the commodity boom was on the downswing, instead of earlier, was too late. For businessmen, there may never be a good time for a tax reform that raises corporate tax contributions, but there can, undoubtedly, be a bad time. The predictable resistance of the economic and politically powerful interests in mining to the tax reform has been accentuated by the downswing of the business cycle, during which it was implemented. Nonetheless, calculations by the Ministry of Finance regarding the impact of the reform on the profitability of the industry vis-à-vis competing jurisdictions do not point to any excess. And, even if the reform is successful, the amount of taxes collected from mining will continue to be minuscule relative to the oil industry.

The launch and implementation of the recent wave of market reforms in Mexico takes place in a context of decades-long economic slow-down, now aggravated by the weak state of the global economy. Indeed, the aftermath of the 2009 financial crisis and the end of the commodity boom put in question the neo-extractivist or *reprimarization* strategies that have been adopted over the last ten years in South America, and which are premised on commodity exports and improved terms-of-trade. These events, coupled with the successful growth and trade performances of China and of South East Asia, also put in question the *maquila* regimes of Central America and Mexico based on the intensive use of low-paid labour to assemble goods with scant value-added generated locally.

The situation faced by PEMEX and the oil industry in general following the reforms is altogether of a different scale and scope. These reforms are an additional, radical extension of the neoliberal reforms launched in the 1980s and deepened with the implementation of NAFTA. By eliminating the monopolistic power of PEMEX and opening its activities to foreign and local investors, the reforms are pushing the state away from its last remaining bastion of economic intervention: the oil industry. The government has sought to reassure public opinion that the reform is intended to increase the nation's welfare. Furthermore, the Executive has identified the oil reform as the crucial element required to push the Mexican economy into a path of high and sustained long-term expansion. These are noble intentions, but ones that will be difficult to fulfil, given Mexico's history of booms and busts related to various commodities. In a way, these sentiments echo (no doubt unintentionally) President López Portillo's (1976–82) oil-financed industrialization drive. His government's development strategy was sustained by the following assumptions: i) Mexico had vast oil reserves; ii) oil prices were expected to increase at more than 2% per year in real terms for the foreseeable future; iii) PEMEX had the technical, financial and political capacity to administer those resources efficiently; iv) fiscal revenues would be significantly boosted by oil policies, complemented by external debt; and v) the government had the capacity and will to use these vast resources to fund an ambitious development plan based on industrialization. Oil for industry was the slogan. As we know, the outcome of the oil boom of the 1970s was not as predicted.

Today, the government repeats the discourse that the oil reform will be the key to boosting Mexico's economic development. The current context and assumptions are notably different: i) Mexico's oil reserves and production levels are on a downward path; ii) prices of oil in the world market are expected to remain weak in the near future; iii) oil revenues will not exclusively accrue to a monopolistic state-owned enterprise, as PEMEX will face intense competition; iv) the fiscal situation of the state is very vulnerable and is not projected to improve in the near future (in fact, as we write, public expenditure is being cut to preserve fiscal stability in the face of a weak oil market); and v) there is no national development plan, or industrial policy for that matter, that offers a serious strategy for channelling oil revenues into investment.

It would be nothing short of a miracle if the oil-centred reform package boosts Mexico's growth potential. And apparently, one was in the making just as the latest reforms were being passed: on 10 June 2015, PEMEX announced the discovery of four new oil fields in the shallow waters of Tabasco, close to the *Cantarell* field. According to PEMEX, by mid-June 2017, they could produce 0.2 million barrels per day (mbd); output 33% higher than the current average production level of any oil field in Mexico (Meana and Sigler 2015). If this target is attained, total oil production in Mexico could reach 2.3 mbd, still considerably lower than the 3.5 mbd reached in 2002–03 when *Cantarell* was at its peak.

The timing of this discovery is very fortunate and extremely surprising. It took place about one month before Round One of bidding on 14 exploration blocks with foreign investors. Incidentally, the result of this Round was very disappointing for Mexico as only two blocks were awarded – in fact to a Mexican consortium – thus falling well short of the US $18 billion in additional investments that the government expected to attract (Webber 2015). Most worrying, when asked about the causes of this failure, J.C. Zepeda, Chief of the National Hydrocarbons Commission in charge of the bidding process, answered: 'What went wrong? We will have to reflect on this'. Indeed, it would be most welcome if in such reflection he is joined by the Minister of Finance in order to design and implement a new fiscal reform that more effectively increases non-oil tax revenues, strengthens the progressive effect of fiscal policy on income redistribution, improves the state's capacity to enact counter-cyclical policies, and launches a much-needed programme of public investment to improve and modernize infrastructure and crowd-in private investment.

For years PEMEX has been underinvesting in exploration, leading to declines in proven reserves, which currently stand at 42.2 billion barrels of crude oil equivalent; their lowest level in decades. During the 2004–14 period oil production has, on average, been falling at an annual rate of 3.7% (Meana 2015). Drilling activities have also been falling for years (Grunstein 2015). In 2014 only 149 wells were drilled, with a success rate of 33%. The collapse of oil exploration, production and drilling in Mexico is not a question of bad luck, by any means. It is the cumulative result of policy decisions by the Mexican government to tightly cap investment by PEMEX, and to use its vast oil revenues to finance either current expenditure or investment in non-oil related activities. With little or no investment for decades it is impossible that PEMEX, or for that matter any company, could remain competitive in the global economy. For some critics, such an outcome is better explained by political economy than economic policy. Milking PEMEX of its revenues and preventing it from investing in its own plants and equipment undermined its efficiency and created grounds for a persistent campaign to strip it of its monopoly and remove the legal restrictions on private participation in, needless to say, very profitable oil activities. While the government's intentions with the reform may well have been to serve the best interests of Mexico's development, its design and implementation are questionable and its outcome remains unclear.

In practice, the reform will certainly benefit a few privileged groups, local or foreign, that will be able to engage in oil activities in Mexico. But in the short and medium term the reform may put pressure on Mexico's macro-economic stability as the relative decline in oil-related fiscal revenues is unlikely to be fully compensated by an increase in non-oil revenues. This outcome is particularly worrying given Mexico's light tax burden and pressing need to boost public investment. In the medium term, Mexico's total oil production will, at best, stop declining. If oil prices do not recover from their recent fall, this poses a challenge for Mexico's fiscal sustainability. To the extent that the fiscal and oil reforms (the whole package) put in place by Peña Nieto succeeds in boosting Mexico's economic growth, the decline in PEMEX's contributions to public revenue, as its monopolistic power is eroded by deregulation, may not turn out to be problematic for fiscal sustainability. However, the results are not promising so far. In 2013–14 the annual average rate of expansion of the Mexican economy was disappointing: only 1.8% growth, half a percentage-point lower than its long-term average, and far below the 4–5% that Peña Nieto promised in his campaign. Due to the relative decrease in oil-related fiscal income, public sector revenue fell from an equivalent of 24.2% of GDP in 2013 to 23.5% in 2014. Furthermore, according to the IMF's June 2015 projections, and barring another round of fiscal reform, public revenue will fall to 22.1% in 2015, to 21.7% in 2016 and will remain below 23% at least until 2020 (Morales 2015). If these projections are correct, the days of Mexico's fiscal pact where tax reforms are systematically blocked may soon be over, and our privileged classes will finally have to contribute with a higher tax burden.

Notes

1 We thank Gabriel Farfán and Eduardo Camero for sharing with us their wisdom on this subject although the opinions here expressed may not necessarily coincide with theirs.
2 *Cantarell,* at the time, besides its massive reserves, permitted oil extraction costs well below those in the USA, Colombia or the North Sea (Puyana 2015). Eventually it became the source of more than half of all oil production in Mexico.
3 Under the 1917 Constitution, *ejidatarios* (peasants) were granted land use rights as members of the *ejido,* a settlement with communal property, i.e. it was not marketable land.
4 See Audley et al. 2004; Blecker 2003; Lederman et al. 2003.
5 SHCP (2012) El Pacto por México, México.
6 The *Pacto* put forward reforms on many sectors and activities, including telecommunications, labour, education, etc. For the purposes of the present paper we restrict our analysis to fiscal reform and the proposed regulatory changes to the oil and mining industries.
7 For detailed information on the priorities for the allocation of such resources and on the scope and functioning of the Oil Revenues Stabilization Fund, the Fund for the Stabilization of the Revenues of the Federal Entities and the Hydrocarbon Extraction Fund see chapter V of the Ley Federal de Presupuesto y Responsabilidad Hacendaria (SHCP 2014).

Bibliography

Audley, J., Polaski, S., Papademetriou, G. and Vaughan, S. (2004). *Nafta's Promise and Reality: Lessons from Mexico for the Hemisphere.* Washington, DC: Carnegie Endowment for Peace, pp.88.

Auty, R. (ed.) (2001). *Resource Abundance and Economic Development.* Oxford: Oxford University Press.

Blecker, R. (2003). The North American economies after NAFTA: A critical appraisal, *International Journal of Political Economy.* 33(3), pp. 5–27.

Cámara De Diputados (2015). *Las finanzas públicas en México: 1980–2010*. Unidad de Estudios de las Finanzas Públicas. México: Republic of Mexico. Available from http://www.diputados.gob.mx/cronica57/contenido/cont11/finanzas.html. [Accessed: 8 July 2015].

Diego Quintana, R. (2014). Actores sociales rurales y la nación mexicana frente a los megaproyectos mineros. *Problemas del desarrollo*, 45(179), 159–80.

Grupo Nuevo Curso de Desarrollo, (2013). *Sobre las Propuestas de Reforma Energética*, UNAM, México, Available from: http://www.nuevocursodedesarrollo.unam.mx/docs/Posicionamiento_Reforma_Energetica.pdf.

Grupo Nuevo Curso de Desarrollo, (2015). *México frente a la crisis. Memorándum ante la situación y la perspectiva económica y social*, UNAM, México, Available from: http://www.nuevocursodedesarrollo.unam.mx/docs/GNCDMemorandumMayo2015.pdf.

Grunstein, D.M. (2015). *Alternativas para la inversión privada en el sector energético en México, Política Energética: motor del crecimiento y del bienestar*. México: Fundación Colosio.

INEGI (Instituto Nacional dd Estadística, Geografía e Infomática) (various years), *La industria petrolera en México*. Mexico: Instituto Nacional de Estadística, Geografía e Infomática.

Lederman, D., Maloney, W. and Serven, L. (2004). *Lessons from NAFTA for Latin America and the Caribbean Countries: A Summary of Research Findings*. Washington, DC: World Bank.

Meana S. and Sigler E. (2015). 'Estos son los nuevos campos de Pemex', *El Financiero*, June 11.

Meana, S. (2015). 'Hallazgo de Pemex no garantiza detener caída en la producción', *El Financiero*, June 12.

México (2012). *Pacto por México*. México; Secretaria de Hacienda y Crédito Público. http://pactopormexico.org/

Morales, Y. (2015). 'Ni en cinco años los ingresos públicos regresarán a los niveles del 2013: FMI', *El Economista*, May 26.

Moreno-Brid, J.C. (2015). 'La economía de México: ayer, hoy y mañana', presented at *Risk Event: Mexico City*, DeLoitte, June 2.

Moreno-Brid, J.C and Ros, J. (2009). *Development And Growth In The Mexican Economy: A Historical Perspective*. London: Oxford University Press.

Moreno-Brid J.C., Rivas, J.C. and Santamaría, J. (2005). Industrialization and economic growth in Mexico after NAFTA: The road travelled, *Development and Change*, 36(6): 1095–119.

Presidencia de la República. (various years). Criterios Generales de Política Económica. Mexico, D.F.: Secretaría de Hacienda y Crédito Público.

Paré, L. (2013). La megaminería tóxica y el derecho a consulta Caballo Blanco y la experiencia latinoamericana. *Nueva Sociedad*, 244, 97–112.

PEMEX (Petróleos MexicanoS). (various years). *Informe Anual*. Mexico: Petróleos Mexicanos. Available from: http://www.pemex.com/informes/descargables/index.html. [Accessed: 24 July 2015].

Puyana, A. (2015). Colombia y México. *La economía política del petróleo en un mercado politizado y global*, FLACSO, México.

Puyana, A. (2008). El manejo del petróleo mexicano: ¿política o economía? *Perfiles Latinoamericanos*, (32), 67–102.

Puyana, A. (2006). Mexican oil policy and energy security within NAFTA. *International Journal of Political Economy*, 35(2), 72–97.

Secretaria De Gobernación (2014). *Programa de Desarrollo [Minero 2013-2018]*, Diario Oficial de la Federación, May 9.

(SHCP) Secretaria de Hacienda y Credito Publico (2015), Nota sobre las contribuciones fiscales del sector minero, unpublished.

(SHCP) Secretaría de Hacienda y Crédito Público (2014). *Ley Federal de Presupuesto y Responsabilidad Hacendaria*, Diario Oficial de la federación, Texto vigente, August 8.

Webber, J. (2015). Historic Mexican Oil Tender Fails to Attract Investors, *Financial Times*, July 15.

World Bank (2015). Commodity Price Data (Pink Sheet). Available from: http://econ. worldbank.org/WBSITE/EXTERNAL/EXTDEC/EXTDECPROSPECTS/0,,contentMD K:21574907~menuPK:7859231~pagePK:64165401~piPK:64165026~theSit ePK:476883,00.html.

9   Resource nationalism and Brazil's post-neoliberal strategy

Jewellord Nem Singh and Eliza Massi

Lula da Silva's 2003 electoral victory marked a period of rising popular expectations towards a reversal of what Rafael Correa once referred to as the 'neoliberal nightmare'. In October 2014, the Workers' Party (PT) secured its fourth electoral victory. In many ways, the Workers' Party gained political legitimacy through an agenda that focused on economic growth alongside programmes aimed at the reduction of poverty and social inequality. While the Brazilian development model offers a particular variety of 'post-neoliberal' model of capitalism, it is important to note that post-neoliberalism constitutes policy continuity with changes (Nem Singh 2010, 2013). Roberts (2011: 18) suggests that the region is experiencing profound political changes reflecting new alignments among states, markets, and socio-political actors. This three-dimensional alignment, in turn, is shaping the globalization strategies of left and left-centre governments in Latin America.

At the heart of this renewed emphasis on state activism in Latin America lies the key question around the governance of natural resources. Our chapter presents the case of Brazil's development strategy, as applied to the mining and oil sectors. In contrast to the rest of the region, whose resource exports have been linked to primary commodity production and the accumulation of domestic revenues, Brazil's mining and oil sectors were and still are central to the country's industrialization strategy, creating linkages to other industries such as automobile, shipbuilding, and petrochemical industries. To explain this, we need understand the relationship between neoliberal reforms and state control over strategic sectors. It is generally assumed that the wave of market-opening policies signalled the failure of state management even in vital industries (Hogenboom 2012; Nem Singh 2013). However, states will most likely exercise direct or indirect forms of control when elites perceive the potential of harnessing their country's comparative advantage through greater state participation. The state coordinates reforms to enhance its role by designing new regulatory frameworks to facilitate the participation of private firms while maintaining state control over the ownership of national enterprises. Put simply, liberal market reforms do not necessarily preclude the possibilities for state-building (Hsueh 2011; Schamis 1999).

Brazil's resource nationalism can be traced back to its *Varguista* legacy, whereby Getúlio Vargas (1930–45) developed an industrialization strategy based on the country's comparative advantages, and in this case, through natural resources (Guimarães 2003). This ideology was guided by a strong political consensus among elites around developmental statism since the post-war years. So despite the fact that the developmentalist state model was in crisis in the 1980s and market liberalization was presented as the only option for Brazil, the developmentalist state was simply too big and too important to the economy to dismantle. This was also reinforced by the strategic importance of mining and oil to industrialization and national security (Nem Singh 2013; Sikkink 1991). The outcome, as the chapter details, is that the state combined partial forms of liberalization with state control. In other words, there was neither the unravelling of the developmental state nor a full shift towards a liberal market model. Instead, Brazil's resource strategy constitutes a remarkable resilience of state control and ownership with limited private sector participation in the domestic market (Diniz and Boschi 2004; Schneider 2014).

Neoliberalism and the unravelling of resource nationalism

In Latin American political economy, neoliberalism was considered hegemonic and states were expected to reconfigure their relationship with the market through strict compliance with the Washington Consensus template (Kingstone 1999; Schamis 1999). In reality, however, this process is far more complex and contradictory. As Steven Vogel (2006: p. 4) remarks, 'market systems are embedded in a complex web of laws, practices and norms ... liberalizing markets involves the transformation of these laws, practices, and norms ... [and therefore] any historical transition towards a market society ... all entails a complex process of building market institutions.' For this reason, he observes, countries fail to converge towards a liberal market-economy model despite pressures for broad macroeconomic liberalization. Market reforms were implemented partially and institutional changes were fragmented, at best incremental. National political economies have retained some of their core features (Hall and Soskice 2001; Streeck and Thelen 2005).

Notwithstanding the complex process of building market institutions, the neoliberal doctrine was perceived as an antidote to rent-seeking that plagued nationalized resource sectors. While natural resources were depoliticized by treating strategic commodities as an average tradable good (Hogenboom 2012), Brazil's mining and oil reforms instead offered an opportunity for elites to renegotiate their relationship with private companies. These sectoral reforms were designed to introduce competition especially between state enterprises and domestic capital without necessarily losing control over the industry (Nem Singh 2013; Thurber et. al. 2011). This was in part a result of the historical legacies of developmentalism that promoted specific policy orientations persisting over time, which overall locked in patterns of reform and the capitalist model in favour of a larger state (Hall and Soskice 2001). In particular, resource nationalism was significant in Brazil and elsewhere, where economic decision-making is shaped by natural resource dependence (Karl 1997; Shafer 1994). In the context of economic globalization, reforms are designed to enable states to obtain secure access to resource rents and strategic control of the industry in order to build new comparative advantages. This typically involves imposing domestic constraints on foreign capital participation or crafting special arrangements between states, private capital and state enterprises (Bayulgen 2010; Luong and Weinthal 2006, 2010). This subsequently results in mixed economic policies that accede to Washington Consensus' style reforms while also giving development space for governments to influence the overall regulation of industries (Heron and Richardson 2008; Nem Singh 2014).

Brazil's resource growth policies cannot be understood without examining the broader changes in its national political economy. Economically, by the 1980s the import substitution model was exhausted and the country was facing macro-economic instability with rampant inflation, rising budget deficits, and a lagging and inefficient industrial sector. Politically, the military government began the *abertura* process that paved the way for the country's return to democracy in 1985. The post-military governments implemented reforms aimed at capital, financial and trade liberalization as the solution to its macro-economic problems. By the early 1990s, international capital flows were liberalized, the financial system was reformed, and the first steps towards privatization were taken. This was followed by measures to reduce import restrictions during Collor de Mello's government (1990–92). Under Cardoso's administration (1995–2003), a full-fledged neoliberal economic strategy was pursued, which combined a macro-economic stabilization plan, the Real Plan, and an ambitious privatization programme.

In this context, reforms in the mining and oil sectors were clear attempts to break away from the protectionist and interventionist past by introducing private sector participation – especially foreign capital – through market opening and privatization of state enterprises. While market opening was directed at attracting private capital and reducing the scope of state participation in the economy, privatization sought to change the relationship between the state and SOEs. These reforms produced quite diverse outcomes in the two sectors. We examine the sector-specific changes in the regulatory framework and trace the post-liberalization trajectories of two key companies, which in many ways are synonymous with the sectors in which they operate – Companhia Vale do Rio Doce (CVRD), also known as Vale, in mining, and Petróleo Brasileiro (Petrobras) in the oil and gas sector. We argue that the visible hand of the state has shaped the behaviour of private capital and state enterprises by enhancing their competitiveness in the international economy. Specifically, we compare the new regulatory frameworks towards private capital participation and the ownership structure of national enterprises in each sector during the Cardoso and Lula da Silva (2003–11) governments.

Cardoso's neoliberal reform strategy

At face value, neoliberal reform appears to be a critical juncture because new legislation finally allowed domestic and foreign capital to operate after decades of market dominance by SOEs, particularly in the oil and gas industry. The 1988

Constitution reinstated the commitment of the Federal Government to encourage domestic firms to operate in resource exploration and exploitation. Cardoso changed this policy in 1995 when he successfully introduced a constitutional amendment to the 1988 Constitution, which removed all restrictions on foreign capital participation. However, there were no changes in law in the oil industry until 1997.

In terms of mineral policy, Brazil's regulatory framework did not go through substantial changes. Mining regulation remained fairly unchanged since its design under the military government. The core guiding policy was codified in the Mining Code of 1967 and the 1988 Constitution. The Mining Code regulates all aspects of the minerals sector, from rights and duties to authorizations and concessions, exploration, production, and use of resources (1988 Federal Constitution; Vilhena Filho 1997). The key principle is that all mineral rights are vested in the national state, which exercises powers to grant authorizations and concessions for mineral exploration and development (1988 Federal Constitution; Vilhena Filho 1997). While foreign companies can develop and exploit mineral resources under the 1995 Constitutional amendment, there are strict conditions regarding how foreign capital operate, notably the rule requiring foreign mining companies to incorporate domestic subsidiaries (1988 Federal Constitution; Constitutional Amendment No. 6 and No. 9 of 15 August 1995; Vilhena Filho 1997: 46). In response to the trend of market liberalization, the Mining Code was amended in 1996 (Law No. 9314) with the intent of providing investment flexibility in the sector, strengthening state capacities, reducing bureaucratic inefficiencies, discouraging speculation, and ultimately, giving private firms a more prominent role in resource extraction (Gurmendi 2010; Vale and Carvalho 1998). Nevertheless, the overall regulation and oversight of mining activities, including policy formulation and coordination, remains under state hands through the Ministry of Mines and Energy (MME). Within the ministry, the National Mineral Production Department (DNPM) is responsible for all aspects linked to coordination, execution, and monitoring of mining policies and activities (Vilhena Filho 1997: 49).

While the mining sector was left relatively open during the reform period, the same cannot be said about the oil and gas sector, which was an exclusive domain of the state through Petrobras. The regulatory framework and the subsequent reforms markedly differ from mining because of the rigid ownership structure and monopoly rights of Petrobras. To begin with, oil nationalization took place in 1952 despite having very little proven oil reserves, leading to restrictions on foreign ownership and operation in the sector. Petrobras exercised its monopoly on the market between 1952 and 1996. It was not until the 1997 Petroleum Law (Decree No. 9478) was passed in Congress that market opening took place. The law broke Petrobras' monopoly rights, opened the sector to domestic and foreign investors, and created a regulatory agency – the National Petroleum Agency (ANP) – to facilitate private sector-led oil exploration and development.

The changes in Brazil's regulatory framework were clear responses to growing pressure for liberalization and other international factors. Throughout the economic restructuring period, mining and oil prices were at low levels and there were pressures for SOEs to become competitive. Privatization was completed in mining but not in the oil industry where Petrobras held monopoly rights. The Petroleum Law was conceived as a way of establishing credible commitment for reforms on the part of the Brazilian government and as a way of introducing economic dynamism, especially in oil exploration and development (or upstream) segment of the industry. In the past, SOEs were viewed as efficient and profitable and the Brazilian government helped in financing the development of sectors (Trebat 1983; Villela 1984; Werneck 1987). With the advent of neoliberalism, state enterprises were increasingly viewed as naturally unproductive. The concessions grant model was adopted in the oil industry precisely to signal Brazil's commitment to open the sector for global capital. The law radically changed the structure of risk sharing between private capital and the state. Under the concessions grant model, firms are allowed to shoulder the high sunk costs of exploration but they also reap the full rewards once oil reserves are found. Cardoso's policy sought to lower risks for private oil firms to explore the reserves. He also attempted to curb the market power of Petrobras. Although this model offers minimal rents to the state – mainly through corporate taxes and royalty fees – it reduces the risk in situations of high uncertainty. Crucially, the model was adopted because at the time Brazil had few proven oil reserves. To put it simply, Cardoso perceived no need for the state to shoulder the risks and costs involved in oil exploration especially during a period of austerity and stagnant growth, not to mention the country's lack of proven oil reserves.

As an outcome of privatization, regulatory agencies were also established to manage the entry of private capital in previously nationalized sectors (Estache et. al. 2001; Mueller and Pereira 2002). In the oil sector, the ANP serves as the regulator of the market and oversees the bidding process. Market reforms were justified in terms of the need to court global capital and change the patterns of sectoral dynamics in favour of private driven models of growth. New institutions were created to establish the credibility of the reforms. There was a conscious attempt to remake politics by changing the economic logic of developmentalism (Jordana and Levi-Faur 2005). This logic is underpinned by the second component of the reform project – the privatization of SOEs – in which state enterprises were increasingly painted and consequently perceived in public debates as inefficient.

The justification for changing the regulatory framework discussed above was premised on the perceived inefficiency of state enterprises, and therefore, the need for private sector participation. Once the economy was stabilized through the Real Plan, the government set up an ambitious programme of corporate restructuring and privatization of state-owned enterprises – the rationale of which was competitiveness and necessity. Petrobras announced a restructuring programme in 1992, during which it reduced operating costs from US$ 4.2 billion to US$ 3.2 billion by decentralizing administrative tasks, reducing the labour force, and selecting subsidiaries for privatization (Randall 1993: 41–6). While Vale was fully privatized and was transferred to domestic capitalists, Petrobras remained under state hands by retaining 51% of its voting capital. Petrobras' ownership structure is, however, a legacy of Vargas, again. His developmentalist model perceived the necessity of creating autonomous SOEs, which served as a 'technocratic and political' solution to address the question of how the government can develop the oil industry without fully relying on foreign capital in 1951 (Philip 1982; Randall, 1993). This means that privatization efforts had varying outcomes in Brazil's mining and oil industries.

The years of macro-economic instability and crisis were still fresh and public attitude towards state monopolies began to wane, allowing Cardoso to build a pro-reformist coalition (Kingstone 1999). With broad public support in his side, Cardoso issued Decree No. 1510 in June 1995, including Vale into the National Privatization Plan, which was carried through in 1997. Unlike other state enterprises, Vale was a large, well-managed, and profitable SOE, which drew its success from several advantages, namely an efficient logistics system, expansion into new projects, joint ventures, political protection, and the fact that it did not face a harsh international competitive environment, given the high quality of Brazilian iron ore reserves (International Directory of Company Histories 2002; Machado 1997; Schneider 2009: 166). Despite its success, Vale experienced a different market environment at the time, during which prices of its main export – iron ore – were much lower and the world was not experiencing a commodity boom.[1] The external pressures and challenges for Vale and Petrobras were also distinctive. While Petrobras was compelled to explore oil reserves offshore that eventually led to the development of deep-sea drilling technology in the 1970s, Vale faced less competitive pressure given its access to abundant and high quality mineral reserves.

Vale's privatization was a source of much controversy, including a legal battle (Goldstein 2009). The Worker's Party challenged Cardoso's policy in Congress, during which the Party argued that the main rationale for privatization – SOEs' inefficiency – did not exist in either company (Hunter 2010). As such, it should not be a surprise that the content of reforms to alter the ownership structure of Vale and Petrobras markedly differ from each other. In terms of capital ownership, Vale's assets were sold at market prices while the state retained indirect control through a golden share. However, when Cardoso introduced reforms in the oil industry, the combined effects of economic slowdown and backlash of Vale's privatization reduced the prospects of privatizing Petrobras.

As Goldstein puts it, 'the challenge of privatization is the design of a new "compact" to regulate the interactions between markets, states, and politics' (1999: 679). Thus, we should expect that the content of market reforms differs substantially between the sectors. This is consistent with studies examining different forms of privatization within sectors, and the ways in which institutional and structural variables, for example domestic electoral competition and coalition politics, have influenced the process of privatization (Kingstone 1999; Murillo 2009; Pinheiro et al. 2004). Governments implemented state divestiture quite differently, recognizing the distinctive role of state enterprises in various national contexts and sectors. In mining, Brazil resolved the principal-agency dilemma by separating ownership and control. That is, the state privatized the company and at the same time retained special voting rights – or golden shares – to ensure state control over the industry (Goldstein 1999; Nem Singh 2013).

To sum up, privatization led to quite different outcomes in restructuring the mining and oil industries. Although political legacies of developmentalism remain strong in Brazil, deeper market reforms still took place in mining while direct state control remains intact in the oil industry. We explain this in terms of policy learning: the privatization of Vale was consequential in forming resistance against the privatization of Petrobras. While labour politics and union opposition to market reforms partly explains this phenomenon given Brazil's corporatist tradition, we suggest that there are practical difficulties in dismantling the *Varguista* legacy of statism in economic policy-making.

Lula da Silva's re-articulation of resource nationalism

It is undeniable that economic reforms introduced a new dynamic into the Brazilian resources sector. Sectoral opening to private domestic and foreign capital brought investments and intensified competition, the restructuring of domestic firms, and integration into global value chains. Yet, market reforms failed to completely dismantle the institutional legacy of the developmentalist period. The shift towards renewed state intervention was marked by the electoral victory of the Workers' Party (PT) in 2003. Developmentalism under PT, however, has not necessarily reneged on Cardoso's liberal reforms. This can be seen in Brazil's new and proposed changes in legislation as well as the structure of the mining and oil sectors in the 2000s.

Under President Luiz Inácio 'Lula' da Silva's government, the Brazilian state sought to reshape the terms of bargaining by introducing new policies aimed at strengthening state enterprises, placing innovation and competitiveness in supporting Brazilian firms, and developing a greater economic role for the state. Given the discussion above, perhaps we should also think of renewed state action under PT as less surprising than most scholarly research has argued. The oil and mining sector reforms under Cardoso demonstrate that neoliberalism was success- fully incorporated in developmentalist policies. While market reforms introduced international competitiveness and SOE efficiency as the new objectives, it is vital to recognize that the core features of state capitalism persist in Brazil.

Lula da Silva's second term (2007–11) was a turn-around in economic policy- making. He consolidated state intervention in the resources sector, and the reasons behind this policy shift are driven by international and domestic factors. Firstly, Brazil benefitted from the commodity boom, particularly the mining and agro-export sector, leading to fiscal surpluses and giving way for more state revenues to finance long-term development projects. Vale and Petrobras, two of Brazil's leading companies, also performed very well during this period, which allowed Lula to renegotiate the relationship between the state and global capital. Lula also received widespread public support for renewed state intervention. While oil has always been strategic for national security, the critical moment was when Brazil's self-sufficiency in oil consumption was achieved at the turn of the

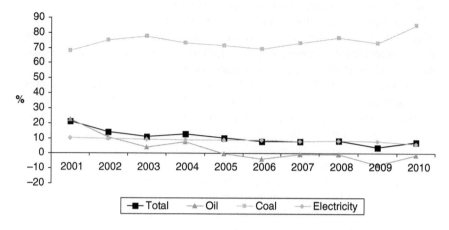

Figure 9.1 Brazil's external dependency on energy, 2001–2010 (%).

Data from Balanço Energético Nacional (Brazilian Energy Balance), 2011, Table 1.8, p. 30.

new century alongside the discovery of new oil reserves in 2008. As Figure 9.1 details, Brazil reduced its external dependency on energy from 21.1% in 2001 to 7.8% in 2010. Crucially, as Figure 9.2 shows, by 2005 Brazil had already eliminated its external dependency on imported crude oil, which put the country in a stronger position to implement changes along the lines of a stronger, activist state.

Secondly, Lula introduced wider institutional transformations at a critical juncture. Brazil had achieved the status of a net exporter of crude oil in 2006. The year after, Petrobras declared the availability of commercially viable oil reserves beneath the salt layer off the Brazilian coast. In the mining sector, the state was

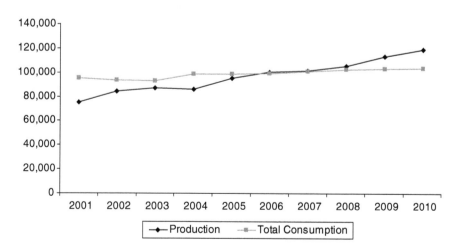

Figure 9.2 Petroleum production and consumption in Brazil, 2001–2010 (10m³).

Data from Balanço Energético Nacional (Brazilian Energy Balance), 2011, Table 2.2, p. 40.

acquiring more resource rents through mineral exports, particularly iron ore, whose prices peaked between 2003 and 2009. The country also escaped the worst effects of the 2008 international economic crisis. Market conditions were thus more conducive for a seemingly radical institutional transformation by increasing the stake of the state in the natural resources sector.

Between 2008 and 2010, Lula da Silva's government introduced a four-prong legislative project in Congress, which was aimed at giving preference to domestic firms over foreign capital. The new regulatory framework was composed of four key policy proposals: (a) the creation of a production sharing regime to manage the pre-salt oil reserves; (b) the establishment of a new state enterprise, Petrosal, to represent state interests; (c) the creation of a national social fund and the passage of a new law that will redistribute the division of royalties between the Federal, state, and oil-producing municipalities; and (d) the market capitalization of Petrobras. While many of these changes are still being debated in Congress and are now temporarily overshadowed by the corruption scandal in 2014 involving Petrobras and top politicians of the ruling party, some have already been approved.

In 2010, Congress passed Law 12.351 that establishes the production-sharing arrangement as applied to the newfound pre-salt reserves while the existing concessions grant model remains in place for blocs considered to be 'non-strategic'.[2] The new law stresses the right of the state over the subsoil and reasserts its ownership of natural resources. The production sharing model limits the role of private companies as service providers while the state increases its risks and costs in oil exploration. Lula justified this reorientation by emphasizing the low uncertainty in the exploration and development of the pre-salt reserves. Furthermore, unlike other Latin American oil producers relying on foreign capital in developing their oil industries, Brazil's Petrobras developed its expertise in ultra-deep engineering technology. An onerous assignment clause in new contracts allocates 30% minimum participation share for Petrobras in all oil activities in the pre-salt reserves. Compared to Cardoso's oil policy, Lula da Silva clearly had greater expectations regarding the capacity of oil to transform Brazil's future.

While the state has far less control in mining due to the absence of a state enterprise, the proposed new mining regulation likewise posits a renewed role for the state. Although still at a discussion stage and subject to changes in Congress, the government has submitted three proposals seeking to modernize the country's mining legislation.[3] From the perspective of the MME, the existing regulatory framework no longer meets the current economic, political, and social environment. Flexibility is the driving force to enhance the competitiveness of the mining industry.[4] Given the high prices of commodities and Brazil's role as a major commodity exporter, the new proposed mining regulatory framework follows the same rationale and similar guidelines as those adopted in the oil sector. These changes involve consolidating the oversight function of the MME and gaining flexibility in setting royalty rates depending on the commodity prices.

Nevertheless, the legislative bill is still under discussion in Congress and has been changed and contested several times. The MME had proposed the reorganization of the mining regulatory framework through the creation of a national council for mining policy and a regulatory agency to replace the DNPM. In an attempt to increase the speed in which mining projects are developed, improve supervision of mining activities, and decrease speculation and sales of rights of mining concessions to third parties, the first draft bill has as its main objective to place time limits on concessions granted to mining firms.[5] In a process similar to the one that occurred in the oil industry, under the suggested draft bill, concessions granted to the mining sector would also provide incentives to the aggregation of value in mining production and development of industrial and service sectors linked to the mining industry, since concession contracts would require or give incentives for the purchase of goods and services locally as well as provide for minimum national content requirements.[6]

To oversee the mining sector, the second proposal seeks to transform the DNPM, which currently overseas mining activities, into an independent regulatory agency – the National Mining Agency (ANM).[7] The move would be similar to that in place in the oil sector with the creation of the ANP and with auction of exploration rights. It also clearly reflects the government's strategy of keeping in place features of neoliberal reforms, such as independent regulatory agencies, and the strengthening of the capacity of the state to regulate and influence private capital. Finally, the third draft law proposes changes in mining royalties. According to DNPM, royalties are one of the main problems of the mining sector. Since their values are fixed, they do not allow for adjustment in times of economic crisis or times of economic boom.[8] In other words, a firm operating during a period of economic boom, such as during a commodities boom, or economic crisis will pay the same. Therefore, an intended objective of the proposed regulation is to allow for flexibility into the regulatory framework.

In other words, the PT government accepted features of a market-based regulatory framework in redesigning statist policies. The state reasserts its position and control over the country's natural resources by securing Petrobras' dominant role in the petroleum sector. However, the PT government under Lula da Silva did not aim to alienate the private sector and return to monopoly rights over natural resource exploration, but instead, recognized the value of private capital in investing in the sector. The state has not only remained an active and influential actor, but it is capable of influencing businesses' choices and the overall development of the resource sectors. In the case of Vale, the government has maintained its golden share after the company was privatized, which provides veto powers for the state over significant changes in any aspect of the company's corporate governance (Schneider 2009; Vale Annual Report 2013).

Furthermore, indirect influence is also exercised through the ownership structure of the company. Despite privatization, the state retains a 6.3% interest in the company (as of 31 December 2013) through the National Development Bank investment subsidiary, the BNDESPAR. Vale's controlling shareholder, however, is the Valepar consortium, which was organized and incorporated with the purpose of holding an interest in the company. As of 2013, the Valepar consortium held 52.7% of Vale's common shares (Vale Annual Report 2013). Valepar, in turn, is controlled by the holding Litel Participações, which has as its main shareholder the government pension fund Previ of the state-owned bank, Banco do Brasil (the BNDESPAR also holds an 11.5% interest in Valepar as of 2013) (Vale Annual Report 2013). Although Previ is not a public entity and does not belong to the state, the government has great political influence over state-owned pension funds. This ownership structure therefore provides the state with the capacity to exert indirect influence over Vale's affairs.

Nothing better exemplifies the continued capacity of the state to influence the company's decisions than the departure of Vale's CEO, Roger Agnelli, in 2011. Under Agnelli's leadership, Vale had been an outstanding performer by becoming the world leader in iron ore production, the second biggest nickel producer, and the world's second largest mining company (Prada and Matthews 2011). From a business and market perspective, Agnelli created the most value for the company's shareholders. However, it was rumoured in the media that the government had lobbied to oust Agnelli due to his failure to comply with the government's desire to create more jobs domestically, complement mining operations with other activities such as steel production, and revive the domestic shipbuilding industry by sourcing Vale's ships domestically – in other words, invest, in the government's view, in Brazilian national industrial development (Prada and Matthews 2011). Although the government cannot directly intervene in the company's decisions, it certainly has indirect influence through the shareholding structure to pressure for change. Even though Agnelli's departure may involve more than politics, the fact remains that while according to market rules a private company should have the interests of its shareholders at heart, Vale has to balance the interests of its private shareholders as well as those of the government. This raises fundamental questions about market reforms and the extent to which neoliberal reforms really dismantled existing patterns of state intervention in strategic industries in the economy. We argue that the Brazilian state consciously refuses to withdraw its control over the resources sector. Despite market reforms, the Brazilian state has historically exercised, and continues to exert, significant influence over the national economy.

Conclusions

Brazil's globalization strategy – the combination of selective market liberalization and statist policies – is shaped by the logic of path-dependency and sectoral considerations. Mining and oil sector reforms, aimed at increasing competitiveness, in the context of post-privatization and the commodities boom, reinforced the existing patterns of state control in the economy. These reforms had important consequences in developing internationally competitive firms. Vale and the mining sector have regained importance in Brazil's economy. As of 2008, the total value of Brazil's mineral production was US$103.1 billion accounting for about 5% of national GDP (Gurmendi 2010: 4.2-4.3). If the measure of success of market opening is whether Brazil has managed to attract foreign investment within the industry, then by all means the mining sector has flourished throughout the 1990s and 2000s. Between 1990 and 2008, over 500 transnational corporations established operations in the country, increasing investments and competitiveness in the sector (Gurmendi 2010: 4.2-4.3). In iron ore production, Brazil ranked second only to China, wherein Vale and companies in which Vale had participation accounted for about 85% of national production (Departamento Nacional de Produção Mineral 2010). In terms of exports, mineral products, crude as well as processed, oscillated between 15 and 30% of total Brazilian exports between 1978 and 1991, averaging approximately 20% of total exports in the period 1994–2008.[9] Exports earnings in turn jumped from US$1 billion in 1994 to US$17 billion in 2008 (Departamento Nacional de Produção Mineral 2010: 11). The combination of high prices and the high quality of Brazilian iron ore provided a niche for Brazilian mining, which has resulted in the successful domestic and international expansion of its former state enterprise. Brazil's mining sector was transformed into a dynamic and highly competitive sector with Vale as a major global player.

In the oil sector, by 2010 there were around 78 companies on exploration and production activities (38 of which were foreign-based), with a solid local industry capable of offering material, equipment and services (Nem Singh 2013). Petrobras remains the dominant player across the upstream, mid-stream, and downstream segments of the oil industry. In oil exploration, Petrobras emerged as the biggest owner of oil blocs after auctions undertaken by the ANP. For this reason, domestic and international oil companies have sought to establish joint ventures, consortia and minority participation with Petrobras. The company also retains its market monopoly in refining, primarily due to the high costs of building refineries and lower rates of return compared to oil exploration. The distribution and sales of oil derivatives is also under the control of Petrobras through its subsidiary, Petrobras Distribuidora. As argued by the SOE competitors, while some thought that Petrobras would weaken and eventually allow more competition, in fact, it benefited significantly from the new environment; it is bigger and stronger than it was before liberalization.[10] As a result of market reforms and increased international competitiveness, Vale and Petrobras have become highly efficient companies. Nevertheless, liberal reforms failed to completely dismantle the production system established throughout years of state intervention. This set the stage for a return of the state in sectoral development.

However, it is vital that we recognize the recurrence of politicization of state enterprises in Brazil, and in Latin America more widely. Despite the post-reform successes of Vale and Petrobras in the natural resources sector, the recent corruption scandal involving Petrobras managers and the PT government raises crucial questions regarding the viability of resource nationalism as a development model. A number of Petrobras executives have been arrested or are under investigation accused of taking payoffs from contractors – mostly construction firms – and kicking back part of the funds to PT as well as other political parties. Their involvement tainted the popular belief that Petrobras is an exceptionally efficient state-owned company that is autonomous from the state. The development strategy also involves high risks that may not be sustainable through state investments.

Petrobras' investment programme is ambitious and grand in scale, and the success of building related industries, notably shipbuilding, relies heavily on the capacity of Petrobras to further develop deep-water engineering technology for offshore oil extraction. The technological challenges and geological risks in the pre-salt reserves are greater and will require far more investments than those made in previous decades. Petrobras alone was expected to invest US$ 128 billion between 2012 and 2015 (BNDES 2012). This, inevitably, leads to increasing domestic demand for machinery and equipment, ships, trade and services. Hence, the paralysis of the company due to the corruption scandal may negatively impact the entire production chain, involving direct and indirect suppliers. For instance, in the shipbuilding industry over 10,000 workers have lost their jobs so far (Moraes 2015). Although the slowdown of the Brazilian economy also contributed to the weakening of the sector, the shipbuilding industry is greatly dependent on orders from Petrobras, which accounts for about 90% of its business (Moraes 2015). The future impacts on the rates of investment in the entire economy could be great. Finally, the company's political autonomy is now in question after Dilma Rousseff (2011–15) used the company as a tool to control gasoline prices by forcing Petrobras to sell its products below market prices. Overall, the once commercially viable development strategy of Petrobras seems to be suffering from state intervention.

The analysis of the two aspects of natural resource sector reforms points to the continuing significance of states in mediating the pace, sequence, and timing of institutional change in strategic industries. Unlike Argentina, Bolivia and Venezuela where re-nationalization projects mobilized opposition from the private sector, in Brazil the domestic capacity of Vale and Petrobras – and their position as international players in the mining and oil industries – have led to more stable state-capital relations. This is similar to the Chilean resource governance model (Nem Singh 2010). But while in Chile significant liberalization in the mining sector took place alongside control over the national copper company, in Brazil the entry of foreign direct investment in strategic sectors was highly regulated from the very beginning, and therefore the role of government control was important in the sequence and pace of market reforms. This reflects political pragmatism of national elites in strong states, hence, making neoliberalism less of an inevitable and homogenous outcome. More broadly, this governance model based on continuity and change between market and statist policies signifies the continuing influence of path-dependency – specifically Vargas' statist developmentalist paradigm – in the process of adjusting to the international economy.

Notes

1 DNPM Deputy Secretary Nogueira da Costa Jr., personal communication, Brasilia, 22 September 2011.
2 The pre-salt area is defined by the state as 'strategic' while other reservoirs with high uncertainty and risk (and less lucrative) have been considered non-strategic.
3 The proposed changes in mining regulation, as well as amendments and additions, have yet to be voted by Congress. In March 2015, a special commission was reinstalled in Congress to debate the bills and their economic, social, and environmental impact For reference, see bills (PL) 37/2011 and (PL) 5807/2013) (http://www.camara.gov.br/proposicoesWeb/fichadetramitacao?idProposicao=581696).

4 Nogueira da Costa Jr., personal communication, Brasilia, 22 September 2011.
5 Nogueira da Costa Jr., op. cit.
6 Nogueira da Costa Jr., op. cit.
7 Nogueira da Costa Jr., op. cit.
8 Nogueira da Costa Jr., op. cit.
9 Iron ore accounted for almost 90% of primary mineral exports (in value) ((Departamento Nacional de Produção Mineral 2010: 11–12).
10 Executive Secretary Felipe Dias, Brazilian Institute for Petroleum, Natural Gas and Bio-fuels, personal communication, Rio de Janeiro, 17 August 2010.

Bibliography

Bayulgen, O. (2010). *Foreign Investment and Political Regimes: The Oil Sector in Azerbaijan, Russia, and Norway*. Cambridge: Cambridge University Press.

BNDES (2012). Perspectivas de investimento na industria: 2012–2015. Visao do Desenvolvimento, No 100, Rio de Janeiro: BNDES.

Cannon, B. and Kirby, P. (2012) *Civil Society and the State in Left-led Latin America: Challenges and Limitations to Democratization*. London: Zed Books.

Departamento Nacional De Produção Mineral. (2010). Sumário Mineral 2009. Brasilia: Ministério de Minas e Energia. Retrieved from: https://sistemas.dnpm.gov.br/publicacao/mostra_imagem.asp?IDBancoArquivoArquivo=4544.

Devin, R., and Moguillansky, G. (2009). Public–private alliances for long-term national development strategies. *CEPAL Review*, 97, pp. 99–102.

Diniz, E., and Boschi, R. (2004). Empresários, interesses e mercado: Dilemas do desenvolvimento no Brasil. Editora UFMG.

Empresa Pesquisa De Energética (EPE) (2011) *Brazilian Energy Balance 2011*. Rio de Janeiro: EPE.

Estache, A., Goldstein, A., and Pittman, R. (2001). Privatization and regulatory reform in Brazil: The case of freight railways. *Journal of Industry, Competition and Trade*, 1(2), pp. 203–35.

Ffrench, D. (2005). Macroeconomía, comercio y finanzas para reformar las reformas en América Latina. ECLAC.

Goldstein, A. (1999). Brazilian privatization in international perspective: The rocky path from state capitalism to regulatory capitalism. *Industrial and Corporate Change*, 8(4), pp. 673–711.

Grugel, J. and Riggirozzi, P. (2012). Post-neoliberalism in Latin America: Rebuilding and reclaiming the state after crisis. *Development and Change*, 43(1), pp. 1–21.

Guimarães, A. (2003). Institutions, state capacity and economic development: The political economy of import substitution industrialization in Brazil. PhD Dissertation, University of Sheffield, United Kingdom.

Gurmendi, A.C. (2010). The mineral industry of Brazil. 2008 Minerals Yearbook. Retrieved from: http://minerals.usgs.gov/minerals/pubs/country/2008/myb3-2008-br.pdf.

Haggard, S., and Kaufman, R. (1995). *The political economy of democratic transitions*. Princeton University Press.

Hall, P., and Soskice, D. (2001). *Varieties of capitalism: The institutional foundations of comparative advantage*. Oxford: Oxford University Press.

Heron, T., and Richardson, B. (2008). Path dependency and the politics of liberalization in the textiles and clothing industry. *New Political Economy*, 13(1), pp. 1–18.

Hogenboom, B. (2012). Depoliticized and repoliticized minerals in Latin America. *Journal of Developing Societies*, 28(2), pp. 133–58.

Hsueh, R. (2011). *China's Regulatory State: A New Strategy for Globalization*. Ithaca: Cornell University Press.

Hunter, W. (2010). *The transformation of the Workers' Party in Brazil, 1989–2009*. Cambridge: Cambridge University Press.

International Directory Of Company Histories (2002). Companhia Vale do Rio Doce. Retrieved from : http://www.encyclopedia.com/doc/1G2-2844700035.html.

Jordana, J., and Levi-Faur, D. (2005). The diffusion of regulatory capitalism in Latin America: Sectoral and national channels in the making of a new order. *The Annals of the American Academy of Political and Social Science*, 598(1), pp. 102–24.

Karl, L. (1997). *The Paradox of the Plenty: Oil Booms and Petro-states*. Berkeley: University of California Press.

Kaufman, R. (2011). The political left, the export boom, and the populist temptation. In Levitsky, S. and Roberts K.M. (eds.). *The Resurgence of the Latin American Left*. Baltimore: Johns Hopkins University Press, pp. 93–116.

Kingstone, P. (1999). *Crafting Coalitions for Reform: Business Preferences, Political Institutions and Neoliberalism in Brazil*. Pennsylvania: Pennsylvania University Press.

Levitsky, S., and Roberts, K.M. (2011). Latin America's 'left turn': A framework for analysis. In Levitsky, S. and Roberts, K.M. (eds). *The Resurgence of the Latin American Left*. Baltimore: Johns Hopkins University Press, pp. 3–30.

Luong, P.J., and Weinthal, E. (2006). Rethinking the resource curse: Ownership structure, institutional capacity, and domestic constraints. *Annual Review of Political Science*, 9, pp. 241–63.

Luong, P.J. And Weinthal, E. (2010). *Oil is not a Curse: Ownership Structure and Institutions in Soviet Successor States*. Cambridge: Cambridge University Press.

Machado, I.F. (1997). The CVRD privatization: A hard victory for the government. *Minerals and Energy*, 12(4), pp. 36–41.

Massi, E. (2014). The political economy of development finance: The BNDES and Brazilian industrialization. PhD Dissertation, SOAS-University of London, United Kingdom.

Moraes, H. (February 6, 2015). Industria naval demite mais de 10 mil metalurgicos. O Dia. Retrieved from: http://odia.ig.com.br/noticia/economia/2015-02-06/industria-naval-demite-mais-de-10-mil-metalurgicos.html.

Mueller, B., and Pereira, C. (2002). Credibility and the design of regulatory agencies in Brazil. *Brazilian Journal of Political Economy*, 22(3), pp. 65–88.

Murillo, M. V. (2009). *Political Competition, Partisanship and Policy Making In Latin America Public Utilities*. Cambridge: Cambridge University Press.

Nem Singh, J. T. (2010). Reconstituting the neostructuralist state: The political economy of continuity and change in Chilean mining policy. *Third World Quarterly*, 31(8), pp. 1413–33.

Nem Singh, J. T. (2013). States, markets and labor unions: The political economy of oil and copper in Brazil and Chile. PhD Dissertation, University of Sheffield, United Kingdom.

Nem Singh, J. T. (2014). Towards a post-neoliberal resource politics? The international political economy (IPE) of natural resources in Brazil and Chile. *New Political Economy*, 19(3), pp. 329–58.

Philip, G. (1982). *Oil and Politics in Latin America: Nationalist Movements and State Companies*. Cambridge: Cambridge University Press.

Pinheiro, A.C., Bonelli, R., and Schneider, B.R. (2004). Pragmatic policy in Brazil: The political economy of incomplete market reform. Retrieved from: http://repositorio.ipea.gov.br/handle/11058/1874.

Prada, P., and Matthews, R G. (24 March 2011). Brazil's push to oust Vale's CEO reflects trend. *The Wall Street Journal*. Retrieved from: http://online.wsj.com/articles/SB10001 424052748704425804576221232291726132.

Randall, L. (1993). *The Political Economy of Brazilian Oil*. Westport, CT: Praeger.

Roberts, K. M. (2011). Substance and methods of a grounded political economy. *Latin American Politics and Society*, 56(1), pp. 17–19.

Schamis, H. (1999). Distributional coalitions and the politics of economic reform in Latin America. *World Politics*, 51(2), pp. 236–68.

Shafer, M. (1994). *Winners and Losers: How Sectors Shape the Developmental Prospects of States*. Ithaca: Cornell University Press.

Schneider, B.R. (2009). Big business in Brazil: Leveraging natural endowments and state support for international expansion. In Brainard, L. and Martinez-Diazm L. (eds.). *Brazil as an Economic Superpower? Understanding Brazil's Changing Role in the Global Economy*. Brookings Institution Press, pp. 159–85.

Schneider, B.R. (2014). *Hierarchical Capitalism in Latin America. Business, Labor and the Challenges of Equitable Development*. Cambridge University Press.

Sikkink, K. (1991). *Ideas and Institutions: Developmentalism in Brazil and Argentina*. Ithaca: Cornell University Press.

Streeck, W. and Thelen, K. (2005). Introduction: Institutional change in advanced political economies. In Streeck, W and Thelen, K. (eds.). *Beyond continuity: Institutional change in advanced industrial economies*. Oxford: Oxford University Press, pp. 1–39.

Thurber, M., Hults, D., and Heller, P. (2011). Exporting the 'Norwegian Model': The effect of administrative design on oil sectoral performance. *Energy Policy*, 39(3), pp. 5366–78.

Trebat, T. (1983). *Brazil's State-owned Enterprises: A Case Study of the State as Entrepreneur*. New York: Cambridge University Press.

Vale, SA. (2013). Annual Report. Retrieved from: http://www.vale.com/brasil/EN/ investors/annual-reports/20F/Pages/default.aspx.

Vale, E., and Carvalho, A. (1998). Brazilian mining code: A mineral economics focus. *Minerals and Energy*, 13(3), pp. 12–17.

Villela, A. (1984). Empresas do governo como instrumento de política econômica: Os sistemas Siderbrás, Eletrobrás, Petrobrás e Telebrás. Rio de Janeiro: IPEA.

Vilhena Filho, C. A. (1997). Brazil's mineral policy. *Resources Policy*, 23 (1-2), pp. 45–50.

Vogel, S. (2006). *Japan Remodeled. How Government and Industry are Reforming Japanese Capitalism*. Ithaca: Cornell University Press.

Weneck, R. (1987). Empresas estatais e política macroeconômica. Rio de Janeiro: Editora Campus.

10 Mining policies in Humala's Peru

A patchwork of improvised nationalism and corporate interests[1]

Javier Arellano-Yanguas

Introduction

Mining has been at the centre of both the exceptional economic growth that Peru has enjoyed during the last decade, and the political disputes that expose the limits of the Peruvian institutional framework to sustain that growth (*The Economist* 2014). The Peruvian economic bonanza has relied on the increased international demand for minerals. While from 2001 to 2011 the country multiplied its GDP[2] by 3.2, the weight of the mining and oil sector in the economy increased from 6.3 to 14.7 per cent (see Table 10.1). This growing economic importance has accompanied the multiplication of social conflicts around the construction of new mines and oil fields, and political disputes over the role of the state in the extractive sector.

The first evidence of a new resource nationalism can be traced to the months leading up to Peru's presidential and parliamentary elections of 2006. In the face of a steady increase in international mineral prices, mining became a hot political topic. Political pundits and some presidential candidates, especially Alan García of the APRA (*Alianza Popular Revolucionaria Americana*) and Ollanta Humala of the Peruvian Nationalist Party (PNP), demanded the revision of the stability agreements, the introduction of a windfall tax, and the payment of royalties by mining companies.[3] The proposals were very moderate, as they did not advocate for radical changes that were being simultaneously implemented in Bolivia and discussed in other Latin American countries. However, as soon as García won the elections and took office, he acquiesced to the mining companies' policy agenda.

In the electoral campaign of 2011 mining policies were again central. Many candidates proposed changes in mining taxation and other regulations such as consultation processes with indigenous and local populations. Humala, the nationalist candidate, was the main challenger to corporate interests. His electoral victory in 2011 provided the legitimacy to advance his political platform on mining. During his initial weeks in power, the new president seemed to take his promises seriously. The negotiation of a fiscal reform for the mining sector was one of the new government's first actions. Moreover, within a few weeks, the president promulgated the long-awaited indigenous consultation law that made it mandatory to seek Indigenous Peoples' consent before going ahead with investment projects that would affect their lives. However, those actions did not herald radical change. In November 2011, the government faced a bitter conflict between the Yanacocha mining company and the regional authorities of Cajamarca over probable severe negative environmental impacts. Humala failed to support the position of his minister of the environment. The event generated the resignation of the Premier of the national government, the shuffling of numerous ministers, and a shift in the government's approach to mining.

Some political analysts consider that since the governmental crisis of December 2011, Humala's mining policies maintained the neoliberal agenda of previous governments (Jiménez 2014; Monge 2012). However, Humala's political background demands a more nuanced understanding of his policies and the political processes informing them. In this chapter, I argue that Humala's policies compose a patchwork of disjointed proposals that respond to the different logics and perspectives that coexisted in the ministerial cabinet. Initially, the government had two objectives. On the one hand, it attempted to increase the participation of the state in mining rents. On the other hand, it wanted to incorporate the voice of local populations into the decision-making process and give more importance to environmental considerations in the process of granting licences for the construction of new mines. However, the priority given to the attraction of new investments in the mining sector watered down the second objective. The 'nationalist turn' in mining policy focused on acquiring more fiscal revenues in order to increase social spending along the lines of the 'new extractivism' implemented in other Latin American countries (Gudynas 2009; Bebbington 2009). Nevertheless, despite this general tendency, Humala maintained in the ministerial cabinet some ministers who defended elements of the original perspective and developed institutions aimed at regulating, not only promoting, the mining sector.

Why did Humala change his original plan? The answer to this question combines contextual and structural factors. The contextual factors relate to the weaknesses of the PNP and Humala's personality. Humala had to rely on diverse political groups to form the government; however, the president's distrust regarding the green-leftist components of the first cabinet influenced changes to his original plans. The structural factors respond to the traditional power of economic groups in Peruvian politics and their capacity to exert ideological influence through technical cadres. Finally, the results of Humala's policies continue to strengthen the primary-export-led growth of the Peruvian economy, deepening economic and political dependency on the extractive sector and on the role of a small group of big companies.

The rest of the chapter proceeds as follows. Taking a historical approach, the second section presents the different policies affecting the mining sector and the main policy changes of the last decade. The third section analyses the main factors that explain resistance to the introduction of more nationalist policies in the mining sector. Finally, the fourth section concludes by assessing the implications of current mining policies for Peruvian politics and the country's developmental model. The analysis presented in this chapter is based on data from interviews with key actors between 2007 and 2013.

Mining policies from Fujimori to Humala

Mining has historically played an important role in Peru's economy. During the Velasco Alvarado administration in the 1970s, the state took direct control over a large part of mining production. The global crisis in the mining industry and poor management plunged these companies into a severe crisis. In the early 1990s, Fujimori's regime implemented significant policy changes and laid the foundations for the current expansion of the mining sector. Subsequent governments maintained these policies; however, the rise to power of Ollanta Humala in 2011 generated expectations for significant changes.

From Fujimori to García: promoting investment by protecting corporate interests

The reform of the mining sector was one of the first tasks undertaken by Fujimori. The General Mining Law of 1992 was designed to attract foreign investment. It addressed four key areas. First, the law mandated the privatization of state-owned companies, providing a strong signal of the business-friendly orientation of the new regime. Second, the law created a new mining cadastre that facilitated the concession and management of mining rights. Third, it proposed a fiscal regime favourable to foreign investment by: (i) simplifying the fiscal regime for mining companies; (ii) eliminating differences between national and foreign capital; (iii) conferring the government with the power to sign stability agreements with companies; (iv) removing restrictive foreign exchange rate policies; and (v) exempting the reinvestment of profits from corporate taxes to be paid by mining companies. Fourth, the law smoothed the relationship between companies, and local authorities and populations by establishing a *canon minero*[4] as the right of jurisdictions where minerals are extracted to receive 20 per cent of the corporate taxes paid by the companies.[5] Moreover, the law was liberal with respect to environmental issues, devoting only 6 of its 226 articles to the topic. Those six articles were mostly formal references to lower level regulations on technical standards. They conveyed a clear message to investors: this is not going to be a problem.

The combination of pro-business policies with the existence of very profitable mineral deposits attracted international companies that came to Peru to explore new business opportunities. As a result, over the last two decades Peru has gained a solid reputation as one of the world's leading mining investment destinations. Simultaneously, mining has multiplied its importance in the Peruvian economy in terms of production, exports, and fiscal revenues (See Table 10.1).

During the 2000s, the Peruvian mining sector had to respond to three types of challenges in the mining sector: (i) tensions with local populations; (ii) political pressures to increase the participation of the state in the mining rent; and (iii) international mandates to develop institutions responsible for the enforcement of environmental regulations. However, until 2011, the policy

Table 10.1 Economic indicators for the Peruvian mining sector

	1994	*2001*	*2011*
GDP (millions of USD)[a]	44,993	52,046	171,262
Mining and Oil as percentage of total GDP	5.6 %	6.3 %	14.7 %
Total Exports (Millions of USD)	4,424	7,026	46,268
Percentage of mining in exports	44.5%	45.6 %	59.1 %
Government total income (millions of USD)	7,782	9,148	37,085
Government income from mining and oil (millions of USD)	DNA	340	5,502
Investment in mining (millions of USD)	254	1,296	7,243

Sources: INEI (2014), Banco Central de Reserva del Perú (2014), SUNAT (2014), Dammert y Molinelli (2007, p. 116).

Notes: [a] in nominal prices.

framework developed by Fujimori saw few changes. As the next paragraphs show, the Peruvian governments during this period responded to these challenges through three policy innovations aimed at defending the interests of mining companies.

The tension with local populations and the pressure for changes in taxation policies were addressed simultaneously by firstly increasing the volume of *canon minero* transfers and secondly promoting a greater involvement of mining companies in developmental activities at the local level (Arellano-Yanguas 2011). The third innovation was the timid development of state institutions responsible for the preservation of the environment.

The first group of policy innovations addresses the territorial redistribution of mining revenues. In 2001, the Peruvian parliament approved the canon law, which raised the canon in the mining sector from 20 to 50 per cent of the corporate income tax paid by companies.[6] Mayors in mining areas had spent many years working to achieve this change without success. However, in 2001 local authorities from mining districts won the support of business leaders who, concerned by the growing local resistance to mining, were interested in local populations benefiting from the incomes generated by the mines (Arellano-Yanguas 2012).

The original law had to be modified several times in 2003 and 2004 to solve the 'unexpected results' caused by the lack of technical precision. When the last reform of the canon was approved in 2004, transfers for mining canons amounted to an additional 308 million soles in 1996 constant prices (US $90 million). In three years, higher mineral prices boosted transfers 13 times greater than their original amounts. That increase affected only a few regions, and few districts within those regions, causing severe inequalities. Several attempts have been made to reform the canon law in recent years with a view to achieving fairer distribution; however, all these attempts have failed. In discussions on reform, mining companies expressed their preference to maintain the established distribution of the canon because of the benefits it brought to the districts hosting the mines.

Regarding taxation, after 2003, the increase in mineral prices and profits awakened critics from different groups. During the 2005 to 2006 period, there were two main attempts to change taxation policies. In 2005, a group of congressional representatives from mining regions presented a draft bill to introduce royalties. In fact, the representatives aimed to benefit their constituents more than to increase the revenues of the state, since the amounts collected as royalties would automatically go to the producing regions.[7] The bill was met with opposition from the powerful MEF (Ministry of Economy and Finance) and the National Society for Mining, Oil, and Energy (SNMPE). However, Congress passed the bill in the end, and President Toledo, who had less than 10 per cent popular support at the time, claimed that he had to enact the law against the opinion of the Minister of the Economy and Finance.[8]

Nevertheless, the reform has had very limited impact, because the payment of royalties affected only old operations that were not protected by stability contracts, and new investments.

The next attempt to reform taxation policies dates to the period ahead of the 2006 presidential elections. Several political groups requested the revision of the tax stability agreements with a view to introducing windfall taxes and payment of royalties for mines that had been exempted from the law passed in 2005. The successful presidential candidate, Alan García, had adopted these concerns as part of his electoral platform. However, as soon as he took office, he acquiesced to the interests of mining companies, stating that palliative measures would be implemented instead of the payment of royalties or windfall taxes. In December 2006, Garcia published the Mining Program of Solidarity with the People (PMSP). The agreement between the government and the mining companies exempted the companies from paying windfall taxes in exchange for a commitment to invest a predetermined amount of money in social development projects in the mining regions for the subsequent five years. Private trusts under company control were to be responsible for the allocation of these resources according to a loose set of rules. This agreement fuelled popular discontent and criticism, because it indicated the clear subordination of the government to mining interests.

The president of the powerful SNMPE was exultant, because the agreement had two favourable outcomes: the companies avoided paying higher taxes and could also use some of the savings to boost their investment in development at the local level.[9] Another leader of the mining industry declared that the 'companies were changing from being defensive regarding environmental conflicts to becoming proactive in the development of communities'.[10]

The need to take into account the impact of mining on the environment was the third challenge. Environmental groups had, for a long time, advocated for the creation of a ministry of the environment. Regarding the mining sector, they claimed the existence of a conflict of interest, because the Ministry of Energy and Mines (MINEM) was simultaneously responsible for promoting investment in new mining operations, and reviewing and approving the environmental assessments that allowed mining companies to move into exploration and exploitation phases (Bebbington 2007). Garcia's government created the Ministry for the Environment (MINAM). Paradoxically, the decision to create the ministry was not a response to internal demands, but a result of the negotiation of the Free Trade Agreement (FTA) with the USA and the negotiation of the Camisea loan. During the FTA negotiations, Peruvian representatives understood that the existence of a ministry for the environment would facilitate the approval of the agreement. The MINAM was set up in May 2008, and the FTA was implemented in February 2009. However, the government made it clear immediately that the new ministry would not assume responsibility for large-scale mining, as that would remain under the supervision of the MINEM.

The García presidency (2006–11) epitomized the market-friendly orientation of Peruvian governments since Fujimori. During García's mandate, the government committed to mining as the main engine of economic development. In 2007, Juan Valdivia, the Minister of Energy and Mines, proclaimed that the 'mining agenda is today the agenda of national development' (Ministerio de Energía y Minas 2007). Moreover, during the negotiation of the PMSP, Jorge Del Castillo, the Premier, asked the SNMPE representatives for their involvement in designing and implementing development projects at the local level, to overcome the limitations of the state in reaching remote rural areas.[11]

President García went beyond his ministers in proclaiming his faith in private investment in the extractive sector as the main driver of development. In a programmatic newspaper article, *El perro del hortelano* (the dog in the manger)[12] (García Pérez 2007), García proposed that increased exploitation of natural resources should drive Peruvian economic development. Consequently, the government should surrender control of land, water, and other resources to private investors. At the same time, García portrayed the leftist opposition, environmental NGOs, defenders of indigenous rights, and local populations resisting extractive activities, as dogs in the manger who wanted to prevent progress in the country. This discourse put García at odds with the majority of the population in rural areas of the Andean and Amazonian regions, who were both insulted and threatened with being dispossessed of valuable assets.

The dramatic increase in social conflict was the most salient result of García's policies. Moreover, the unrestricted support to mining companies eroded the legitimacy of the state, as the government was seen to be acting in collusion with corporate interests. The political support for mining also damaged the mining companies' public image and fuelled radical discourses calling for either the nationalization of natural resources or the imposition of severe restrictions on new mining operations. Paradoxically, radical pro-business policies were threatening the viability of the expansion of the mining sector.

Humala's patchwork

Prior to the 2011 presidential elections, candidates and mining companies acknowledged that changes were inevitable in order to relieve public pressure against the expansion of the mining sector.

Regarding taxation, a few months before the elections, the MEF and the SNMPE hired experts to ensure they had proposals ready to submit to the newly elected government (Otto 2011). Nevertheless, nationalist candidate Humala's victory caused concern among mining companies. President Humala knew that his administration would start with actions related to mining taxes, but also that prudence was necessary. On one hand, he had to show voters that he was willing to demand greater commitment to the country's development from companies. On the other hand, he had to win the companies' trust and keep foreign investment flowing into the country.

Humala attempted to achieve balance in appointing his cabinet. In the first electoral round, Humala had a landslide victory in rural Peru and his showing was especially strong in mining regions and places in which the population had mobilized against government policies and private sector projects. In preparation for the second round, Humala moderated his electoral platform and teamed up with centre-left political groups in order to defeat Keiko Fujimori, the right-wing populist daughter of Alberto Fujimori. Once in office, and given the lack of capable political cadres within his own party, Humala relied on two ideological lines. On one hand, he partnered with 'Citizens for the Change' (CpC), a loose centre-left political platform constituted by professionals who had historically participated in leftist political parties. Humala's first premier, some ministers, and numerous senior ministerial professionals, belonged to CpC. On the other hand, Humala chose continuity for the economic ministries. For instance, he appointed Miguel Castilla, Deputy Minister of Economy in García's cabinet, as the new Minister of Economy, underlining to the business community the idea of the continuity of the pro-market policies.

A few days after taking office, Premier Salomón Lerner began negotiations with the SNMPE regarding the taxation of mining activities. The government stated that its objective was to collect at least an extra 3,000 million new soles (US $1,100 million).[13] Top-level meetings were held, often attended by the Premier, Minister of Economy and Finance, the SNMPE president, and representatives of leading mining companies. An agreement was reached in under two weeks (See Table 10.2). The law was passed in Congress with support from pro-government parliamentary deputies and conservative groups that had received the go-ahead from the mining companies.[14] The government and the companies were satisfied with the result. The government announced higher tax collection and publicly highlighted its skill in forcing mining companies to pay more without breaching the stability agreements.[15] The companies replaced ad valorem royalties approved in 2005 with royalties according to profits, and managed to minimize the effects of this on their profit and loss accounts.

During the negotiation of the new tax regime, mining companies indicated their concern over the end of the PMSP and their decreased ability to participate in development activities at the local level as a result. The companies demanded the right to manage 20 per cent of the new taxes to implement social projects. The new government did not respond to these concerns because this type of arrangement was very unpopular. However, after some months the MEF and the

Table 10.2 New mining taxes introduced in 2011

	Companies without stability contracts		Companies with stability contracts
Tax	Royalties	Special mining tax	Special levy on mining
New terms	Replaces the previous royalties	New	New
Base figures	Operational profit	Operational profit	Operational profit
Rates according to operating margin bracket	From 1% to 12% (minimum 1% of sales)	From 2 to 8.4%	From 4% to 13.12%
Accounting treatment	Deductible as expenses in the calculation of income tax		

companies started to use Law N° 29230, also called 'projects for taxes' that had been enacted in 2008 during the García administration. The law enabled private companies to execute decentralized public investment projects through agreements with local authorities. The money invested by the companies was discounted from corporate taxes.[16]

Humala's second promise on mining was the approval of a law on prior consultation with indigenous populations on projects that affected their lives. By September 2011, the elected president had honoured that promise. Humala promulgated the law in a symbolic ceremony in the village of Imaza (Amazonas), territory of the Awajun people who were the protagonists of the *Baguazo* in 2009, the most emblematic clash between the indigenous population and the Peruvian government for several decades. Humala's determination brought fresh hope to the indigenous population for the inauguration of a new era in their relationship with the Peruvian state. However, after some months the implementation of the law stalled, generating consternation and discontent. Conflicts in the initial stages of the process among senior officials of the Ministry of Culture and pressure from the SNMPE for a restrictive interpretation of the law were among the factors explaining the delay in the implementation of the law (Schiling-Vacaflor and Flemmer 2013).

Humala's ideas for the future of the MINAM was the third area under the scrutiny of the business community. The initial appointments were daring. The deputy ministers had a long history of activism and commitment to the environment and were determined to build a capable ministry.

Finally, regarding the *canon minero*, Humala announced that the reform of the canon law was one of his priorities. A minor reform was implicit in the new tax system. Under the new system, the amount that companies pay as a special mining tax could be deducted from their corporate income tax; accordingly, that part is not included in the canon to be distributed. This 'recentralizing' skirmish was part of President Ollanta Humala's bigger plan. The MEF hired several international consultants and spent months designing technical proposals to be used as the outline for the reform. The government could have found support for equalizing reforms in non-producing districts; however, it preferred to postpone the reforms due to conflicts in some mining regions and predicted resistance from the people of producing districts and mining companies.

In summary, Humala tried to be faithful to three streams of nationalism that had inspired the political discourse of the previous six years: (i) a peripheral nationalism represented by the historically neglected demands of indigenous people and peasants who claim to be the genuine Peruvians; (ii) an orthodox-leftist nationalism that aspires to strengthen the role of the state in the economy; and (iii) a nationalism inspired in the 'environmentalism of the poor' (Martinez-Alier 2002) that defends the livelihoods of rural populations. Humala incorporated people and groups representing these three streams in his first government.

However, Humala's honeymoon with these groups was extremely short. The outbreak of a conflict over the Conga Mine project in Cajamarca in October 2011 disrupted the government and conditioned the future of Humala's presidency.[17] The García administration approved the project and granted the legal permits to begin the construction phase. However, local communities and the regional government believed that the mine would threaten the headwaters of the watershed. The conflict put Humala in a difficult position. In an election rally in Cajamarca he had openly backed local protests against mining expansion by asking rhetorically: 'What is more important, water or gold? You don't drink gold, you don't eat gold'.[18] However, the candidate became President and had to make decisions about one of the biggest investments in the country's history. Humala asked the MINAM to review the EIA, but when the MINAM's report was due, the President blocked its publication, disavowed the Ministry, and contradicted his electoral promises. The Minister of the Environment and the deputy ministers resigned, and in a few weeks the Premier and the cabinet also stepped down. In four months, mining had generated a cabinet crisis and a change in the future of the government.

In the new cabinet after the crisis, Humala maintained some ministers with a progressive profile. The main challenge was to find a candidate for the MINAM. Manuel Pulgar Vidal, a prestigious lawyer with a long professional career in the SPDA, an environmentalist NGO, assumed the position. Pulgar is one of the few ministers to endure in government over the 2011 to 2014 period. During his tenure, the MINAM developed institutions responsible for monitoring and sanctioning the mining sector, providing them with the necessary resources to fulfil its mandate. However, it is also true that with the rapid turnover of ministerial cabinets, the pro-market orientation of the MEF has progressively gained leverage within the government. Miguel Castilla, the Minister of Economy, was in 2014 the only remaining representative from Humala's first cabinet. Most Peruvians recognized Castilla as the actual Premier.

Regarding the mining sector, the results of the 2011 to 2014 period comprise an ambiguous patchwork. There have been relatively important changes in taxation policies and advances in the institutionalization of the MINAM, and in the implementation of regulations over prior consultation. However, these policy reforms are far from Humala's campaign promises, and are far from the expectations that he set during his first weeks in office. Why?

Understanding the resilience of radical market-friendly policies

The tide of resource nationalism in other Latin American countries and the clear popular mandate for change provided Humala with the political backing to promote significant policy reforms and to develop state institutions able to regulate the mining sector. Understanding the reasons for his frustrated attempts reveals important features of Peruvian politics. In order to explain Humala's political decisions on mining, it is helpful to differentiate between contextual and structural factors. To facilitate the analysis, this section deals with both types of factors in turn. However, as the analysis reveals, those factors are intertwined in the political process of policy-making.

Contextual factors: presidential solitude, distrust, and lack of a long-term plan

Humala rose to power with a very weak party, without a clear government plan, lacking a team ready to staff senior positions in the government, and with very limited knowledge of economics and other key policy areas. He built his first government on a diverse group of people. When problems emerged, the diversity of opinions within the cabinet was interpreted as a lack of cohesion, and Humala decided to trust Miguel Castilla, the Minister of the Economy, who had articulated a developmental narrative that was conservative but clear.

Before the 2011 elections, the PNP was little more than the Humala-Heredia clan. In the last months of 2010, Humala personally interviewed dozens of social leaders from the Peruvian regions, asking them to head the electoral rolls of the PNP in their regions.[19] He also partnered with a group of small leftist parties and brought together a group of like-minded academics for the design of the electoral platform (Durand 2012).[20] In preparation for the second electoral round, Humala convened a wider group of professionals and academics to redesign the electoral manifesto. He aimed to attract moderate voters who did not trust the democratic credentials of Keiko Fujimori. One of those academics, who was later part of the team that prepared the transition from García to Humala, highlights three personal features of Humala: he initially knew very little about economics, he was open to listening and learning, and he was extremely reserved about his own conclusions.[21]

The appointment of the first ministerial cabinet revealed some of his perceptions. After listening to different people, including business leaders, Humala decided to entrust the responsibility of his government to CpC, which had endorsed Humala's electoral programme. However, he reserved some key positions in the economic area for technocrats who had held important responsibilities in previous governments. This was the case of Miguel Castilla, responsible for the MEF. As soon as the Conga conflict arose, Humala started to distrust most of the cabinet members from the CpC. The government faced a difficult situation. Yanacocha had fulfilled its legal requirements, and if the government were to block the construction of the new mine, the Peruvian state might have had to answer to formal complaints from investors before international authorities. In this context, Humala felt that the cabinet lacked unity and that some ministers and senior officials, especially those close to the CpC, had an independent agenda. Moreover, he did not recognize a viable and coherent policy agenda in their proposals. In contrast, the liberal ranks of the government, led by Castilla, put forward a plan that Humala could understand more easily: (i) promote investment; (ii) generate employment and increase state fiscal revenues; and (iii) invest state revenues to implement policies that foster social inclusion. The idea was to leave the economic model untouched to guarantee state income and to be more progressive in spending.[22] After the increase in the tax regime of the mining sector, the attraction of new investments and the quick start-up of new mines were the main conditions for maintaining the model.

Initially, this model did not conflict with the development of new institutions and regulations by the MINAM or with the commitment to implement the law on prior consultation. For Humala, these were issues that could advance in parallel. However, little by little Castilla gained more power and capacity to influence Humala, and the rest of ministers and their policies were increasingly subordinated to the promotion of investment, especially in the mining sector (Reuters 2014).

For example, the implementation of the law on prior consultation, which mining companies disliked, was repeatedly postponed and trimmed in scope. In the case of environmental policies, the most apparent case of subordination happened in 2014. The Peruvian rate of economic growth decreased drastically, putting at risk state income, government popularity and, more generally, the stability of the economic model. The MEF and the MINEM promoted a set of policies aimed to speed up the construction of some mines that had been in the project portfolio for a long time.[23] The policies relaxed some of the environmental regulations introduced in the last two years by the MINAM. These policies tried to: (i) unlock investment in some projects, generating employment and economic activity; and (ii) accelerate the entry into the production phase of some mines, multiplying the mining GDP (Ministerio de Energía y Minas 2014). These results could have a positive impact in the short term, improving the image of the government in the last two years of Humala's term. However, they threatened to erode the environmental institutions developed by the MINAM under the leadership of Pulgar and deepen dependency on the mining sector.

Structural factors: the historical power of the economic elite and its access to the state through lobbyists, technocrats, and international connections.

The capacity of the Peruvian economic elite, especially mining companies, to shape the state and its role in blocking the development of institutions that should enable the democratization of the country and the diversification of the economy beyond the extractive sector has been masterfully attested and analysed (Thorp 2012; Thorp and Bertram 1978). The arrival of Humala, who had no connections with the economic elite and whose discourses announced significant changes, brought hope for a different balance of power in the country. However, the elite anticipated the new scenario and used different means to minimize negative impacts on their interests.

In the next paragraphs, I analyse how private business managed to exert influence over Humala through lobbying, the colonization of the MEF and MINEM by neoliberal technocrats, and the inclusion of international interests within the state apparatus.

The National Confederation of Private Business (CONFIEP) did not wait for the results of the election to sit and discuss plans with Humala. Leading up to the second round, a delegation from CONFIEP met with the candidate. They asked him to maintain the economic model and keep within his economic team professionals with experience from previous governments, emphasizing the presidency of the Central Bank and the MEF. Apparently, these business representatives were very persuasive. Once in office, Humala confirmed continuity in the appointment of the president of the Central Bank, and selected Castilla, the previous Deputy Minister of Economy and Finance, as head of the MEF. Political analysts gave two reasons for this quick adjustment to business preferences: to assure investors of the commitment of the new government to the market economy, and to pay back the financial support of some economic groups for his electoral campaign (Durand 2012: 20–1).

The negotiation of the reform of the mining tax policy in the first weeks of government was the second opportunity for private business to extract a commitment from the new president. Mining companies had already discounted the introduction of tougher taxation policies. The SNMPE, by far the most powerful business association in the country, prepared a proposal that minimized the risks from the introduction of new taxes. In the negotiations, they put forward the proposal and convinced the new government of the need to publicly support mining investment. They would pay more, but in exchange they wanted unrestricted government support in the case of social conflicts that put important investments at risk.[24] This commitment of the President to the protection of investments in the mining sector explains the reaction of Humala to the Conga conflict some weeks later.

Finally, law firms and lobbyists often broker the interaction between the mining companies and the government, but are not always transparent in their operations.

The cases of Cecilia Blume and Eleodoro Mayorga illustrate the influence of those groups and the means through which they operate. Blume is a brilliant lawyer. She held important official positions in the Toledo government, acting as a main advisor to Pedro Pablo Kuczynski, Premier and Minister of Economy and Finance. Kuczynski was also the Minister of Energy and Mines in the 1990s during the Fujimori administration and maintained a professional relationship with oil companies. After leaving the government, Blume became one of the main advisors to mining companies. She and Del Castillo crafted the PMSP, and she was also initially involved in the process of preparing the SNMPE's proposal for the negotiation of the new taxation regime with the Humala government.[25] Surprisingly, Blume did not lose her access to the government when the administration changed. Her partner at C&B Consult was Carolina Castilla who had been, among other important roles, Manager of Corporate Affairs of Yanacocha and the General Manager of CONFIEP. Carolina Castilla is also the sister of Miguel Castilla, the powerful Minister of Economy and Finance. Eliodoro Mayorga, the Minister of Energy and Mines between February 2014 and February 2015, also exemplifies the access of extractive companies to the state. From 1991 to 2009, he worked for the World Bank as a specialist in the energy, oil, and mining sectors.[26] From 2011 until his appointment as minister in February 2014, he was a partner in Laub & Quijandría, the main Peruvian firm specializing in advisory services for oil and energy companies.

These two cases also reveal the existence in the MEF and the MINEM of a professional culture permeated by a strong pro-market ideology, which in Peru means a pro-mining bias. Since the 1990s, professionals with a clear pro-market orientation have staffed these ministries, and most of the senior officials came from private companies and will ultimately return to the private sector. Moreover, many young public servants aspire to get jobs in the private sector.[27] These officials have nurtured a well-oiled rotating door in which ideological conviction and the pursuit of personal careers reinforce the continuity of pro-market policies. Thus, state bureaucracy creates an economic orthodoxy favourable to mining companies. Often they dismiss alternative policies by portraying apocalyptic scenarios that are tirelessly publicized by the media. In this context, it will be difficult for the incoming president to challenge old policies, particularly if he does not have a sound alternative plan and is bound by short-term popularity ratings.

The final point refers to the inclusion of international interests in the state apparatus through bilateral aid programmes. Here I put forward two examples. The first is the Peru-Canada Mineral Resources Reform Project, also call 'PERCAN'– a bilateral agreement between the Canadian International Development Agency and the MINEM. Through the agreement the Canadian Government donated CAN $ 17.7 million to generate institutional capacity at the MINEM. The project also contemplated the provision of technical support to improve mining policies in different areas. Here it is important to note that Canadian mining companies account for 15 per cent of the confirmed Peruvian mining investment portfolio, and that most of the junior companies exploring in

Peru come from Canada (Ministerio de Energía y Minas 2014). An academic analysis of PERCAN suggests that the project was designed to cover the needs of the companies without paying enough attention to other stakeholders (Campbell et al. 2011). The second example is less public and even more problematic. An aid programme directly managed by the Swiss embassy in Lima paid the salaries of some senior advisors of the MEF. Those advisors are reputedly professionals with successful careers in the public sector and international organizations. However, their salaries exceeded the amounts officially approved by the Peruvian Government.[28] Thus, in order to retain the service of those professionals, bilateral and multilateral aid agencies hire and pay them as consultants through technical assistance programmes, although they continue working directly for the Ministry.[29] In the case of Switzerland, a potential conflict of interest emerges because Swiss companies have important investments in the mining sector and in other sectors in which the MEF and other state agencies can play an important regulatory role.

Conclusion and likely developmental outcomes

As has occurred in other Latin American countries, the increase in mineral prices in the 2000s fuelled investment in the mining sector and the emergence of popular demands for greater state participation in mining rents and in the regulation of the sector. The content of the demands was less stringent than those in neighbouring countries, as radical statist policies were not on the agenda. The rise to power of Ollanta Humala in 2011 generated expectations that policies would be implemented that would incorporate these popular demands. During his first weeks in office, Humala's government introduced new taxes and promoted long-awaited regulations. However, over the course of a few months, Humala modulated his administration's policies, prioritizing the attraction of private investment in the mining sector and subordinating all other policies to that objective. The weakness of the PNP, the features of the political groups with which Humala partnered, and the historically-proven capacity of the Peruvian economic elite to exert influence on policy-makers are among the factors explaining Humala's change of perspective.

Humala's accommodation of conventional policies reinforces Peruvian dependency on the primary-export-led economic model and on the crucial role of private mining companies. Humala seemed to be locked in the logic of private interests: (i) the Peruvian economic bonanza is, to an important extent, based on private investment in the mining sector; (ii) the state should facilitate the activities of private mining companies in the country; (iii) the state should benefit from increased economic activity and more revenues; but (iv) companies will grow more powerful and economic diversification will become more difficult.

Moreover, Humala supported the policies of previous governments that gave up playing any significant role in planning the development of the country. Despite belonging to a 'nationalist' party, Humala has substituted the idea of development – crucial for nation building – with 'inclusion'. This conveys the idea of satisfaction with the current economic model, which fails to incorporate some groups into the current processes of development. However, the current model gives mining companies the power to make decisions on two types of parameters that determine the direction of national development.

First, the mining companies are de facto planners of the country. They plan the territory, because all other activities are subordinated to the presence of mining operations. They also determine the level of extraction at any given time and the amount and timing of investments. Unsurprisingly, the coordinated action of a handful of mining companies in moderating production can significantly reduce the national GDP, exports, and fiscal revenues, putting pressure on the government. Second, the state has also transferred the capacity to decide how to spend mining revenues. In fact more than 50 per cent of all mining revenues goes to subnational governments, which use the money to finance a myriad of small investment projects with very limited capacity to diversify the economy. Furthermore, the government has granted to the mining companies the capacity to decide how to invest public revenues through schemes such as the PMSP and 'projects for taxes'. The result is the reinforcement of the role of the mining companies vis-à-vis the state and increased dependency on the mining sector.

Notes

1 The research on which this chapter is based has been supported by the Ford Foundation through the grant n° 1115-0635, as part of the research project: 'Extractive industry, decentralization and development: an Andean comparative study', and by a Marie Curie Career Integration Grant from the European Research Executive Agency (PCIG10-GA-2011-303631).
2 In nominal prices and calculated in $US (INEI 2014).
3 All mines built between 1992 and 2004 were exempted from the payment of royalties.
4 In Peruvian Spanish, *canon* has come to mean 'a rule for the devolution to sub-national governments of revenue collected by central government'.
5 The law fulfilled Article 121 of the Peruvian Constitution, which recognizes that right but does not fix a percentage.
6 Law n° 27506.
7 Formula for distribution of mining royalties: 20% to the municipality of the producing district; 20% to the municipalities of the producing provinces; 40% to the municipalities of the producing regions; and 20% to the regional government.
8 Interviews with Eduardo Carhuaricra, one of the promoters of the law (Lima, October 2011) and Cecilia Blume at that time advisor at the MEF (Lima, October 2011).
9 Personal interview with Ysaac Cruz (Lima, September 2008).
10 Personal interview with Raúl Benavides (Lima, June 2007).
11 Personal interviews with senior manager of a mining company (Lima, June 2007).
12 A reference to Aesop's fable about a dog that does not allow the cattle to eat hay, because it cannot eat hay.
13 See Table 10.1 to compare with the total amount collected previously.
14 Personal interview with official parliamentary deputy (Lima, October 2011).
15 Although negotiators mentioned an additional 3,000 million new soles, the actual figure was lower, despite the inclusion of new mines expected to go into operation in the next few years.
16 In 2013 Law 30138 modified the law of 2008 to facilitate its use by companies.

17 Conga is a 4.8 billion dollar project of Yanacocha – a company owned by Newmont (US-based), Buenaventura (Peru), and the International Financial Corporation of the World Bank.
18 Recording of the original speech available at https://www.youtube.com/ watch?v=lslloKzTEpE. [Accessed 7 July 2015].
19 Interviews with two persons who were contacted by Humala (Lima, November 2011).
20 The Socialist Party of Javier Diaz-Canseco was the most important among those parties.
21 Interview in Lima in October 2011.
22 Interview with former advisor to the Premier (Lima, February 2013).
23 In 2014, MINEM (2014) reported a portfolio of project investments close to $US 62 billion.
24 Interview with two senior managers of mining companies who participated in the negotiation of the new taxes (Lima, November 2011).
25 Personal interview with Cecilia Blume (Lima, October 2011).
26 Eliodoro Mayorga was one of the specialists who participated in the privatization of the Peruvian state-owned oil and energy companies in the early 1990s.
27 Interview with General Director of Mining Production in the MINEM (Lima, November 2009).
28 In 2006 Garcia's government introduced legislation reducing salaries in the high levels of the public sector.
29 Interview with official of the Swiss Embassy (Lima, April 2012) and with consultant of the National Authority of the Civil Service – SERVIR (Lima, April 2012).

Bibliography

Arellano-Yanguas, J. (2012). Mining and Conflict in Peru: Sowing the Minerals, Reaping a Hail of Stones. In Bebbington, A. (ed.). *Social Conflict, Economic Development and the Extractive Industry: Evidence from South America*. London: Routledge.

Arellano-Yanguas, J. (2011). ¿Minería sin fronteras? Conflicto y desarrollo en regiones mineras de Perú. Lima: IEP y PUCP.

Banco Central De Reserva Del Perú. (2014). *Estadísticas*. [Online] Available from: http:// www.bcrp.gob.pe/bcr/Cuadros/Cuadros-Anuales-Historicos.html. [Accessed: 18 August 2014].

Bebbington, A. (2007). *Mining and Development in Peru*. London: Peru Support Group.

Bebbington, A. (2009). 'The new extraction? Rewriting the political ecology of the Andes?' *NACLA Report on the Americas* 42(5), pp. 12–20.

Campbell, B., Roy-Grégoire, E., and Laforce, M. (2011). Regulatory Frameworks, Issues of Legitimacy, Responsibility, and Accountability: Reflections Drawn form the PERCAN Initiative. In Sagebien, J. and Lindsay, N. (eds.). *Governance ecosystems: CSR in the Latin American Mining Sector*. Basingstoke: Palgrave Macmillan.

Dammert, A. and Molinelli, F. (2007). *Panorama de la minería en Perú*, Lima: Osinergmin.

Durand, F. (2012). El Señor de los Anillos. *Quehacer* (185). p. 9–23.

García Pérez, A. (2007). El síndrome del Perro del Hortelano, *El Comercio*. 28th Octobre. p. A4.

Gudynas, E. (2009). Diez Tesis Urgentes Sobre el Nuevo Extractivismo. In Schuldt, J. and Acosta, A. (eds.), *Extractivismo, política y sociedad*. Quito: CAAP.

INEI. (2014). *Perú, Compendio Estadístico 2013*. Lima: Instituto Nacional de Estadística e Informática.

Jiménez, F. (2014). Ollanta Humala: la Continuidad de la Modernización neocolonial. [Online] 14 July. Available from: http://felixjimenez.blogspot.com.es/2014/07/ollanta-humala-la-continuidad-de-la.html. [Accessed: 25 March 2015].

Martinez-Alier, J. (2002). *The Environmetalism of the Poor.* Cheltenham: Edward Elgar Publishing Limited.

Ministerio De Energía Y Minas. (2014). *Cartera de Proyectos Mineros.* Lima: MEM.

Ministerio De Energía Y Minas. (2007). Empresas Mineras deben Promover Turismo, Agronegocios, Textiles, y Ganadería. [Online, press release] 19th July. Available from: http://intranet.minem.gob.pe/AppWeb/AppIntranet/Notihoy/notihoy_3412.pdf. [Accessed: 27th August, 2014].

Monge, C. (2012). Humala y las Industrias Extractivas: Poca Transformación Y Mucha Continuidad. In Toche, E. (ed.). *La Gran Continuidad.* Lima: Desco.

Otto, J. (2011). *Analysis of Peruvian Mineral Sector Fiscal Reform Options.* Lima: Ministerio de Economía y Finanzas.

Reuters. (2014). Luis Miguel Castilla, el omnipotente ministro que marca el rumbo económico de Perú. [Online] 2nd May. Available from: http://gestion.pe/economia/castilla-omnipotente-ministro-que-marca-rumbo-economico-peru-2096107 [Accessed: 12 June 2015].

Schiling-Vacaflor, A., and Flemmer, R. (2013). *Why is Prior Consultation Not Yet an Effective Tool For Conflict Resolution? The Case Of Peru.* Hamburg: GIGA.

SUNAT. (2014). *Ingresos Tributarios por Actividad Económica.* [Online] Available from: http://www.sunat.gob.pe/estadisticasestudios/nota_tributaria/cdro_31.xls. [Accessed: 18 August 2014].

The Economist. (2014). Peru's Italian Job: Economic Success Cannot Indefinitely Co-Exist With Political Weakness. *The Economist.* 12 April, p.50.

Thorp, R. (2012). The Challenges Of Mining-Based Development in Peru. In R. Thorp, R., Battistelli, S., Guichaoua, Y., Orihuela, J.C and M. Paredes (eds.). *The devopmental challenges of mining and oil: lessons from Africa and Latin America.* Basingstoke: Palgrave Macmillan.

Thorp, R., and Bertram, G. (1978). *Peru 1890–1977: Growth and Policy in an Open Economy.* London: The MacMillan Press.

11 Resource nationalism in the plurinational state of Bolivia

Lorenzo Pellegrini

Introduction

The electoral success of Evo Morales – sworn in as president in January 2006 – coincided with numerous departures from recent Bolivian history. The Morales Administration has been hailed as revolutionary, anti-hegemonic and globally influential (Dunkerley 2007; Escobar 2010). Two distinguishing features of the recent transformation in Bolivia are the nationalization of natural resources and the ensuing increase in government revenues that finance high levels of public investment and expanded social policies. Underpinning these processes is a discourse of resource nationalism, which claims that colonial patterns of foreign exploitation are being broken and the benefits of extracting natural resources are accruing to the Bolivian population at large. At the same time, and similarly related to anti-imperialist struggles, the country has been re-founded with a new constitution based on alternative development models, which acknowledges the plurinational character of the country, and endorses indigenous autonomy (Tockman and Cameron 2014). However, the indigenous territories where autonomy should be exercised often coincide with the areas where the extractive frontier is expanding and intensifying. This overlap creates tensions between some indigenous organizations and the very government that institutionalized their right to autonomy. These organizations – acting as resistance movements – are also using a discourse draped in natural resource nationalism, to defend their autonomy and resist foreign-led exploitation of natural resources. This chapter investigates the tensions generated by the extractive process and the way these are legitimized by and resisted through nationalist discourses.

We view a 'discourse' as a group of statements in the Foucauldian sense (Foucault 1972; Peet 1996). In fact, by examining the exercise of governmental power beyond the use of force, we interpret the nationalist discourse employed by state authorities as 'governamentality': shaping citizens as subjects that are functional to the state's grand objectives (Foucault 2008). Thus, a discourse can be used by the state to discipline its citizens and generate obedience without the use of force. In other words, a discourse may serve to assert (state) leadership by promoting worldviews that become common sense, and ultimately contribute to consensus around a political programme (Gramsci 1975). At the same time, state policies can also be resisted by groups that employ variations of the same (nationalist) discourse to legitimize their actions and engender counter-hegemonic opposition.

The discourse we focus on here is resource nationalism. Giddens' definition of nationalism helps us to see how nationalism can apply to natural resources: 'the definition of practices, programmes and policies that are in the "general interest", as opposed to those that favour the sectional interests of groups or classes. The more the state becomes administratively unified, the greater the degree to which government must appeal to the "general interest" (in some formulation or other) in order to sustain a basis for its rule' (Giddens 1985: 220).

In fact, some degree of nationalism is part and parcel of the process of modern state-building and also at the root of definitions of self and otherness (i.e., Sand 2010; Pellegrini and Tasciotti 2014). In the case of Bolivia, the public discourse is replete with references to the influence of foreign interests and their desire to exploit the resources belonging to the Bolivian people (Pellegrini 2015). This nationalist discourse is a response to a colonial history marked by the domination of foreign powers, foreign intervention (the Chaco War), and foreign influence that characterized the first half of the twentieth century, when, for example, the director of the oil and mining department was from North America, and the commanders in chief of the Bolivian army were first French and then German (Zavaleta 1986: 234–54). Nationalist sentiment has re-emerged as central to Bolivian politics, and was epitomized by the events of the so-called 'gas war' when popular protest, following an agreement to export gas through construction of a pipeline in Chile, led to the resignation of President Sanchez de Lozada in 2003 (Dangl 2007), and continues to mark the discussion on natural resources and extractive policies.

The chapter begins by providing a broad overview of the role of extractivism and alternative development models in the Bolivian Constitution and the National Development Plan. The following section discusses concrete policies in the extractive sector and the way in which the government and opposition movements have used resource nationalism as a discourse to promote their ideas. Subsequently, we examine Bolivia in the international context by juxtaposing prominent positions on climate change with infrastructural investment for regional integration. The chapter concludes by linking the debates about resource nationalism to the concepts of governmentality and discourse.

'Living well' and extractivism

To understand the role played by natural resource nationalism in Bolivia we need to frame it within the broader politics of the period following the election of President Evo Morales. The radical political and policy changes of this period are epitomized by the new Constitution (2009) and the National Development Plan (PND 2006). The Constitution fundamentally transformed the structure of the state and made significant political, social and symbolic changes to existing state-society relations (Schilling-Vacaflor 2011). The PND was the first comprehensive planning document produced by the Morales' administration. Its enactment coincided with the increase in state revenues that resulted from the hydrocarbon nationalization (2006), and it provided a broad framework for the use of these revenues. In fact, both the Constitution and National Development Plan were based on, and reinforced the underlying logic of the nationalizations: extractive activities would provide financial resources to the state; in turn, the state would use these resources to fuel an industrialization drive expected to further increase demand for extractive industries. Despite the focus on extractives, the Constitution and the National Development Plan also included several references to alternative development models.

The new Constitution re-founded Bolivia as a 'plurinational' state and recognized indigenous cosmology and autonomous organizations based on indigenous territories. In this regard, it underlined a historical bifurcation with the past 'in a country that has long exalted its mestizo character [...], and looked to the North for its model of development' (Walsh 2010: 18). In the Constitution, the overall objectives and values of the Bolivian state and society were redefined to embrace a development model that was presented as an alternative to the western one. One of the main points of departure was the recognition of the concept of *vivir bien* (living well) as an alternative to *vivir mejor* (living better). *Vivir bien* captures the idea of living a satisfactory life in all of its spheres, rather than striving for continuous material improvements, and is sometimes translated as 'collective wellbeing'. The concept originated in the cosmology of the indigenous people of the Andean Region and denotes a way of living 'based on the communion of human beings and nature and on the spatial-temporal-harmonious totality of existence. That is, on the necessary interrelation of beings, knowledges, logics, and rationalities of thought, action, existence and living' (Walsh 2010: 18).

With regard to the non-developmental objectives intrinsic to *vivir bien*, David Choquehuanca, Minister of Foreign Affairs of Bolivia, suggested that the 'living well' paradigm differed radically from 'living better', which is central to the western concept of development. He also marked the difference between a capitalism that emphasized accumulation and a socialism that focused on people's needs and societal wellbeing. 'Living better translates into egoism, individualism, indifference towards the others and a one-sided focus on profit. The capitalist doctrine promotes people's exploitation that concentrates wealth in few hands, while living well promotes a simple life' (*La Razón*, 31 January 2010). These considerations echoed the Constitution:

> The state embraces and promotes as moral-ethical principles of the plural society: ama qhilla, ama llulla, ama suwa (don't be lazy, don't be a liar, don't be a thief), suma qamaña (living well), ñandereko (harmonious life), teko kavi (good life), ivi maraei (land with no evil), and qhapaj ñan (noble life).
> (Bolivia 2009)

The recognition of these indigenous values was part of changes embodied in numerous rhetorical and practical initiatives that aimed to culturally and socially emancipate the indigenous majority. In this emancipatory process, new values that resonated with the traditional indigenous cosmology, including a harmonious relationship with nature, were promoted by the state (*Upside Down World*, 19 February 2015). Official recognition of these values was coupled with the endorsement of indigenous peoples' right to control and manage their territories according to their own autonomous forms of organization. These rights and autonomies were central to President Morales' political project, and were mentioned in the first article of the Constitution, while implementation was enshrined in the second (Bolivia 2009).

Notwithstanding these changes, the revolutionary agenda of the Constitution was predicated on the continued extraction of natural resources and their industrialization, and more generally, on the expansion of activities based on the primary sector. The ultimate objective of the sectoral policies was to capture a larger proportion of the value-added by processing primary goods (Bolivia 2009). It was intended that the state would play a leading role through state-owned companies that retained 'strategic control' of these value chains. In this regard, the process of industrializing natural resources and diversifying the economy was set as a priority.

It is worth noting that the project to develop industrial activities based on natural resources has a long history in Bolivia and was also topical during the 1952 Revolution. An exemplary depiction of this resource nationalism is powerfully represented in a 1958 mural –*The History of Bolivian Petroleum*. The Bolivian artist, Walter Solón, depicted a future in which the extraction and processing of hydrocarbons would produce dividends through investments in education and technology, and spur the take-off of national economic development (Pellegrini 2015).

The prominence, in the Constitution, of the industrialization of natural resources, showed this issue was back on the centre stage of Bolivian politics. While the extractivist aspects of the Constitution created tensions with *vivir bien*, they complemented the neo-developmentalist model whose main tenets were to promote the extraction of natural resources and the appropriation of the revenues by the state in order to support social programmes and investments in socio-economic development (Zabala Vásquez 2006; Mendonça Cunha and Santaella Gonçalves 2010; Costoya 2010). Essentially, this model endorsed a re-allocation of resources, benefiting the national economy and especially the poor at the expense of foreign multinational companies, but without changing the fundamental structure of the economy. In contrast, the *vivir bien* discourse was a radical break with mainstream development models, due to its objective of improving rights and dignity at the individual and collective level.

However, the tension between the *vivir bien* and neo-developmentalist discourses was partly transcended by resource nationalism: nationalization of the hydrocarbon sector generated revenue for the state, but was also seen as a necessary step to achieve sovereignty and break from the colonial past. The nationalization process was a popular measure that was consistent with nationalist sentiment regarding natural resources and provided popularity and democratic

legitimacy to the government (Gudynas 2010, 2012). This sentiment was historically rooted in the widely held, if contentious, belief that the disastrous Chaco
War (1932–35) was a proxy war that the Bolivian state fought for the US-based
multinational company Standard Oil (see Dunkerley 1984; and Klein 2011). The
war demonstrated the lack of preparedness of the state and the army, resulting in
enormous casualties and the loss of most of the Chaco region to Paraguay. These
events marked the 'Chaco generation' and created a persistent and widespread
consensus that the country was in the hands of a corrupt elite manipulated by
foreign interests to the detriment of the national population. The natural wealth
of the country played a central role in this thesis: it was the source of foreign
greed and was appropriated by foreign interests instead of improving the lot of
Bolivian people who were the legitimate owners of this wealth. It is worth noting
that this view did not question extraction *per se*, but rather, radically questioned
the distribution of benefits generated by extractive activities.

The paradox of promoting both *vivir bien* and a development model based on
the extraction and industrialization of natural resources was also evident in the
main planning document of the Morales administration: the National Development
Plan (PND), announced in April, and published in June 2006 (Sanjines 2006;
Gobierno de Bolivia 2006).[1] The *vivir bien* discourse is apparent in the PND
sections on the new development model that opens the plan, while the neo-
developmentalist discourse emerges in the sections of the PND pertaining to the
'strategic sectors' of the Bolivian economy. The PND proposed an expansion of
extractive activities coupled with an industrialization of natural resources, with
the objective of generating added-value, and moving beyond Bolivia's past as an
exporter of raw materials (Gobierno de Bolivia 2006).

Extractive activities and nationalism

Beyond policy documents, the prominent role played by extractive industries in
the Bolivian economy is demonstrated by exploratory activities, the granting of
new concessions and contracts with investors, and the arrival of mega-projects,
which are pushing the extraction frontier outward. As extractive industries
expand into non-traditional areas (i.e., outside the eastern lowlands), the concessions increasingly overlap with indigenous territories and national parks (Ribera
2010). One particularly vivid example of the tensions generated by contending
visions of development is the overlap between hydrocarbon exploration activities
around Palos Blancos, and the territory of the Mosetén people. Exploratory activity in this area, carried out in 2009 and 2010, was commissioned by the company
Petroandina, a joint venture of Yacimientos Petrolíferos Fiscales Bolivianos
(YPFB), the Bolivian state-owned oil company, and Petróleos de Venezuela
(PVDSA), the Venezuelan state-owned oil company (Pellegrini and Ribera
Arismendi 2012). This company is emblematic of the state-state and South-South
partnerships that are becoming increasingly common throughout Latin America,
especially among countries that have leftist governments and large extractive
industries (Hogenboom and Fernández Jilberto 2009). Exploration activities,

however, were conducted by a US company and included cutting seismic lines: straight paths were cleared of vegetation and explosives were implanted and detonated in order to record seismic waves that reveal the extension of hydrocarbons deposits. Analysis of the seismic data gave evidence of a commercially-viable deposit, permitting the project to move forward to exploratory drilling.

The exploration venture resulted in some environmental damages associated with the clearing of the paths in ecologically sensitive areas and with the use of explosives.[2] More prominently, in terms of social impacts, the activities also resulted in a series of conflicts with and within indigenous organizations. The Organization of Indigenous Mosetén People (OPIM – *Organización del Pueblo Indígena Mosetén*), the local indigenous organization that represented the people living in the Mosetén indigenous territory, complained that the company directly negotiated access to lands with individuals and funded parallel organizations with the aim of delegitimizing OPIM.[3] That is, the company appeared to use a 'divide and conquer strategy' that, according to other authors, has been used by multinational oil companies since they started to operate in the region (i.e., Sawyer 2004). For example, evidence suggests that the consultation and compensation rights of the Mosetén people were not fully implemented due to the subdivision of consultation into small groups of people, and the exclusion of the organization that represented Mosetenes people as a whole (*Erbol*, 28 March 2010).

The exploration activities also had a remarkable economic impact on the local community because of the employment opportunities that were created. These opportunities included formal employment contracts that were very rare in this economically marginal area and also employment for community leaders who were hired as 'facilitators' of the company's operations. Furthermore, smaller but significant handouts were provided to the population (such as work tools, meals, etc.), and compensation at the community level included a number of 'public' works: squares, meeting rooms, electricity generators and wiring. The distribution of costs and benefits associated with exploration activities also engendered conflicts that include threats, physical violence and attacks on private and communal property. These conflicts pitted the members of OPIM –who wanted to negotiate more comprehensive compensation for the whole Mosetén people – against community members who negotiated more limited, but direct, compensation and favoured the start of exploratory works as soon as possible (see Bolivia 2011; LIDEMA 2010: 61–74; Pellegrini and Ribera Arismendi 2012).[4] The process contradicted the government discourse and the provisions included in the Constitutions regarding the recognition of indigenous territories and indigenous forms of autonomy and self-government, and commitments to engage in activities affecting indigenous territories only after a consultation process carried out in 'good faith'.[5]

Resource nationalism surfaced several times during the dispute and was visible in the discourse of both proponents and opponents to the project. Thus, proponents denounced those opposed to the project for being in the pockets of the 'gringos' and rejecting a project owned by the Bolivian government and advancing decolonization and the national interest. In fact, this accusation was painted on the walls of OPIM's offices in graffiti: 'OPIM of the gringos'.[6] This allegation is reminiscent of discourses on 'green imperialism' which claim that developing countries are having their natural resources expropriated by rich countries asserting their control primarily through international environmental conventions and transnational NGOs (i.e. Driessen 2005). In this view, opposition to extractive activities was a form of imperialism that prevented the development of the area, betterment of local living standards, and deprived Bolivians, once again, from the benefits of their own natural resources (Pellegrini and Ribera Arismendi 2012).

The opposition camp retorted that the involvement of PVDSA and Venezuelan financing in the project was itself another twist of neo-colonialism, as was the exploration contract to a US-based company, and the extraction and sale of Bolivian hydrocarbons in international markets that reinforced the country's dependency on commodity exports (LIDEMA 2010). In this view, the modern Bolivian state was repeating its neo-colonial mission: to facilitate the extraction of natural resources by multinational companies. It should be noted, however, the direct involvement of the state in extractive activities (primarily through the state-owned oil company, government agencies and MAS (*Movimiento al Socialismo*)-led municipalities) made resistance to extraction, such as that by the Mosetén people, more difficult, because it reduced the opportunities for local communities to find support in state organizations.

A widening of the extraction frontier was also envisioned by Supreme Decree 675 of October 2010 that opened a number of new areas, including parkland, to exploration. These parks included the Madidi National Park and the adjacent Pilon Lajas Reserve (*Oecoamazonia* 21 March 2011), which were ranked twice by National Geographic as among the top-ten ecotourism destinations worldwide. The importance of the tourism industry in this region, and the presence of relatively strong indigenous organizations, suggest that socio-environmental conflicts could occur as a result of hydrocarbon exploration.

Interestingly, Vice-president Álavaro García Linera promoted the expansion of the hydrocarbon frontier to the National Parks by questioning the very existence of the parks, and arguing that they were mostly established by neoliberal governments in the 1980s and 1990s in order to keep resources out of reach from the national population, and set them aside for foreign interests (*Economía Bolivia*, 23 May 2013). In response to these declarations, the progressive think-tank CEDIB (Bolivian Centre for Documentation and Information) observed that while foreign oil companies controlled up to 13 million hectares of the Bolivian territory in 1999, by 2007 this area had diminished to less than 3 million ha; and after 5 years of Morales government this area had reached the all-time high of 22 million ha. These figures underlined the increased appropriation of Bolivian national resources by foreign companies, even after nationalization (*Hidrocarburos Bolivia*, 31 May 2013).

Similar tensions can be identified when juxtaposing the posturing of the Bolivian government on the international environmental scene with its support for the rapid development of South American economic infrastructure. The next section examines the use of the discourse of resource nationalism in the realm of climate change and infrastructure development.

Morales on the global stage: environment and integration

President Morales has been on the centre stage in the international environmental movement, especially with respect to climate justice. At the Copenhagen Climate Change Conference in 2009, he called on the world leaders: 'Our objective is to save humanity and not just half of humanity. We are here to save Mother Earth. Our objective is to reduce climate change to [under] 1 degree centigrade'. Limiting warming to 1 degree is a radically ambitious proposal since most of the representatives were aiming at much more modest objectives – between 2 and 4 degrees. He further added that 'The real cause of climate change is the capitalist system. If we want to save the earth then we must end that economic model. Capitalism wants to address climate change with carbon markets. We denounce those markets and the countries [which promote them]. It's time to stop making money from the disgrace that they have perpetrated' (*The Guardian*, 16 December 2009).

The tensions between alternative development models and the extractivist model were also reflected in the international arena where President Morales has been an active proponent of grassroots initiatives to tackle global environmental issues. Bolivia's profile on climate change became even more prominent since the Morales administration promoted and hosted the 'World People's Conference on Climate Change and the Rights of Mother Earth' in April 2010, Cochabamba. The conference was inaugurated by President Morales who set the tone of the discussion by proclaiming that 'either capitalism dies, or Mother Earth dies' (*Agencia Boliviana de Información*, 26 February 2010). The conference conclusions were equally unambiguous, stating that in order to tackle climate change, capitalism – its root cause – would also have to be addressed. Beyond some broad statements regarding the need to live in harmony with nature, some parts of the declaration applied specifically to the situation in Bolivia and Latin America as a whole, and deserve to be cited at length.

> We […] denounce the way in which the capitalist model imposes mega-infrastructure projects and invades territories with extractive projects, water privatization, and militarized territories, expelling indigenous peoples from their lands, inhibiting food sovereignty and deepening socio-environmental crisis. We demand recognition of the right of all peoples, living beings, and Mother Earth to have access to water, and we support the proposal of the Government of Bolivia to recognize water as a Fundamental Human Right.
>
> (People's Agreement, 2010)

The whole declaration was wholeheartedly endorsed and defined a 'triumph' by President Morales (Guerrero 2010).

The tensions between the governmental discourse on the international scene and domestic policies became apparent when Bolivian activists made their dissent heard in the World People's Conference at the 18th roundtable, the conclusions of which were excluded from the meeting's formal documents. The 18th roundtable focused precisely on the violations of Mother Earth's rights and the socio-environmental impact of extractive activities in Bolivia, including those carried out during President Morales' administrations (*Upside Down World*, 7 July 2010). The case of the TIPNIS (National Park and Indigenous Territory Isiboro Sécure)[7] was included in the list of twenty cases of violation of nature and indigenous rights explicitly mentioned in the final declaration of the roundtable, and is emblematic of the contradictions between competing discourses and policies that are being promoted by the Morales administration.

The construction of the TIPNIS road was an emblematic case that attracted both national and international attention (BBC, 15 August 2011). A planned 300 km road that would cut the Natural Park and Indigenous Territory Isiboro Sécure in half met with resistance from local indigenous groups that feared environmental impacts in their territory and increased pressure on their land by settlers from the highlands. The settlers' argument was particularly controversial both because such land invasions are the source of ongoing conflicts among indigenous groups in Bolivia, and because the settlers are staunch supporters of the MAS government (Fontana 2014). President Morales himself was a former settler, as were the coca farmers that he represented as trade union leader. The settlers' unions in the Isiboro Sécure area and throughout the lowlands were the main supporters of the road that was intended to facilitate the transportation of agricultural crops (BBC, 24 September 2011).

The position of President Morales on the TIPNIS road was unambiguous: he declared that environmental impacts were an unavoidable side effect of developmental activities and that the local indigenous populations opposing the road were being manipulated by obscure interests and by European NGOs.[8] The charge that European NGOs were trying to establish a transnational conservation regime over the Amazon, thus expropriating Bolivian wealth, was another call-out to the nationalist discourse on natural resources, previously discussed as 'green imperialism'.

Opposition to the construction project and lack of negotiation opportunities were the leading reasons for the organization of the 8th march of indigenous people in 2011, of some 600 kms from the Amazonian Beni department to La Paz. The march was opposed by settlers along the route and was joined by other indigenous people, protesting the polarization marking Bolivian indigenous movements. The lowland indigenous people marched to demand respect for their territories, autonomy and consultation rights recognized by national and international law. On the latter point, President Morales retorted that, in any case, consultation rights did not include the right to 'say no' to an initiative – such as the TIPNIS road – that was necessary for the development of the country. In another remarkable twist, the Brazilian government was financing the road construction (80% of the investment through a low interest loan) as part of the Initiative for the Integration of the Regional Infrastructure of South America (IIRSA), another manifestation of the new South-South cooperation patterns, but also a fresh opportunity to invoke nationalist sentiments, this time by the opposition groups.[9]

Thus, nationalist sentiment can be leveraged in similar but opposite discourses in order to support or to oppose extractive activities. In the former case, nationalism is used to juxtapose the interests of the nation versus 'green imperialists'. In this view the interests of the nation are defended by a legitimate national government that uses the revenues generated by extractive activities to finance social policies and public infrastructure. Interestingly the Bolivian government, apart from the resource nationalism, has also embraced a discourse on alternative development – *vivir bien* – and in the international arena has stressed its opposition to global capitalist dynamics that are patently the ultimate cause of environmental disruption. These positions, if contentious and conflicting, are a reflection of the different groups and their diverse ideologies that are represented by the MAS government and can also be interpreted as an attempt by the governing party to occupy the political space that otherwise could develop into fertile ground for opposition. The environmental and indigenous groups that oppose extractive activities also use a nationalist discourse to highlight the foreignness of companies and capital used in the extractive industries and to stress that commodities are feeding global markets. They argue that the national interest is undermined – rather than pursued – through extractive activities.

Conclusions

In this study we surveyed some of the most contentious issues concerning natural resources management, and public policies more generally, in Bolivia. The discussion examined the 2009 Constitution, the 2006 National Development Plan, as well as concrete examples of extractive and infrastructure projects, and the government's international positioning on climate change. Extractivism and alternative development models both compete and coexist within government programmes in Bolivia. In terms of the policies and management of the extractive sector, state institutions are using the discourse of resource nationalism to legitimize the expansion and deepening of extractivist activities. We can interpret the use of the resource nationalism discourse as an exercise of governmentality; in other words as an attempt to shape the mentality and rationality of the Bolivian citizenry in ways that are compatible with governmental strategies (Foucault 2008). Similarly, but conversely, social movements, are basing their anti-hegemonic approach to extractivism on a discourse that also leverages resource nationalism. That is, they employ the hegemonic discourse of resource nationalism to construct anti-hegemonic resistance to extractivist policies (Gramsci 1975: 19, 67–69). Resource nationalism is a hegemonic discourse that is instrumentally used both by proponents of redoubled extractive activities as well as by groups opposing extraction and promoting a transition towards alternative models of development. That is, contrasting social groups are leveraging nationalist discourses to pursue their objectives, suggesting that in the Bolivian context, resource nationalism *per se* is not a strategy, but rather a rhetorical instrument used to garner political support and legitimize views and actions.

Notes

1 For an in-depth analysis and comparison with previous planning documents from a participative perspective, see Pellegrini 2012.
2 Interview with Marco Ribera Arismenti (LIDEMA, La Paz).
3 Interviews carried out by the author in July 2011 with current and former OPIM leadership.
4 At the time of writing, the operations to drill the Liquimuni well had been started, but were taking place in an area just outside the indigenous territory.
5 These rights are also part of the International Labour Organisation's Convention No. 169 and the UN Declaration on indigenous rights that are enshrined in the Bolivian legal system and have been adopted by the Congress.
6 In Spanish, it read 'OPIN (sic.) de gringos'.
7 TIPNIS stands for *Territorio Indígena Parque Nacional Isiboro Sécure*.
8 In this charged atmosphere the leader of the pro-government trade union CSUTCB (*Confederación Sindical Única de Trabajadores Campesinos de Bolivia*), Roberto Coraite, bluntly stated that the construction of the TIPNIS road would improve the life of the indigenous residents and allow them to 'cease living like savages' (*La Razón*, 7 September 2011).
9 This conflict continues to develop at the time of writing of this chapter, and its conclusion cannot be foreseen. Nevertheless, the conflict offers a striking example of the tensions that mark the Morales government's administration of natural resources.

Bibliography

Agencia Boliviana De Información (26 February 2010). Evo Morales: Muere el capitalism o muere la Madre Tierra. Agencia Prensa Rural. Available from http://www.prensarural. org/spip/spip.php?article3655. [Accessed: 8 June 2015].

BBC (15 August 2011). Indigenous Bolivians march against Amazon road. Available from: http://www.bbc.co.uk/news/world-latin-america-14536163. [Accessed: 8 June 2015].

BBC (24 September 2011). Bolivia Amazon road protesters break police blockade. Available from: [http://www.bbc.com/news/world-latin-america-15048897]. Accessed: 8 June 2015.

Bolivia, Plurinational State Of (2009). Constitution. La Paz, Presidencia de la República

Bolivia. Tribunal Constitucional Plurinacional (2011). Sentencia Constitucional 0429/2011-R. 18 April: Sucre, Bolivia. Available from http://buscador.tcpbolivia.bo/ (S(hg0vpzfqyustwuilnu3uej2a))/WfrJurisprudencia.aspx. [Accessed: 6 July 2015].

Costoya, M. M. (2010). Politics of trade in post neoliberal Latin America: The case of Bolivia. *Bulletin of Latin American Research*, 30(1), pp 80–95.

Dangl, B. (2007). *The Price of Fire: Resource Wars and Social Movements in Bolivia*. Oakland, CA: AK Press.

Dunkerley, J. (1984). *Rebellion in the Veins: Political Struggle in Bolivia, 1952–1982*. London: Verso.

Dunkerley, J. (2007). *Bolivia: Revolution and the Power of History in the Present*. London: Institute for the Study of the Americas, University of London.

Economía Bolivia (23 May, 2013). Se cae el discurso "pachamamista"; ahora se irá en busca del petróleo de las reservas naturales protegidas. Available from: www. economiabolivia.net/2013/05/23/se-cae-el-discurso-pachamamista-ahora-se-ira-en-busca-del-petroleo-de-las-reservas-naturales-protegidas/. [Accessed: 8 June 2015].

ERBOL (28 March, 2010). Petroandina no quiere indemnizar a mosetenes por exploración petrolera. Available from: http://www.ftierra.org/ft/index.php?option=com_content&view=article&id=2289:rair&catid=98:noticias&Itemid=175. [Accessed: 8 June 2015].

Escobar, A. (2010). Latin America at a crossroads: alternative modernizations, post-liberalism, or post-development? *Cultural Studies*, 24(1), pp. 1–65.

Folgarait, L. (1998). *Mural Painting and Social Revolution in Mexico, 1920-1940: Art of the New Order*. Cambridge: Cambridge University Press.

Fontana, L. B. (2014). Indigenous peoples vs peasant unions: land conflicts and rural movements in plurinational Bolivia. *Journal of Peasant Studies*, 41(3), pp. 1–23.

Foucault, M. (1972). *The Archeology of Knowledge*. New York: Harper.

Foucault, M. (2008). *The Birth Of Biopolitics: Lectures At The Collège De France, 1978–1979*. New York: Palgrave Macmillan.

Giddens, A. (1985). *A Contemporary Critique of Historical Materialism: The Nation-state and Violence*. Berkeley: University of California Press.

Gobierno De Bolivia (2006). Plan Nacional de Desarrollo. La Paz: Government of Bolivia.

Gramsci, A. (1975). *Quaderni del carcere*. Turin: Einaudi.

Gudynas, E. (2010). El nuevo extractivismo progresista. *El Observador del OBIE*, 8, pp. 1–10.

Gudynas, E. (2012). Estado compensador y nuevos extractivismos: Las ambivalencias del progresismo sudamericano. *Nueva Sociedad*, 237, pp. 128–46.

Guerrero, M.M. (22 April 2010). Evo Morales: Cumbre de Cochabamba es triunfo de los pueblos. Havana: Agencia Cubana de Noticias. Available from http://www.ain.cu/2010/abril/22egevo.htm. [Accessed: 8 June 2015].

Hidrocarburos Bolivia (31 May 2013) CEDIB: ampliación de áreas hidrocarburíferas pone en riesgo sistema de àreas protegidas de Bolivia. Available from: http://www.cedib.org/post_type_titulares/cedib-ampliacion-de-areas-hidrocarburiferas-pone-en-riesgo-sistema-de-areas-protegidas-de-bolivia-hidrocarburos-bolivia-31-5-13/. [Accessed: 8 June 2015].

Hogenboom, B., and Fernández Jilberto, A.E. (2009). The New Left and Mineral Politics: What's New? *European Review of Latin American and Caribbean Studies*, 87, pp. 93–102.

Klein, H.S. (2011). *A Concise History of Bolivia*. Cambridge, Cambridge University Press.

La Razón (7 September 2011). Coraite pide carretera para que indígenas no vivan más como "salvajes". Available from: http://www.enlacesbolivia.com/sp/noticias_proc.asp?Seleccion=751. [Accessed: 8 June 2015].

La Razón, (31 January 2010). Canciller de Bolivia señala los 25 postulados para "Vivir Bien". Plataforma Buen Vivir. Available from: http://www.plataformabuenvivir.com/wp-content/uploads/2012/07/Vivir-Bien-Bolivia-Choquehuanca.pdf. [Accessed: 5 July 2015].

LIDEMA (2010). *La situación ambiental desde las percepciones locales: Testimonios de la gente de las regiones del país*. La Paz, Bolivia, Liga de Defensa del Medio Ambiente (LIDEMA).

Mendonça Cunha, C., and Santaella Gonçalves, R. (2010). The National Development Plan as a Political Economic Strategy in Evo Morales's Bolivia. *Latin American Perspectives*, 37(4), pp. 177.

OECOAMAZONIA (21 March, 2011). Bolivia transforma parque en la Amazonia en zona petrolera. Available from: http://old.kaosenlared.net/noticia/bolivia-transforman-parque-amazonia-zona-petrolera. [Accessed: 8 June 2015].

Peet, R. (1996). A sign taken for history: Daniel Shays' memorial in Petersham, Massachusetts. *Annals of the Association of American Geographers*, 86(1), pp. 21–43.

Pellegrini, L. (2012). Planning and natural resources in Bolivia: Between rules without participation and participation without rules. *Journal of Developing Societies*, 28(2), pp. 185–202.

Pellegrini, L. (2015). Imaginaries of development through extraction: the "History of Bolivian Petroleum". ISS, Erasmus University. The Hague: The Netherlands.

Pellegrini, L., and Tasciotti, L. (2014). Bhutan: Between happiness and horror. *Capitalism Nature Socialism*, 25(3), pp. 103–109.

Pellegrini, L., and Ribera Arismendi, M. (2012). Consultation, compensation and extraction in Bolivia after the "left turn": The case of oil exploration in the north of La Paz Department. *Journal of Latin American Geography*, 11(2), pp. 101–118.

People's Agreement Of Cochabamba. (2010). People's Agreement of Cochabamba. World People's Conference on Climate Change and the Rights of Mother Earth. Cochabamba: Bolivia. Available from https://pwccc.wordpress.com/2010/04/24/peoples-agreement/. [Accessed: 6 July 2015].

Ribera, M. O. (2010). *Hidrocarburos: Análisis general, zona tradicional y norte de La Paz*. La Paz: Liga de defensa del Medio Ambiente (LIDEMA).

Sand, S. (2010). *The Invention of the Jewish People*. London: Verso.

Sanjines, E. (2006). Resumen: Plan Nacional de Desarrollo: Bolivia Digna, Soberana, Productiva y Democrática Para Vivir Bien. Fundación Tierra. La Paz.

Sawyer, S. (2004). *Crude Chronicles: Indigenous Politics, Multinational Oil, and Neoliberalism in Ecuador*. Durham [N.C.], Duke University Press.

Schilling-Vacaflor, A. (2011). Bolivia's new constitution: Towards participatory democracy and political pluralism? *European Review of Latin American and Caribbean Studies/Revista Europea de Estudios Latinoamericanos y del Caribe*, 90, pp. 3–22.

The Guardian (16 December 2009) Evo Morales stuns Copenhagen with demand to limit temperature rise to 1C. Available from: http://www.theguardian.com/environment/2009/dec/16/evo-morales-hugo-chavez. [Accessed: 8 June 2015].

Upside Down World (19 February, 2015). Decolonizing Bolivia's History of Indigenous Resistance: An Interview with Elisa Vega Sillo. Available from: http://upsidedownworld.org/main/bolivia-archives-31/5216-decolonizing-bolivias-history-of-indigenous-resistance-an-interview-with-elisa-vega-sillo. [Accessed: 8 June 2015].

Upside Down World (7 July 2010). Reflections From Bolivia: Water Wars, Climate Wars and Change From Below. Available from: http://upsidedownworld.org/main/bolivia-archives-31/2583-reflections-from-bolivia-water-wars-climate-wars-and-change-from-below. [Accessed: 8 June 2015].

Walsh, C. (2010). Development as Buen Vivir: Institutional arrangements and (de) colonial entanglements. *Development*, 53(1), pp. 15–21.

Zabala Vásquez, J. L. (2006). Lineamientos estratégicos del plan nacional de desarrollo de Bolivia. Monografias.com.

Zavaleta, R. (1986). *Lo nacional-popular en Bolivia*. México D.F.: Siglo XXI.

12 Resource nationalism and the Bolivarian revolution in Venezuela

Daniel Hellinger

Introduction

In 1998, Hugo Chávez Frías, a former lieutenant-colonel cashiered for an attempted coup in 1992, was elected president of Venezuela. Chávez earned a reputation as champion of resource nationalism and critic of neoliberalism in Latin America and the Third World beginning with his hosting the Second Summit of Heads of State and Government of the Organization of Petroleum Exporting Countries (OPEC) in Caracas in 2001. In that same year he decreed a new law that took aim at the *apertura petrolera* (oil opening), a set of policies by which executives of Petróleos de Venezuela S.A. (PDVSA), the state oil company, brought foreign investment back into Venezuela's oil fields for the first time since nationalization in 1975. In 2006 and 2007 foreign companies in joint ventures and operating agreements were required to 'migrate' to comply with new laws requiring majority ownership by PDVSA, in a so-called 're-nationalization' of the oil industry.

Yet one can question just how radical was the turn toward resource nationalism under Chávez. The president never sought return to the pre-*apertura* policy of state monopolization of basic facets of oil exploration, production, and distribution. Most foreign companies complied (however reluctantly) with the mandates to 'migrate' to the terms of the new laws, influenced in part by major new proven reserves that stood at nearly 300 billion barrels, exceeding that of Saudi Arabia in 2014 (according to International Energy Administration estimates). By the time of Chávez's death in early 2013, Venezuela was increasing its reliance on foreign capital, technology and financing in the oil sector. What had changed were the terms on which capital could enter the subsoil to extract hydrocarbons.

Resource nationalism in Bolivarian Venezuela took the form of a reaction to the *apertura*, which was a neoliberal project linked to the global transnationalization of capital. Transnationalization is more than just the expansion of trade and investment flows across national boundaries. As William Robinson puts it, 'Transnationalization occurs when national capitals fuse with other industrializing national capitals in a process of cross-border interpenetration that disembeds them from their nations and locates them in a new supranational space opening up under the global economy' (2004: 14). Before Chávez, PDVSA's executives had sought to 'disembed' Venezuela's subsoil resources from the national space and relocate them in a 'supranational space', that is to treat minerals and hydrocarbons as free gifts of nature to all who would exploit them. Their careers and professional identity had taken shape in the bosom of the transnational oil industry, specifically in the three major foreign companies that dominated extraction in the era before nationalization. They took advantage of the decay of Venezuela's 'pacted democracy' in the wake of the OPEC oil boom of the 1970s to advance their agenda to boost production through the *apertura*.

Chávez also, of course, took advantage of political decay, but he and his Bolivarian comrades rejected PDVSA's attempt to link Venezuela's position as an oil exporter to the interests of consuming countries, rather than the exporting nations of OPEC. As Justin Dargin puts it, 'Chavez [sought] to reverse the humiliating energy policies of an earlier era (the *apertura*) which he viewed as a "giveaway" to Western IOCs [international oil companies]' (2010: 39). His plans for oil were not otherwise well formulated upon taking power, but nationalism and suspicion of the country's elites rapidly moved him toward policies that sought to maintain ownership of subsoil resources within the territorial space of the Venezuelan nation, not 'supranational space'. Dargin captured the Bolivarian attitude well, which saw natural resources as integral to the national territory, and believed 'the sovereign disposition of such resources is part and parcel of the inalienable right of a people's national self-determination' (2010: 6).

This chapter begins with a brief review of the concessionary era and nationalization in Venezuela so that we can better understand: (i) why nationalization did not mean the final triumph of national sovereignty over foreign capital; (ii) how nationalization weakened rather than strengthened state capacity to regulate extraction and maximize appropriation of rents generated by oil exports; and (iii) why the old international regime of production and trade in minerals and hydrocarbons is unlikely to be reborn in the age of transnational capital. We next examine the forces that first gave impetus to the *apertura petrolera*, but which ultimately produced a nationalist reaction in the Chávez era. In the last section we examine how the failure to develop the domestic productive capacity of Venezuela's oil industry leaves Chávez's achievements vulnerable to the forces of transnationalization.

Nationalism and oil in the concessionary era

Oil nationalism in Venezuela is linked closely to the career of Rómulo Betancourt, the country's most important twentieth-century politician and founder of *Acción Democrática* (AD), the country's dominant political party. From 1928 until 1945 he railed in populist style against *imperialismo petrolero*, arguing that the concessions granted to the foreign companies during the dictatorship (1908–1935) of Juan Vicente Gómez were unjust and obtained through corruption. Betancourt's writings (especially Betancourt 1978) portray Venezuelan oil nationalism as the exclusive province of democratically elected governments and, in particular, those headed by AD.

In fact, the earliest stirrings of oil nationalism in Venezuela were visible in the Gómez era. Even then, sectors of Venezuela's financial, commercial, and intellectual elite took notice that the liberal fiscal regime enjoyed by concessionaires in Venezuela, contrasted with the higher royalties and taxes prevailing in the US, where companies were producing mainly for a domestic market, not for export (see Beth 2002; Mommer 1983). The liberal, but unelected, President (General) Isaías Medina Angarita took advantage of a favourable international context (Mexico oil nationalization of 1938; World War II) to legislate the oil reform law of 1943. The most important features of that law established Venezuela's sovereign right to raise taxes on the oil companies, which hitherto had been limited by contracts made in the Gómez years. The reform pushed the state's share of company profits to 60% in 1945, but AD stridently criticized an inducement offered by Medina to gain the company's acceptance of the reform, namely, his extension of the companies' leases for 40 years.

With the conclusion of World War II, prices fell, and with them Venezuela's share of profits. The task of responding to this challenge fell to AD, which had come to power through a coup in late 1945. By this time Betancourt had evolved from firebrand nationalist to reformist democrat, developing a close friendship with Standard Oil's Nelson R. Rockefeller. Rather than relying on the state's sovereign power of taxation, Betancourt negotiated a *modus vivendi* with the three majors, whereby each party agreed to a '50-50' split of profits. Standard took the lead in the negotiations, not least because it could promote '50-50' as a norm in the Middle East, where American companies were competing for concessions with the Europeans.

A coup in 1948 put an end to the *trienio* government, which was beset by domestic political polarization not unlike that prevailing in the Chávez era. A decade of dictatorship induced most elites to compromise on their differences. Betancourt would win Venezuela's first presidential election of December 1958, but beforehand he and other leaders negotiated a series of political pacts that laid the basis for four decades of liberal democratic politics – the 'Punto Fijo' regime, after the name of the villa in Caracas where a power-sharing agreement among non-Communist parties was signed.

AD's '50-50' deal is often portrayed as a nationalist breakthrough (Alexander 1982: 257; Karl 1997: 112). Betancourt always insisted that the Medina reform of 1945 was 'watered down' and 'negotiated behind the back of the people' (1978: 70, 74). But Betancourt had also compromised, promising the companies that royalties and taxes would not be raised without prior consultation. That agreement only became known in 1958 when the interim civilian-military junta that took power after the fall of the dictatorship of General Marcos Pérez Jiménez unilaterally raised oil taxes over the objection of the companies, who made public their 'gentleman's agreement' with Betancourt.

In 1960, responding to the threat raised by increased oil production in the Middle East, and after a fruitless effort to work out a deal with the US to guarantee continued access to its market, Betancourt sent Juan Pérez Alfonzo, Venezuela's oil minister, on a mission to the Middle East. There he gained the support of Saudi Arabia and other Middle Eastern exporters to create OPEC, a cartel of landlord states that have collaborated, with varying degrees of success over time, to defend prices and regulate global supply, much as the companies constituting the famed 'Seven Sisters' were able to do in the middle decades of the twentieth century.[1]

OPEC's economic power became evident after the October 1973 Arab-Israeli War and the Arab oil embargo (Venezuela maintained exports to the West.) The oil companies no longer controlled production levels and pricing over their subsidiaries in OPEC countries. By 1974, in Venezuela, the state was already collecting 80 cents of every dollar of oil exported; the government could freely levy export taxes, leaving the companies with a regulated profit. Also, the largest concessions were due to expire in 1983, and even if renewed, new investments would be needed in fields that were past their peak productivity. The three majors (Standard, Shell and Gulf) approached (outgoing) President Rafael Caldera (1969–1973) to propose compensated nationalization. The new president, Carlos Andres Pérez (1974–1978) oversaw the nationalization law of 1975, and in 1976, PDVSA was created as a holding company with subsidiaries corresponding to each of the old companies, each marketing its production to its former owner, and each managed by the same Venezuelan executives as before.

Before late 1973, no Venezuelan politician or intellectual of any significance had advocated nationalization. The most radical position had been articulated by a maverick Communist, Salvador de la Plaza, a name that few Venezuelans would recognize today. De la Plaza criticized both Medina's reform and Betancourt's 50-50 arrangement, arguing that oil was 'the non-renewable capital of the nation', a natural resource for which the Venezuelan nation should be compensated by royalties for its exhaustion (1996: 135; original, 1958). That position that would form a major part of oil policy in the Chávez years, not least because its architects had studied De la Plaza's writings at the University of the Andes in the state of Merida. One of them was Adán Chávez, brother of Hugo.

Neoliberalism and the 'oil opening'

After Pérez proclaimed that '*el petroleo es nuestro*' (the oil is ours), the state became sole shareholder of PDVSA, the only company authorized to extract oil. The interests of the landlord state and extractive capital began to blur. In the concession era, foreign companies bargained not only over royalties and taxation, but also over exploration rights, import taxes, labour regulation, etc. Much as Vernon (1971) and Moran (1983) have argued for host states, Venezuela had steadily gained sophistication in negotiating with and regulating foreign investors. A consensus had developed in the 1960s not around nationalization but around using expiring concessions (reversion) to develop a domestic industry, both state and privately owned, coexisting with foreign capital. That is, it was anticipated that some of the concessions due to revert to the state in 1983 would not only be subsequently exploited by a state corporation, but also be newly conceded to domestic and foreign capital, most likely in partnership with a state corporation, christened the Venezuelan Petroleum Corporation (CVP). This plan was discarded in favour of the chimera of nationalization in 1975. The nationalization law seemed to rule out foreign capital in the industry; few took notice that the law left a camel's nose in the tent by virtue of Article 5, allowing some partnerships and contracted services with private companies. Meanwhile, the oil ministry's capacity, built over 50 years, to monitor the industry began to atrophy.

Nationalization took place at a highly favourable international conjuncture, the OPEC boom years (1973 to 1983). The boom obscured the failure of the state and company to invest in new fields or in revitalizing older ones. The priority of President Pérez was not the oil industry but a rapid transformation whereby capital from oil would be invested in the metallurgical sector and other capital intensive industries (i.e., automobiles) that would serve domestic but also overseas markets (Coronil 1997). Venezuela would become the Ruhr of Latin America.[2] Space does not permit full exposition of what went wrong; suffice to say that by the end of the administrations of Pérez and his successor, Luis Herrera Campíns (of the main Christian Democratic opposition party), the country had borrowed extensively against future oil export earnings and the new heavy industries were failing to compete in global markets.

The OPEC boom faded in the face of (i) falling demand due to the global recession of 1978–1982; (ii) conservation and technological developments that helped decrease energy demand; and (iii) the opening of the oil spigot in non-OPEC countries. OPEC responded, ultimately unsuccessfully, with a quota system. Venezuela was among the cartel members most eager to defend prices by cutting production. PDVSA's executives chafed at the limits.

The upsurge in production outside of OPEC not only raised the global volume of production but also introduced a neoliberal model for the industry, one embraced by Venezuela's oil men. Especially important was the fiscal regime initiated by Prime Minister Margaret Thatcher. The North Sea was opened to exploitation with virtually no royalty and with many other incentives to stimulate capital investment and production. Overall, production from the North Sea increased from negligible in 1975 to 3 million bpd (barrels per day) by 1982; it would continue to climb to 6 million bpd by 1998—the year prices collapsed. Alaska's policies were similar to Britain's; that state's production rose from less than 200,000 bpd in 1976 to 1.8 million bpd in 1981.

In Venezuela, the reality of the shift in global market conditions came crashing down on February 18, 1983, Black Friday, when the bolivar was devalued. It marked the beginning of a socio-economic catastrophe. In the industrial sector, wages stagnated in real terms, rising just 1.2% on average per year through 1988. Then the country experienced what Javier Corrales has called its 'second lost decade' (1999: 26). From 1988 to 1998, real wages fell by an average of -5.5% per year, from Bs. 2900 to Bs. 1100 (in 1984 bolivars). In 1999 they were only 33% of what they had been in 1978, the peak year of the OPEC boom. There had been some recovery of growth in the early 1990s, but by 1999, the gross domestic product had fallen, when adjusted for inflation, to its 1992 level again. Poverty jumped from 36 to 68% between 1984 and 1991, extreme poverty from 11 to 34% (Di John 2009: 51; Lander 1996: 65; see also Martel 1993).

The impact of this catastrophe was made worse by the performance of the political class, which not only showed itself incapable of responding with an economic policy to ameliorate the deteriorating social conditions, but also failed to curb corruption. Corruption at all levels of society – manipulation of the tiered currency rate, pyramid schemes in the banking sector, petty bribes needed to obtain passports, telephone service, etc. corroded public confidence in government. The net effect was the decline of the middle class and rise of a sense of social and economic exclusion (Lander 2007). This explains the failure of the population to rally to the *Punto Fijo* democracy after Chávez's coup attempt of 1992 against the President, Pérez, who had been returned to office in the 1988 election.

In his *Plan de Barranquilla* of 1931, Betancourt had posited that political democracy was required to confront *imperialismo petrolero* and to 'sow the oil' in economic development for the benefit of all. After nationalization, no longer could Venezuela's quest for development be linked ideologically to confrontation with *imperialismo petrolero*, i.e., an 'unjust' exploitation of national wealth. So, as the majority of Venezuelans slid deeper into penury, who was to blame? There were plenty of deserving culprits among the political class and the bourgeoisie, but initially at least, the PDVSA executives were not among them.

However, PDVSA's managers were not nationalists preoccupied with maximizing rent for the Venezuelan treasury. Many were engineers by training, skilled at finding, extracting and processing oil. Their goal was maximizing production, not conservation or limiting supply. Their peers and colleagues were not Arab oil sheiks but button-downed executives of European and US oil companies. One PDVSA president went so far as to argue that Venezuela's linguistic and historic ties to Spain made the developed, consuming countries more suitable associates for business than Third World OPEC nations (Sosa Pietri 1996). Political corruption and economic catastrophe gave them additional motivation to break away from state control. The emblematic episode of mismanagement of PDVSA occurred when Herrera Campíns in 1982 forced the company to repatriate $5.5 billion from abroad, only to devalue the bolivar in February 1983. The Venezuelan president might well have simply burned the company's dollar reserve in a bonfire.

Company executives embraced the label of 'meritocracy', suggesting that the company constituted an island of efficiency, rationality and rectitude in a society where everything else was falling apart. In 1986 company executives already began envisioning a return of private capital to the *aguas abajos*, basic productive activities. PDVSA executives began to take control over oil policy from the state. The company's Department of Strategic Planning rationalized the shift as 'a change in the oil-society relationship. It is a change in the rentier model by which the industry provides resources to the Treasury, which distributes them to society in a very inefficient manner, plagued by corruption, clientelism, etc.' (quoted in Azpúrua 1996: 24).

From the view point of PDVSA, these plentiful resources were fruits of the company's professional management. But the meritocracy's quest for autonomy went far beyond management of the industry – i.e., productive activities, including exploration, drilling, transportation, marketing, etc. It also sought management of the natural resource itself, that is, levels of production, fiscal arrangements with foreign capital, and international dispute resolution.[3] For PDVSA executives, state control over such matters was political interference with the industry; to the handful of nationalists in Congress who tried to block the *apertura*, this was intrusion of the company into matters properly the province of the state.

The *apertura petrolera* proper was proclaimed as policy in 1994, the culmination of a project of transnationalization of PDVSA underway since the mid-1980s. Major features of that project were:

- *Internationalization*. Arguing that it should acquire refineries and distribution networks abroad, PDVSA made several purchases, most notably CITGO (1986) in the US and Veba (1992) in Germany. Critics (i.e., Boué 2004) argue that the company overpaid in the case of CITGO and that assets abroad allowed the company to engage in transfer pricing to shelter profits from the reach of the state. They also exposed Venezuela to a possible seizure of assets should the country renounce international dispute resolution.
- *Elimination of the Calvo Clause*. The Calvo Clause is a diplomatic convention by which foreign investment disputes, resulting from joint ventures and operating or service agreements, must be resolved in national courts.
- *Production in excess of OPEC quotas*. The company failed to reach the ultimate goal of inducing Venezuela to leave the landlord cartels, but Venezuela routinely exceeded its quotas. The company also was successful in convincing the cartel to exclude extra-heavy oil from production statistics, even though so-called 'bitumen' competes with oil on the market.
- *Foreign companies re-enter production*. PDVSA negotiated service, operating agreements, and joint ventures, all of which allowed foreign capital to re-enter base facets (*aguas abajas*) of production on terms so generous that their profit margins would exceed those of the concessionary era (see Mommer 2001). The company facilitated this not only by progressively widening Article 5 of the nationalization law, but also by obtaining a Supreme Court ruling to that effect. One example was elimination of a provision, dating to before the Medina era, under which the state reserved for itself ownership of a large portion of oil deposits newly discovered by private exploration. The Court's derogation of existing laws was written by a former company lawyer who afterwards left the Court and returned to the company (Arrioja 1998: 61–80). The company also evaded the nationalization law's requirement for majority control of joint ventures by merely requiring that ventures have a control committee with power to review and veto management decisions, but not actually run the enterprise.

It is impossible to know whether the *apertura* would have culminated with privatization of the company. In some ways, state ownership was useful to transnational capital as it returned to the fields, as contracts usually held the state, as owner of PDVSA, liable for any costs that might arise from new taxation or environmental damage. Still, in 1991 one prominent executive advocated a 'total opening of the State toward private investment ... toward state enterprises' (1991: 188), including the raising of new capital for expansion through the issue of stock.

Ironically, while the mass urban uprising of 1989 (known as the *Caracazo*) was viewed as a popular revolt against neoliberal structural adjustment policies, in some way it facilitated the *apertura* by further weakening the political elite – as did the two coup attempts of 1992. President Pérez, who was forced from office by Congress in early 1993, had opposed some of PDVSA's plans to internationalize and to turn exploration and production over to foreign contractors. Ramón Velásquez, the interim president in 1993, by contrast, was weak and posed no obstacle to PDVSA (Mommer 2003:137).

Rafael Caldera won the December 1993 election promising to find an alternative to the neoliberal economic policy, but a major banking crisis almost immediately derailed his plans. He appointed Luis Giusti, former head of the Shell subsidiary, as president of PDVSA. Giusti convinced Caldera that the *apertura* was Venezuela's best chance for economic recovery. The meritocracy had developed powerful allies in the leadership of AD and other parties desperately clinging to power in the faltering *Punto Fijo* regime (Arrioja 1998). The only opposition came in Congress from the small delegation of the *Causa R* (Radical Cause) congressmen, a leftist party that had emerged from regional social and labour movements, and a few dissenters within AD. Some of the *Causa* deputies had been part of the Merida circle and would (after divisions in the party) occupy influential posts in PDVSA and the oil ministry under Chávez.

Bolivarianism and resource nationalism

Chávez's most popular appeal in 1998 was his promise to call a Constituent Assembly to write a new constitution, but his candidacy was also aided by collapsing oil prices and renewed economic distress. While the global recession touched off by the Asian financial crisis was a major a factor in the price collapse, a contextual factor was global oversupply, fed in part by Venezuela's chronic violation of its OPEC quota. Between 1985 and 1997 Venezuelan production rose from 1.68 billion barrels to 3.28 billion barrels. In the presidential campaign, Chávez did not address oil policy so much as decry the compensation and lifestyle of PDVSA executives. Oil and other economic policies were secondary on his agenda in 1999 and 2000 as he concentrated on calling the Constituent Assembly, passing the new constitution, and evicting the old political guard through comprehensive 'mega-elections' in July 2000.

The new charter included many guarantees on social and economic rights at odds with neoliberal economic policy. On the surface it also seemed to repudiate neoliberalism in the extractive sector. Article 302 stated, 'The State reserves to itself, through the pertinent organic law, and for reasons of national expediency, the petroleum industry and other industries, operations and goods and services which are in the public interest and of a strategic nature.' Article 303 guarantees that 'the State shall retain all shares of Petróleos de Venezuela, S.A. or the organ created to manage the petroleum industry', but it adds, 'with the exception of subsidiaries, strategic joint ventures, business enterprises and any other venture established or coming in the future to be established as a consequence of the carrying on of the business of Petróleos de Venezuela, S.A.' Hence, the charter did not invalidate the *apertura*.

Chávez's early appointments to head PDVSA were men selected for their loyalty to his person, with little regard for their views on oil policy. However, the ministry was staffed with oil nationalists, such as Alí Rodríguez, who would move him toward policies that challenged the men entrenched in the company's executive suites, and also its technical and managerial cadre. The goals included:

- *Revitalization of OPEC.* Chávez took the initiative to organize the second summit of OPEC Heads of State in Caracas in 2000, the first since 1975. Nothing about the meeting specifically reversed the *apertura*, but it sent a clear signal that Venezuela was recommitting to the defence of prices over supply and that the meritocracy's goal of withdrawing Venezuela from the organization would not be attained as long as Chávez was in power.
- *Reforming the fiscal regime.* In November of 2001 Chávez, using decree powers granted by the National Assembly, issued a new hydrocarbons law whose most important provision imposed a 30% royalty (reducible to 20% for mature reservoirs, 16.7% for extra-heavy oil). The income tax rate was lowered slightly to 50% (some private companies operating under service contracts were subject only to a 34% rate), although this was more than offset by the new royalty rates, which were levied on gross, not net revenues. The law also limited private participation in joint ventures to 49% of ownership; that is, it insisted on majority state ownership of all joint ventures in oil exploration and extraction, reversing the mere requirement for a management committee emblematic of the *apertura*.
- *Migration to joint ventures.* In 2006 the Chávista controlled legislature passed a law requiring companies with operating agreements to 'migrate' to the provisions of the 2001 law requiring majority state ownership of joint ventures. This was followed in February 2007 by a Decree Law that required joint ventures and operating agreements in the extra-heavy oil sector (the Orinoco Belt) to migrate (with compensation) to the provisions for majority state ownership – what has become known as 're-nationalization'.
- *Re-establishment of the Calvo Clause as standard practice.* The 2006 law restored the principle of final resolution of conflicts in national courts. In 2008, Venezuela gave notice to Netherlands of its termination of the bilateral trade treaty requiring international dispute resolution. Most foreign investment in the oil sector had been made by dummy corporations set up in the Netherlands for this purpose. Chávez's policy had clearly shifted from 1999, when the Bolivarian-controlled National Assembly passed the Law for the Promotion and Protection of Investments, which contained provisions similar to the Netherlands bilateral treaty (Eljuri and Pérez 485–9).

PDVSA executives reacted to the 2001 Decree Law by openly aligning with the opposition. A mass protest that touched off the short-lived coup of April 2002 was called to resist 'politicization' of the company (see Aharonian 2002). In December 2002 the meritocracy tried to drive Chávez from office through a three-month shutdown[4] of the oil industry. Its defeat resulted in the firing of 18,000 to 20,000 employees, mostly technical and managerial personnel. Afterwards, production levels returned to nearly pre-shutdown levels, but the loss of so many professional employees significantly handicapped expansion of production ever since.

The defeat of what Chávistas call the 'oil sabotage' further radicalized oil policy, leading to the 2006–2007 renationalization and re-establishment of the Calvo Clause. Not coincidentally, 2006 marks the high point of Chávez's popularity and support, which culminated in his open declaration of an intention to implement 'twenty-first century socialism' in Venezuela. However, even at this time no prominent Bolivarian voice advocated exclusion of private and foreign investment from the oil sector. Far from relying on PDVSA to undertake new exploration and production, the Venezuelan state has relied heavily on foreign companies, with national oil companies (NOCs), i.e., CNOC (China), STATOIL (Norway) and Total (France), leading the way, but with participation of private majors (i.e., Chevron) as well. Most foreign companies complied in 2007 with the negotiated 'migration' to majority Venezuelan ownership. The principal exceptions were Exxon-Mobil and ConocoPhillips, both of which invoked international arbitration. As of October 2014 neither had achieved compensation greatly above that originally offered by the government (see Boué 2014).

Oil nationalism and development

Bolivian Vice President Álvaro García Linera once ruminated about his homeland, '…The [Bolivian] state is the main wealth generator in the country. That wealth is not valorized as capital; it is redistributed through society through bonuses, rents, direct social benefits to the population, the freezing of utility rates and basic fuel prices, and subsidies to agricultural production' (in Burbach et al. 2013: 83). This observation also applies to Venezuela under Chávez and his chosen successor, President Nicolás Maduro (2013–present).

The combination of fiscal reforms and surging global oil prices provided the financial means for Chávez to expand and sustain popular social programmes, especially in health care, nutrition subsidies, and education. Poverty rates, unemployment, and other socio-economic indicators registered significant improvements (for a summary, see Robertson 2014), which undoubtedly contributed to Chávez's repeated electoral successes. Less successful were efforts to use oil rents to found the new socialism through 'endogenous development', consisting of programmes to encourage micro-enterprises, cooperatives, worker-run nationalized companies, and worker participation schemes in large state enterprises (i.e., in the metallurgical sector).

Chávez linked distribution of rents to his vision of 'twenty-first century social-ism', specifically toward the creation of a communal state. The communes were envisioned as networks of communal councils tied to leaders of social move-ments, state-financed 'missions' and endogenous development projects. For more radical sectors in the Bolivarian movement, such a communal state would be more democratic in allocating rents than the institutions of representative democ-racy. To the Venezuelan opposition, the councils and communes were simply a way for the Chávez to centralize control over rents and to bypass elected state and municipal officials.

Chávez began to involve PDVSA directly in endogenous development and social programmes for three reasons. First, even after the personnel losses of 2003, PDVSA remained, with the military, the largest repository of professional skill in the county. Second, the company was in a position to stimulate growth in the endogenous sector by buying goods and services (i.e., valves, food for employees, transportation) from the new cooperatives, micro-enterprises, and worker co-managed or self-managed industries. Third, the company could be used to sequester funds from the professional politicians (including those in Chávez's own party) and from the Central Bank.

Much of oil rent after 2005 was retained in PDVSA's own development fund (FONDEN) or in funds directly controlled by the Executive. In 2012 alone, the company directed $23 billion to various social missions, and another $15.6 million to FONDEN. The total for 2001 to 2012 amounted, respectively, to $106.2 billion and $174.2 billion (PDVSA 2012). The plunge in oil prices in the second half of 2014 will undoubtedly be reflected in significant decreases in these totals.

The wisdom of using PDVSA to promote endogenous development has been criticized not only by opposition critics but also by some analysts sympathetic to Chávismo who are doubtful that socialism can be achieved through small-scale enterprise and without globally competitive industrial enterprises (i.e., Purcell 2011). However, there can be little dispute that involving the company directly in popular social programmes did reinforce collectivist attitudes about national sovereignty over subsoil resources and support for Chávista oil policy.

A good indication of this success became evident when Manuel Rosales, the main opposition presidential candidate in 2006, tried to sell Venezuelans on the idea of directly distributing PDVSA profits on a per capita basis by issuing each household a black debit card. Rosales ran ads featuring Afro-descendant men and women from the poor barrios proudly showing off '*Mí negrita*', some planning to use their money to start a small business, others anticipating how their 'negra' would resolve their problems. Undoubtedly, there were many reasons for Rosales' resounding defeat (63 to 37%), but the trope, a central strategy of his campaign, utterly failed.

Revolutionary internationalism and oil nationalism: strange bedfellows

The opposition had more success criticizing Venezuela's petro-diplomacy, including its oil discount programmes and other initiatives to integrate energy production (refineries, electrical grids, etc.). For Chávez, these were the embodiment of the country's proud heritage as the birthplace of Latin American integration and its commitment to Third World solidarity (Fox 2006). For the opposition, the government was giving away the natural patrimony.

The major components of Bolivarian oil diplomacy were: subsidies and investments for member-countries of the Bolivarian Alliance for the Americas (ALBA); Petrocaribe, a programme of discounts for Caribbean and Central America; a separate programme of 33,000 bpd provided to Cuba on terms separate from ALBA; and PetroAmérica, which offered discounts across Latin America along with ambitious plans to foster integration through mega-projects, such as an energy pipeline stretching from Venezuela to Argentina.

It is almost impossible to calculate the true cost of Venezuela's subsidies abroad because they take the form of barter arrangements and deep discounts on financing, varying according to global oil prices. Petrocaribe nations paid in part through commodity exports, some of which were then distributed to Venezuelans through PDVSA's role in providing discounted food (PDVAL). It is especially difficult to calculate the return to Venezuela of Cuba's provision of medical personnel and other human resources in exchange for oil.

If we use a very high estimate of a cost of production of $15 per barrel for Venezuelan oil, based on heavy oil production and service contracts, the cost of oil exchanged through Petrocaribe would approximate $602 million. It may be much less if we use the $7 general cost of production from the 2012 *PDVSA Annual Report*. In that report PDVSA claims that Venezuela received $868 million in commodities in exchange for 111,000 barrels per day (i.e., 40.1 million bpd for the year) from Petrocaribe countries, excluding Cuba. By those figures, the exchange would be favourable for Venezuela. However, there is also an opportunity cost that figures into the way the opposition estimates the cost of the programmes, i.e., using total export earnings forgone. At the basket price of $103, Venezuela's exports to Petrocaribe totalled approximate $4.1 billion for 2012, suggest a cost for this programme alone of $3.4 billion. One report sympathetic to Chávismo estimated the total cost of all oil discount programmes at $5 billion per year (Ives 2013).

By far the most virulent criticism by the opposition targets Venezuela's oil lifeline to Cuba. However, the resonance of that criticism has been attenuated in the poor *barrios* by the thousands of Cuban doctors and nurses providing health care in exchange. That may change if the government proves unable to sustain social and economic support programmes in the wake of the oil price declines that began in late 2014. By March 2015 the price was below $50; it rebounded to $60 by May, the price on which Maduro's government predicated its 2015 budget. By late 2015 the price had fallen again to almost US $40. Maduro avoided drastic cuts to social spending, but the country's economic woes were visible and felt by almost all Venezuelans.

Besides oil set aside for international discount programmes and barter arrangements, Venezuela now dedicates a certain amount of oil, not yet fully disclosed, to repayment of loans, including approximately $40 billion borrowed from

China[5] between 2008 and 2014 (though some has been paid back). Based on PDVSA's 2012 *Annual Report*, my rough estimate is that if we take repayment to China and the petro-diplomacy programmes into account, PDVSA has not been paid directly and fully for 43% of barrels exported in recent years. This burden has grown more onerous because PDVSA has failed to achieve expansion goals set by the Chávez administration. In 2014 total production remained at approximately 2.9 million bpd, far below the 5 million bpd set six years before. Accentuating this problem is the rising domestic consumption of oil, sold below the cost of production, which totalled 800,000 bpd in 2012 – or 36% of production.

With Maduro's approval rating hovering around 20% in 2015, and the opposition deeply divided around a strategy to recapture the state, it is difficult to predict the direction of oil policy in the next few years. Henrique Capriles, the opposition candidate against Chávez in 2012 and the narrow loser of the 2013 election against Maduro, promised in his campaign to respect existing legislation and guaranteed that 'we will maintain full state ownership of PDVSA: the oil belongs to all Venezuelans'. Capriles' platform also included the promise, 'We guarantee the managerial, financial, and operational autonomy of PDVSA' (Capriles 2012). Both statements are empty signifiers, the first suggesting continuity with resource nationalism, the second echoing the meritocracy's rejection of state control of oil policy as 'politicization' of company business.

Venezuela's indebtedness and failure to curb domestic consumption create pressure for significant and rapid increases in production, the same lure that favoured the *apertura petrolera* in the last days of the *Punto Fijo* regime. That process may have already begun. In May 2013, PDVSA signed an agreement with Chevron for a $2 billion loan to cover the company's share of investment in a joint venture. According to reports, the agreement includes international arbitration and, though the venture will still be majority owned by PDVSA, it grants more managerial flexibility for Chevron (Neuman 2014).

Conclusion

After nationalization, executives of PDVSA stepped into a vacuum of state power left by the collapse of the *Punto Fijo* regime to transnationalize the company and implement the *apertura petrolera*. Their goal was to fuse PDVSA and its subsidiaries to foreign transnational oil companies, both state and private, through fiscal incentives, foreign managerial control over joint ventures, acceptance of international adjudication in dispute resolution, and the separation of Venezuela from OPEC. This agenda was far advanced but not complete when Hugo Chávez won the election of 1998. He set out to wrest control of oil policy from PDVSA, but he did not seek to return to monopoly state control of extraction and associated activities.

Of course oil policy cannot be simply reduced to a clash between transnational capital and the landlord state. Within each host nation is a constellation of social, economic and political forces whose interest in natural resources varies. Indigenous groups, environmentalists, unions and business elites outside the oil sector are just a few of the social forces interested in oil policy. Most of the Venezuelan bourgeoisie opposes Chávismo, but outside of oil the business sector is very heavily weighted toward commerce and finance, and both have historically depended directly (though subsidies and exchange policies) and indirectly (through consumerism generated by circulation of oil rents) upon the petrostate. It is difficult to see how they can be 'rent seeking' and not also to some degree espouse natural resource nationalism.

Just as the tension between the landlord state and capital did not disappear with nationalization or the neoliberal *apertura*, nor is it likely to be resolved by the hybrid, neo-extractivist policy that Chávez bequeathed to Maduro upon the former's death in 2013. The steep slide in oil prices in late 2014 magnified serious deficiencies in oil policies and governance now in the hands of Maduro. Regardless of whether the Chávistas or the opposition prevails in the highly polarized politics of contemporary Venezuela, the legacy of Chávez's resource nationalism remains vulnerable to reversal and to the global forces set in motion by transnational capitalism.

Notes

1 The 'seven sisters' were Anglo-Persian (British Petroleum); Gulf Oil, Standard Oil of California (SoCal); Standard Oil of New Jersey (Esso); Standard Oil of New York (Socony); Shell; Texaco (Chevron).
2 We should take note that Venezuela's developmental project, unlike most of the larger countries of Latin America, was less tied to be import substitution. Certainly, the domestic market would be served, but these industries were not to replace an existing market so much as serving a rapidly expanding one.
3 For a defence of the *apertura*, see Azpúrua 1997; a general critique is Luzardo 1995.
4 I say 'shutdown' because the action was not clearly a 'strike' or a 'lockout', though it had elements of both.
5 India actually surpassed China in 2013 as Venezuela's largest Asian market for oil.

Bibliography

Aharonian, A.R. (2002). Hamburgers, Cured Ham, and Oil. *Proceso*. 1st May.
Alexander, R. (1982). *Rómulo Betancourt and the Transformation of Venezuela*. New Brunswick, NY: Transaction Books.
Arrioja, J. (1998). *Coientes negros: Petroleos de Venezuela bajo la genercación de Shell*. Caracas: Los Libros de El Nacional.
Azpúrua Sosa, J.C. (1997). *La apertura petrolera venzolana*. Maracaibo: Petróleo YV. Available from: http://www.petroleoyv.com/website/uploads/aperturapetroleraweb.pdf. [Accessed: 4 December 2014].
Betancourt, R. (1935). *Plan de Barranquilla*. Available at constitucionweb.blogspot. com/2010/07/el-plan-barranquilla-romulo-betancourt.html. [Accessed: 27 May 2015].
Betancourt, R. (1978). *Venezuela: Oil and Politics*. Boston: Hughton-Mifflin.
Boué, J.C. (2004). *The Internationalization Program of Petróleos de Venezuela S.A. Commission by PDV-United Kingdom*. Caracas: Ediciones del Ministerio de Energía y Minas de la República Bolivariana de Venezuela (Fondo Editorial Darío Ramírez). Available from: http://www.academia.edu/7707864/THE_INTERNATIONALISATION_

PROGRAMME_OF_PETR%C3%93LEOS_DE_VENEZUELA_S.A._PDVSA. [Accessed: 8 December 2014].

Boué, J.C. (2014). *Enforcing Pacta Sunt Seervanda? Conoco-Phillips and Exxon-Mobil versus the Bolivarian Republica of Venezuela and Petróleos de Venezuela.* Working Papers Series 2, No. 1. Cambridge: University of Cambridge and Centre of Latin American Studies.

Burbach, R., Fox, M., and Fuentes, F. (2013). *Latin America's Turbulent Transitions: The Future of Twenty-first Century Socialism.* London: Zed Books.

Coronil, F. (1997). *The Magical State: Nature, Money and Modernity in Venezuela.* Ann Arbor: University of Michigan Press.

Corrales, J. (1999). Venezuela in the 1980s, 1990s, and Beyond. *ReVista, Harvard Review of Latin America,* (Fall), pp. 26–29. Available from: http://revista.drclas.harvard.edu/book/venezuela-1980s-1990s-and-beyond. [Accessed: December 2014].

Dargin, J. (2010). *Investor-State Relations in the Chávez Age: the Nature of Resource Nationalism in the 21st Century.* Cambridge: Harvard University-Kennedy School of Government. Available from: http://belfercenter.ksg.harvard.edu/publication/20527/investorstate_relations_in_the_chavez_age.html.

Di John, J. (2009). *From Windfall to Curse? Oil and Industrialization in Venezuela, from 1920 to the Present.* University Park: Pennsylvania State University Press.

Eljuri, E., and Victorino Tejera Pérez, J. (2008). 21st Century Transformation of the Venezuelan Oil Industry. *Journal of Energy and Natural Resources Law,* 26 (4), pp. 475–98.

Fox, M. (2006). President Chávez Hosts 141st OPEC Meeting in Caracas. Venezuelanalysis. com (2 June) [Accessed: 10 June 2015].

Ives, K. (2013). Hugo Chávez's Legacy in Haiti and Latin America Venezuelanalysis.com. March 17, 2013. Available from http://venezuelanalysis.com/analysis/8263. [Accessed: 5 October 2015].

Karl, T.L. (1997). *The Paradox of Plenty: Oil Booms and Petro-States.* Berkeley: University of California Press.

Lander, E. (2007). Venezuela Social Conflict in a Global Context. In Ellner, S., and Tinker Salas, M. (eds.). *Venezuela: Hugo Chávez and the Declie of an 'Exception Democracy.* Lanham MD: Roman and Littlefield, pp. 16–32.

Lander, E. (1996). The Impact of Neoliberal Adjustment in Venezuela, 1989-1993. *Latin American Perspectives,* 23 (3), pp. 50–73.

Luzardo Parra, G. (1997). *De la nacionalización a la apertura petrolera. Derrumbe de un esperaza.* Maracaibo, Venezuela: Universidad de Zulia.

Martel, A. (1993). *Metodologías de estimación de la pobreza en Venezuela.* Caracas: COPRE.

Mommer, B. (2003). Subversive Oil. In Ellner, S. & Hellinger, D. (eds). *Venezuelan Politics in the Chávez Era: Class, Polarization and Conflict.* Boulder CO: Lynne Rienner Publishers, pp.131–46.

Mommer, B. (2001). Fiscal Regimes and Oil Revenues in the UK, Alaska and Venezuela. Oxford UK: Oxford Institute for Energy Studies, WPM No. 27. Available at http://www.oxfordenergy.org/tag/fiscal-regimes. [Accessed: 5 December 2014].

Mommer, B. (1983). *Petróleo, renta del suelo, e historia.* Merida, Venezuela: CORPOANDES.

Moran, R. (1983). *Multinational Corporations and Politics of Dependence in Chile.* Princeton: Princeton University Press.

Neuman, W. (2014). Venezuela, in Quiet Shift, Gives Foreign Partners more Control in Oil Ventures. *New York Times,* October 9.

PDVSA (2012). *Annual Report, 2012.* Caracas: Bolivarian Republic of Venezuela.

Capriles Radonski, H. (2012). Plan 'Petróleo para el progreso'. Available from: https://henriquecapriles.wordpress.com/2012/08/05/petroleo-para-el-progreso/. [Accessed: 8 July 2015].

Purcell, T.F. (2013). The Political Economy of Social Production Companies in Venezuela. *Latin American Perspectives*, 40 (3), pp. 146–68.

Robertson, E. (2014). Is Poverty Still Falling in Venezuela? Venezuelanalysis.com (June 17th) [Online]. Available from: http://venezuelanalysis.com/analysis/10749. [Accessed: 8 July 2015].

Robinson, W. (2004). *A Theory of Global Capitalism: Production, Class, and State in a Transnational World*. Baltimore: The Johns Hopkins Press.

Sosa Pietri, A. (1998). Venezuela, el 'Tercermundismo' y la OPEP. *Venezuela Analitica* [Online.] Available from http:www.analitica.com. [Accessed: March 2002].

Vernon, R. (1971). *Sovereignty at Bay: the Multinational Spread of US Enterprises*. New York: Basic Books.

Conclusion

13 Towards a theory of resource nationalisms

Paul A. Haslam and Pablo Heidrich

Introduction

This book began with the challenge of understanding Latin America's resource *nationalisms*. Part of this challenge involved identifying and categorizing the range of policies used under the moniker of resource nationalism; and part of it involved explaining these choices. Both of these questions are logically prior but, ultimately, essential to understanding how resource nationalism affects the development potential of the region. Our methodology has been to examine a number of possible causes of resource nationalism, organized in Part 1 of the book; followed by the examination of six country-cases in Part 2. The country-cases were organized into three groups that represent different positions on the capture and use of resource rents from 'limited', to 'moderate', to 'radical' – reflecting the diversity of policy responses found in the region. By organizing the countries in this way, we improve our ability to make meaningful comparisons: we can see which causal variables are shared between countries with broadly similar outcomes in resource nationalist policies; as well as which variables differ between the countries with dissimilar outcomes.

Our focus on the policy choices that countries are making with regards to the management and regulation of extractive industries is distinct, but not opposed, to the wider preoccupation of the resource curse literature with the consequences of natural resource abundance for development. We take on the challenge of understanding how resources are leveraged for development, not through the large-n studies typical of the resource curse literature, but through a nuanced examination of how specific countries formulate their sectoral policies and developmental objectives in the challenging context of today's globalized economy. It is our belief, that it is first necessary to understand how the extraction of natural resources is managed and regulated, before we can examine how economic development is supported or stunted by resource abundance. Sectoral policies are therefore, an intermediate step of consequence, and by examining them we treat governments as agents that are working within a set of opportunities and constraints, allowing for movement in the slow process of policy learning and institution-building. In this regard, the analysis goes beyond the resource curse literature's standard dichotomization of cases into failures and successes.

In that context then, the range of cases included in this volume takes on greater significance. The more radical cases of Bolivia and Venezuela are not simply those countries which have used a wider range of policies and more aggressively bargained with private firms, but also those that have made stronger bets on improving the developmental capacity of the state, within national projects that aim at maximizing rent extraction for social transformation and political/economic/ethnic inclusion. The moderate cases of resource nationalism, Brazil and Peru, are quite diverse, having distinct institutional and policy capacities. Nonetheless, policy in both countries has been informed by the need to balance the appropriation of rents with the maintenance of incentives for private investors to expand extractive industries. Unlike the radical countries, they have sought to use resources to gradually improve social and economic conditions. And, although limited resource nationalism might seem to be an oxymoron, Colombia and particularly Mexico, show that even in governments not necessarily concerned with leftist ideologies or progressive social goals, further regulation of extractive industries has eventually taken hold. In these countries, moderate reforms have sought to maintain a fiscal status quo in which the state is funded by the surplus from extractive industries instead of general taxation. Reforms have created the incentives for foreign direct investors to expand the extractive frontier, seeing this as the best way to maintain and increase resource revenues to the state.

This chapter draws together the observations made by the authors united in this volume about the causes of the region's resource nationalisms within the broad categories of 'limited', 'moderate' and 'radical'. As a first step, we examine and categorize the diverse policy choices that are included within these resource nationalisms. Following the structure established in Chapter 1, we consider three categories of actions: the maximization of public revenue; the assertion of strategic control over the sector by the state; and governmental efforts to enhance the developmental spillovers resulting from extractive activity. Secondly, we address the causes of this variation in resource nationalism, by organizing the factors identified by the thematic and country specialists as variables, which at low values constrain, and at high values constitute opportunities for resource nationalism. Our analysis shows that the variation in resource nationalisms in the region is indeed explained by these international, industry and national-level variables. The limited resource nationalisms of Colombia and Mexico face more constraints than opportunities, while the converse is true for the radical cases of Bolivia and Venezuela, with the moderate cases of Brazil and Peru the result of contradictory incentives.

The policies of resource nationalism in Latin America

In Table 13.1 we outline the major policy options used across the region by resource nationalist governments, dividing them into three categories that reflect the principal objective of the policy measure: the maximization of public revenue; assertion of strategic control over the sector; and the enhancement of developmental spillovers. We have limited our discussion to those measures that directly affect firms, leaving aside the important question of the social use of resource

Table 13.1 Resource nationalist policies by category

Policy category

Maximization of public revenue
- Increased royalties
- Additional taxes and duties
- Extra-legal pressures to increase voluntary financial contributions
- Forced divestment of shares to the state (without effective control)
- Limitation of tax exemptions and deductions
- Increased rent collection through efficient management of existing state-owned enterprise

Assertion of strategic control over the sector
- Constitutional assertion of state's ownership of subsoil resources
- Replacement of concession system with contracting /licencing regime
- Forced divestment to the state of shares (majority ownership, with control)
- Creation or renovation of state-owned enterprise
- Full nationalization (and operational control)
- Develop state-owned enterprise with operational capacity

Enhance developmental spillovers from extractive projects
- Require devolution of (tax) revenue to subnational jurisdictions
- Require community engagement and corporate responsibility programming
- Enhance responsiveness of consultation processes within environmental licencing regime
- Foment supplier development (local-content requirements; technological transfer)
- State-owned enterprise spearheads industrialization through contracting

Source: Compiled by the authors.

revenues, which is discussed in depth by Eduardo Gudynas in Chapter 6. Within each of these three categories, we have roughly ranked the policy options used in the region by the institutional capacity needed to realize them, from low (at the top) to high (at the bottom).

The most basic requirement for a policy measure to contribute to resource nationalism is that it increases the state's ability to capture rents from the extractive sector. In this regard, maximizing government revenue from natural resources has been the fundamental objective of Latin America's resource nationalisms: most governments have increased royalty rates or established mining-specific taxes based on the value of production (Bolivia, 2005 on hydrocarbons, 2007 on mining; Brazil, 2010 in petroleum; Mexico, 2014 on mining; Peru, 2005 and 2011 on mining; Venezuela, 2001, 2006, and 2008, on petroleum). A notable exception to this trend was Colombia, which established a variable royalty rate for oil and gas (2002) intended to incentivize exploration and production. Although profit-based taxes should better balance revenue with investment incentives (Hogan et al. 2010: 11–14), royalties tend to be preferred by resource nationalist governments, since the former, in practice, allows numerous deductions and loopholes that reduce tax collection (see Riesco 2008: 7–9). In addition, some countries, notably Peru in the PMSP (2005) and Special Levy (2011), opted to pressure companies into making 'voluntary' financial contributions to local development, in lieu of establishing formal increases in taxation.[1]

The forced divestment of shares is another policy option that has been widely used in the region to increase the 'government take', especially among more radical governments. It is generally understood to include the coerced sale of a private ownership stake in an enterprise, including the effective or indirect expropriation that may occur in the process of contract negotiations or regulation (Kobrin 1980: 68–9). Bolivia's nationalization programme (2006) required oil and gas companies to transfer 51% of their ownership to the state; as did Venezuela's Hydrocarbon Law (2001), increased to 60% in 2006. Brazil's production-sharing framework for the pre-salt reserves, which applies to new investments and in that sense did not require divestment, set a 30% minimum for state ownership.

The key issue in forced divestment is whether the policy is in practice, an attempt to gain direct access to profits of the enterprise through an ownership stake, or to assert strategic control of the industry. There is good reason to believe that the ownership requirements in Bolivia, Brazil and Venezuela are principally revenue-grabs, rather than an attempt by the state to impose its direction and management on the sector (for example, see Kaup 2010: 132–3). In the Bolivian case, the importance of these ownership stakes in extractive industries to government revenue is clear: in 2005, prior to nationalization, the state captured $US 858 million from taxation, and $US 77 million from hydrocarbon sales; by 2012, taxes brought in $US 357 million, and sales, a massive $US 5.8 billion (Anderson 2014: 3.1–2).

The second category of policies we consider are those that are intended to assert the state's strategic control over the sector – meaning that the state moves to make important decisions about investments, strategic priorities, and the development of supporting industries or infrastructure (including human capital). This often begins with the assertion of the legal right of the state to own and control the nation's subsoil resources, and the shift from a concession to a contract-based system for resource exploitation. Venezuela and Bolivia legalized this perspective during constitutional reforms (1999 and 2009, respectively) and Brazil re-asserted its control over the subsoil in its legislation requiring production-sharing agreements to develop its pre-salt reserves (2010). In so far as the state does re-assert its strategic control of the sector, this is usually done through the establishment of new, and the renovation of existing, state-owned enterprises (Petrosal created in Brazil, 2010; existing SOEs were renovated elsewhere: YPFB and COMIBOL, 2006; ECOPETROL, 2007; PETROPERÚ, 2004; CVG, 2008–2011; PEMEX, 2014).

In the more wide-ranging nationalization programmes in Bolivia and Venezuela, the state has acquired operational capacity through the purchase or expropriation of mostly foreign-owned firms. At the level of political discourse, as Pellegrini reminds us in Chapter 11, this is a state-building project that aims to industrialize natural resources. However, it remains unclear if such companies have (or will have) the ability to independently identify, develop and run extractive projects – has occurred in Brazil. On the one hand, both Bolivia and Venezuela have bought turn-key operation from private companies on the global market (Anderson 2014: 3.6; Gurmendi 2014: 15.2–3; Hennart 2012: 177). Other political agreements provide technical support, including PDVSA–YFPB collaboration, and

Venezuela's agreements with China and Russia worth $US 16 billion and $US 21 billion respectively to develop the eastern Orinoco Belt. One must allow for the possibility of institutional learning, but doubts remain as to whether such companies can learn to operate without foreign expertise.

The last category of resource nationalist policies is the enhancement of the developmental spillovers made by extractive industry. The least institutionally demanding of these policies, are requirements to distribute tax revenues to subnational jurisdictions, or via direct contributions by firms to nearby communities, often as part of corporate social responsibility programmes. As Arellano-Yanguas notes in Chapter 10, these mechanisms have been widely used in Peru, via the *canon minero*, the MPSP programme (2005), and more recently in the 'infrastructure for taxes' programme (2013). Direct decentralization of revenue has also been tried in Bolivia (2005, 2007), Brazil (1989, under consideration in 2015), Colombia (1994, 2011), and Mexico (2014). Governments have also experimented with trust/development funds which aggregate resource revenue (royalties and taxes) before distributing them to various sub-funds and activities, often including activities to diversify beyond the extractive economy, and social spending (corresponding with Gudynas' observations on the Compensatory State). These funds have been created in all the countries examined in this book.

More challenging has been the conversion of extractive activities and revenues into a broader industrialization, which remains a central concern for many governments of the region. As previously indicated, efforts have been made by the state to industrialize natural resources (particularly in Bolivia and Venezuela), however, in both cases, the state is forced to rely on the purchase of technology and management expertise from private, and mostly foreign companies. Of the countries discussed in this book, only Brazil has really developed autonomous domestic capacity in the extractive sector, most notably in the ultra-deep drilling technology used to discover and exploit the pre-salt reserves. As Nem Singh and Massi argue, industrialization has been at the core of the resource nationalist enterprise in Brazil, since the 1940s. In contrast, Colombia, Mexico, and Peru have eschewed the deliberate linkage between resource nationalism and industrialization, despite recent attempts to modernize SOEs through private investment. Industrialization, however, has not been an explicit part of this agenda.

Resource nationalism: between constraints and opportunities

The authors united in this book have brought together a unique set of arguments regarding the factors that drive resource nationalism. Drawing on the chapters, we have identified a number of factors that influence the likelihood of a country adopting more or less radical versions of resource nationalism. We have organized these factors (variables) according to level of analysis: those that originate in the relationship between the country and its international environment; those that are specific to industry characteristics; and those related to the domestic level of analysis.

Rather than considering power resources separately from constraints, as is typical of the obsolescing bargain literature (see Vivoda's analysis in Chapter 3; Kobrin 1987: 618; Eden et al. 2005: 256), the factors we have identified have a range of values that at bottom end act to constrain governments from pursuing a resource nationalist agenda, while at the top end of the scale they create incentives for governments to seize an opportunity. Obviously, the recourse to resource nationalism is multi-causal, and the chapters in this collection clearly show that just because there are opportunities available (in terms of recourse rents), does not mean they are seized, known in the bargaining approach as the gap 'between potential power and its implementation' (Kobrin 1987: 611). Overall, the framework suggests that as these factors tend towards creating more opportunities and fewer constraints, the commitment to resource nationalism will become increasingly radical.

The chapters identify three factors that correspond to the relationship between the international environment and the country. Perhaps, the most fundamental is the role played by commodity prices. As commodity prices rise, the mineral rent potentially available for capture increases, creating incentives for states to act. Gayi and Nkurunziza in Chapter 2 suggest that resource nationalism is cyclical and associated with the upswing phase in commodity prices. Consistent with the 'time-inconsistency' problem, as economists call it, dramatic increases in commodity prices cause governments to re-evaluate the terms they had offered to investors under less favourable conditions. Vivoda, in Chapter 3, shows that rising commodity prices have been a key contributor to the declining bargaining power of international oil companies vis-à-vis host governments.

Another important factor in the international environment is the changing nature of Latin America's international economic integration, particularly, its trade and investment dependence. As Heidrich explains in Chapter 5, Latin America's international insertion has changed in significant ways since the 1990s. Although countries have become both more dependent on natural resource exports (as a proportion of total exports by value), they have also become more diversified in terms of the nationality of inward FDI and export destinations. Previous periods of resource nationalism occurred during an era of regional dependence on the United States, for both capital and exports, which allowed the US to pressure and punish nationalizations. The resource nationalisms of the 2000s occur in a more diversified environment: the corporate victims of nationalization are as likely to be Brazilian, British, Australian, Canadian, Mexican or Spanish, as American; exports are assured of markets in Asia, regardless of expropriations; and US ideological and material influence in the region is in sharp decline. The openness of the Chinese markets to extractive exports, and the availability of Chinese investors and technical cooperation is not unimportant to ensuring that should ideologically-inclined investors decide to depart the region, substitutes can be found (as Vivoda and Hellinger demonstrate in the Venezuelan case). In other words, most countries face fewer substantive constraints from the international environment, than they did in the past.

In addition to international and national-level factors, industry (sectoral) factors are also of key importance. The existence of known (or probable) reserves in combination with the economic importance of the sector to the economy, are two of the most important factors influencing the occurrence of resource nationalism. Sectoral liberalization of the 1990s occurred in a context of low prices and low reserves, and was intended to transfer the risks and costs of exploration and exploitation activities to the private sector, in exchange for larger share of the rewards. In contrast, when sizable reserves are known, and there is little immediate concern over locating more reserves, the calculation for the state shifts to appropriating a larger share of the available rents. When these sectoral activities constitute an important percentage of economic activity, or state revenue, these incentives are multiplied.

Where resource nationalism was most radical, as in Bolivia and Venezuela, private companies operating under a generous incentive regime had previously expanded the known reserves. Hellinger notes that in Venezuela, after bitumen reserves worth 300 billion barrels had been proven in the Orinocco Delta, the government's hand was strengthened, resulting in the annulment of the generous tax regime that had prompted the exploration activities in the first place. In Bolivia, the nationalizations of 1 May 2006, came on the heels of a decade of private investment in exploration that had increased the country's proven and probable reserves of gas to 48.7 trillion ft^3 from 5.7 trillion ft^3 in 1997 (Haslam 2010: 227). In the intermediate cases, Brazil and Peru, increased reserves clearly allowed a revival of resource nationalism. In Chapter 9, Nem Singh and Massi suggest that the 1997 petroleum reforms, which liberalized the petroleum sector, and established a concession system that transferred risks and rewards of exploration to private firms, were done in a context of economic crisis and absence of proven reserves. Conversely, the resource nationalist production-sharing regime created for the pre-salt reserves, was justified by Lula in terms of the low levels of uncertainty about the existence of reserves. Although similar incentives existed in Peru, Arellano-Yanguas points out in Chapter 10 that the government found itself constrained by important domestic pressures. In the least resource nationalistic countries in our study, Colombia and Mexico, the availability of reserves was fundamental. As Caballero Argáez and Bitar (Chapter 7), and Moreno-Brid and Puyana (Chapter 8) point out, the failure to prove reserves under a more statist regime, led both to adopt an incentive structure that encouraged private investment in exploration and exploitation.

Another important industry-level factor is the availability of alternative sources of financing and technology necessary to develop and exploit natural resources. Where there are few alternatives, governments must be careful not to alienate foreign investors. However, the period of resource nationalism covered by this book corresponds with the increasing availability of alternatives, in part due to the rise of multinational oil companies from emerging economies. But, even without China, most of the technology and management expertise needed to exploit a resource can be bought on international markets (Hennart 2012). In Chapter 3, Vivoda points to the changing circumstances for international oil companies, which face increased competition from national oil companies (NOCs), both in terms of accessing reserves (in developing host countries), and in downstream activities, including consumer markets. Vivoda argues that IOCs no longer even have a technological advantage, as NOCs can rely on technology purchased off the shelf, or from other NOCs from developing countries. The sum of these industry-level changes is that IOCs have lost much of their bargaining power with host governments. Although the resource nationalist model, in even its most radical forms, remains dependent on privately-owned capital, technology, and expertise, few companies have firm-specific assets to offer that are not substitutable on the international market.

National-level factors are examined in the six country-cases included in this volume, which show that decisions about how to pursue resource nationalism depend on national politics, institutions and cultures. The political culture (left/right divide) of the governing party and the civil service undoubtedly plays an important role. The left turn towards progressivism brought with it a different worldview that prioritized social justice, economic inclusion, participatory democracy, and an enlarged role for the state, national ownership of resources and anti-imperialism, but also failed to entirely break with the neoliberal model that preceded it (Castañeda 1993: 18; Panizza 2005: 727; Haslam 2010: 210). The chapters by Heidrich (Chapter 5), Gudynas (Chapter 6), Pellegrini (Chapter 11) and Hellinger (Chapter 12) underline the importance of the left turn for changing ideas about what was possible as resource nationalism. Indeed, we find that the most ideologically radical countries, Bolivia and Venezuela are also those that have pushed furthest; while those that have least embraced resource nationalism are those with strong liberal political traditions: Colombia and Mexico. Arellano-Yanguas shows that Peru is an interesting intermediate case where strong bureaucratic ideologies and interests against resource nationalism have undermined the state's ability to pursue it. In this regard, the relationship between progressivisms (as Gudynas terms it) and resource nationalisms does seem to matter.

Certainly, political ideas about what the state should or should not do have changed in a way that favours the left over the neoliberal right, even in the mainstream. Hira, in Chapter 4, examines the change in economic ideas about industrial policy. He describes an emerging economic policy consensus described as 'industrial policy lite', based on the new institutional economics, which envisages a role, albeit limited, for the state. In this regard, economic theory has legitimized the reinvigoration of state policy in areas of existing comparative advantage, an approach that is, at least theoretically, compatible with the new resource nationalism. More generally, as Pellegrini shows in Chapter 11 on Bolivia, resource nationalism is a versatile idea that plays on anti-imperialist sentiment, and which can be used by both proponents and opponents of specific projects to promote their vision of development.

Eduardo Gudynas, in Chapter 6, is the only contributor in this volume to consider extractivst models in terms of both production and consumption. He shows that insofar as extractivisms are *necessarily* destructive of the environment and disruptive of social relations, they *require* compensation to affected parties, and to the broader society. Furthermore the state justifies and legitimizes its recourse to extractivism by social spending, further intensifying this relationship.

Gudynas draws attention to how societal expectations regarding the reduction of poverty, development and social inclusion are intrinsically associated with resource nationalism – and indeed, constitute push factors that require the state to perpetually chase higher revenues. In this regard, as political demands for inclusion intensify, the pressure on the state to turn to resource nationalism is greater. There is little doubt that these pressures to tax undermine the incentives established to encourage private investment in the first place. Arellano-Yanguas, in Chapter 10, shows how Peru has been caught in this contradiction, leading to a moderate (and incoherent) form of resource nationalism.

Few of the other chapters directly address, the way social expectations compound pressures to increase the government take from resources, but Gayi and Nkurunziza, in Chapter 2, point out that increases in public spending associated with the resource boom, cannot be easily rolled back in periods of bust. Bolivia and Venezuela offer good examples of these redistributive pressures, and their contradictions. Both aggressively taxed the resource sector, principally for redistributive purposes, resulting in declining private sector investment activity, which subsequently required that the state step in with more nationalizations to capture more rents, and assure ongoing industrial activity (Anderson, USGS 2011: 3.3; Anderson 2014: 3.7). Both countries show how the contradictions of resource nationalism have led to its intensification.

A final consideration is the role of state capacity in explaining resource nationalism. Intrinsically it makes sense to think that a more capable institutional apparatus would be better placed to pursue resource nationalism. However, state capacity does not obviously map on to resource nationalism. If we were to rank the countries in our study by state capacity, using the six indicators of the World Bank's Worldwide Governance Indicators, they would be ranked, from most to least capable: Brazil, Mexico, Colombia, Peru, Bolivia, Venezuela. However, ranked from most to least resource nationalist, the list is as follows: Venezuela, Bolivia, Brazil, Peru, Mexico, Colombia (World Bank 2015).[2] As the earlier discussion of policy demonstrated, relatively low-capacity Bolivia and Venezuela have pursued the most transformative set of policies that imply a growing, and increasingly sophisticated role for the state in extraction and related industrialization.

However, institutional capacity does seem influence the success in converting resources into industrialization. The only country that has successfully combined resource nationalism with an industrialization strategy is Brazil. In Chapter 9, Nem Singh and Massi point to the importance of the Varguista legacy in Brazil, where, despite a partial liberalization under Cardoso, the tools to ensure ongoing state control were maintained, because of the broad consensus that oil was of strategic importance to the developmental state. The resource nationalism associated with the development of the pre-salt reserves is a testament to Brazil's institutional and corporate capacity, particularly Petrobras' autonomously-developed technological capacity to exploit ultra-deep offshore reserves. In contrast, Hellinger, in Chapter 12, points to the limits on Venezuelan development, despite the state's increasing control over the real economy, resulting from the politicization of PDVSA and its relatively unsuccessful developmental mission.

In this regard, there seems to be a pattern regarding how the existence of constraints and availability of opportunities maps onto the degree of radicalism of resource nationalism in Latin America. When we look at the radical cases (Bolivia and Venezuela), we see that these countries faced the greatest opportunities and weakest constraints. Opportunities included massive increases in the price of oil and gas, recently proven increases in reserves, the diverse nationality of investors, declining power of oil and gas companies, and the availability of alternative political allies, investors and technology on the international market. Both Chávez and Morales' political support was based on the economically excluded, and as a result, were attentive to their political demands for inclusion and redistribution of resource wealth. In that regard, they faced strong political pressures to increase the government take, and were able to overcome domestic interests opposing such a move. Furthermore, left ideology generated a world-view that was critical of foreign capital, and opened up a new set of international allies that were generally supportive of the resource nationalist project. The only serious constraint these countries faced was low state capacity. Here, we see the principal reason for the moderation found even in Latin America's most radical resource nationalist experiments. Both Bolivia and Venezuela were unable to fully replace the private sector, relying on it for technology, management expertise, and investment capital. This prevented the radical cases from turning to full nationalization.

The cases of moderate resource nationalism, Brazil and Peru, are much more diverse, and the logic behind the policy options taken is completely distinct. The pre-salt reserves have allowed Brazil to move forward in a more statist direction that connects with the powerful intellectual tradition of *desenvolvimentismo*, which sought complementarity between state and private sector roles. Ideas and state capacity distinguish Brazil's resource nationalism from all others, making it a unique case. In Peru, despite obvious opportunities for resource nationalism, efforts to increase the government take were constrained by ideas and interests. Peruvian bureaucratic culture was favourable to private enterprise (especially in the Ministry of Energy and Mines), and responsive to pressures from a strong domestic lobby in favour of liberal mining policies. Growth and employment were seen as directly related to inflows of FDI, leading to fears that increased taxation of mining companies may not compensate for lost growth. Furthermore, Peru was not capable of substituting for lost investment with an activist state. In this regard, while some of the factors discussed in Table 13.2 would predict a resource nationalist response, there were strong constraints at the domestic and sectoral level.

In Colombia and Mexico, although limited resource nationalism was ideologically more attractive, as both countries had experienced relatively right-wing governments over the preceding decade, and were more dependent on relations with the United States than the rest of South America, it is important to underline that the objective conditions also constrained them. While they benefited from the same international factors that led to higher hydrocarbon and mineral prices, both countries faced the double problem of high governmental budget dependence on petroleum revenues, and declining reserves, which are forerunners to declining

Table 13.2 Factors that affect resource nationalism

Constraint	Factors	Opportunity
International		
Low	Commodity prices	High
High	Trade and investment dependence	Low
Few	International allies	Many
Industry		
Small	Known (proven) reserves	Large
Small	Economic importance of sector	Large
Unavailable	Alternative investment and expertise (to FDI)	Available
National		
Right	Left/right political culture	Left
Low	Political demands for inclusion	High
High	Powerful local mining interests	Low
Low	State capacity	High

Source: compiled by authors.

production and revenue. In response to unsustainable resource revenues, both countries liberalized the investment climate for hydrocarbons, transferring the risk and rewards of exploration (and exploitation) to the private sector, and incentivizing more activity than the state was capable of undertaking by itself.

Future directions

This book has brought together group of scholars characterized by their diversity in terms of theoretical approaches, disciplinary backgrounds, and country-knowledge, to reflect on the challenge of understanding Latin America's resource nationalisms in the early twenty-first century. Their contributions permit a nuanced exploration of both particular drivers of resource nationalism (Part 1), and the complex political-economy of resource nationalism in each of the country-cases (Part 2). Considered together, these chapters permit us to identify and classify the major policy initiatives that define resource nationalism in the region. Most importantly, we have drawn on the chapter analyses to identify a series of factors that, depending on their values, can constitute either constraints or opportunities for resource nationalism. There is logic to the resource nationalisms we examine, with the more radical efforts facing fewer constraints that the most limited, and the moderate cases caught between opportunities and constraints. Although our approach is qualitative in nature, these factors could be the foundation for a quantitative analysis that extends the generalizability of our findings to the entire Latin American region and the rest of the world.

A crucial theme, which has received relatively little attention in this volume, but which ought to be taken up by researchers in the immediate future, is the sustainability of resource nationalism over time, particularly as we enter what seems to be an extended period of lower commodity prices in the global economy.

As Gudynas points out in his chapter, resource nationalism is a balancing act in which the state encourages environmentally destructive activities for their revenue-generating potential, allowing it to address social demands for inclusion and compensate for the negative externalities of extractivism. Although crises are bound to occur as resource nationalism confronts international price volatility, increasing environmental costs and social protests, the state finds itself on a treadmill where it cannot risk not covering its social and political commitments.

In a similar manner, we should ask if the embrace of resource nationalism entails now, in the critical juncture of lower global commodity prices, a logic that propels Latin American countries down a path of even greater reliance on resource rents or to a change of course. By analogy, the structural disequilibria of the neoliberal model during the 1990s (of inequality, unemployment, insufficient competitiveness, indebtedness) were interpreted by policymakers at the time to require a doubling-down of deeper liberalization. Do we see the same logic in the more radical cases of resource nationalism?

In this regard, the sustainability of resource nationalism depends to a significant extent on its transformational potential. Will it lay the foundation for institution-building, diversification (into industry and services), and professionalization, including stronger internationalized SOEs like Petrobras? Or will the displacement of private firms by the state, in the absence of learning and capacity development, lead to inefficiency, dependence on rents and locked-in social spending that is highly vulnerable to shocks that convert opportunities into constraints? Even if further research at the firm-level is needed to answer this question, this book has shown that many of the resource nationalist policies adopted in the region do aim at this deep institutional transformation. At the same time, our cases of limited resource nationalism, show how fiscal reliance on resource rents, in a context of declining production and reserves, and the failure to build professional and internationalized SOEs, pushes governments back to liberal solutions. The success of Latin America's experiment with resource nationalisms ultimately depends on whether its state-building is mostly a cover for rent appropriation, or whether it is a first step on long journey of institutional learning capable of complementing and regulating private enterprise.

Notes

1 Anecdotal evidence suggests that this practice may be widespread in the region, especially in subnational jurisdictions, such as the Argentine provinces.
2 Authors' calculations based on a sum of their ranking on the WGI indicators, 2013 values.

Bibliography

Anderson, S.T. (2014). *Bolivia. 2012 Minerals Yearbook*. Washington, DC: U.S. Geological Survey, 3.1-3.18. Available from: http://minerals.usgs.gov/minerals/pubs/country/sa.html. [Accessed: 28 April 2015].

Anderson, S.T. (2011). *Bolivia. 2009 Minerals Yearbook*. Washington, DC: U.S. Geological Survey, 3.1-3.16. Available from: http://minerals.usgs.gov/minerals/pubs/country/sa.html. [Accessed: 28 April 2015].

Eden, L., Lenway, S., and Schuler, D.A. (2005). From the Obsolescing Bargain to the Political Bargaining Model. In Grosse, R.E. (ed.). *International Business and Government Relations in the 21st Century*. Cambridge, MA: Cambridge University Press, pp. 251–272.

Castañeda, J. (1993). *Utopia Unarmed: The Latin American Left after the Cold War*. New York: Knopf.

Gurmendi, A.C. (2014). *Venezuela. 2012 Minerals Yearbook*. Washington, DC: U.S. Geological Survey, 15.1-15.9. Available from: http://minerals.usgs.gov/minerals/pubs/country/sa.html. [Accessed: 28 April 2015].

Haslam, P.A. (2010). Foreign investors over a barrel: Nationalizations and investment policy. In Cameron, M.A., and Hershberg, E. (eds.). *Latin America's Left Turns: Politcs, Policies & Trajectories of Change*. Boulder: Lynne Rienner, pp. 209–30.

Hennart, J-F. (2012) Emerging market multinationals and the theory of the multinational enterprise. *Global Strategy Journal*, 2, pp. 168–87.

Hogan, W., Sturzenegger, F., and Tai, L. (2010). Contracts and investments in natural resources. In William Hogan and Federico Sturzenegger, eds. 2010. *The Natural Resources Trap: Private Investment without Public Commitment*. Cambridge MA: The MIT Press. pp.1–43.

Kobrin, S.J. (1987), Testing the bargaining hypotheses in the manufacturing sector in developing countries. *International Organization*, 41(4), pp. 609–38.

Kobrin, S.J. (1980). Foreign enterprise and forced divestment in LDCs. *International Organization*, 34(1), pp. 65–88.

Panizza, F. (2005). Unarmed Utopia Revisited: The Resurgence of Left-of-Centre Politics in Latin America. *Political Studies*, 53(4), pp 716–34.

Riesco, M. (2008). On 'Mineral Rents and Social Development in Chile'. Draft Working Document prepared for UNRISD project on Social Policy in Mineral-Rich Countries. Geneva: United Nations Research Institute for Social Development (UNRISD).

World Bank (2015). Worldwide Governance Indicators [Online]. Available from: http://data.worldbank.org/data-catalog/worldwide-governance-indicators. [Accessed: 24 July 2015].

Index

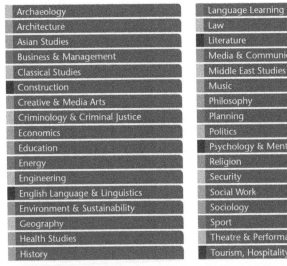

For Product Safety Concerns and Information please contact our EU
representative GPSR@taylorandfrancis.com
Taylor & Francis Verlag GmbH, Kaufingerstraße 24, 80331 München, Germany

www.ingramcontent.com/pod-product-compliance
Ingram Content Group UK Ltd.
Pitfield, Milton Keynes, MK11 3LW, UK
UKHW021617240425
457818UK00018B/603